ACUPRESSURE AND ACUPUNCTURE THERAPIES

DIAMOND POCKET BOOKS PRESENTS
HEALTH SERIES

M. Subramaniam
- 'Unveiling the Secrets of Reiki 195.00
- 'Brilliant Light 195.00
  (Reiki Grand Master Manual)

Sukhdeepak Malvai
- *Natural Healing with Reiki 100.00

Pt. Rajnikant Upadhayay
- *Reiki (For Healthy, Happy & Comfortable Life) 95.00
- *Mudra Vigyan (For Health & Happiness) ... 95.00

Sankalpo
- Neo Reiki 125.00

Dr. Shiv Kumar
- *Aroma Therapy 95.00
- *Causes, Cure & Prevention of Nervous Diseases 75.00
- *Diseases of Digestive System 75.00
- *Causes and Cure of Stress 95.00

Dr. Satish Goel
- *Causes & Cure of Blood Pressure .. 75.00
- *Causes & Cure of Diabetes 60.00
- *Causes & Cure of Heart Ailments ... 75.00
- *Pregnancy & Child Care 95.00
- *Ladies Slimming Course 95.00
- *Acupuncture Guide 50.00
- *Acupressure Guide 50.00
- *Acupuncture & Acupressure Guide 95.00
- *Walking for Better Health 95.00
- *Nature Cure for Health & Happiness 95.00
- *A Beacon of Hope for the Childless Couples 60.00
- *Sex for All 75.00

Dr. M.K. Gupta
- *Causes, Cure & Prevention of High Blood Cholesterol 60.00

Dr. Shiv Kumar
- *Asthma-Allergies (Causes & Cure) 75.00
- Eye-Care (Including Better Eye Sight Without Glassess) 75.00

Acharya Bhagwan Dev
- *Yoga for Better Health 95.00
- *Pranayam, Kundalini aur Hathyoga 95.00

Dr. S.K. Sharma
- *Add Inches 60.00
- *Shed Weight Add Life 60.00
- *Alternate Therapy 95.00
- *Miracles of Urine Therapy 60.00
- *Miracle of Pranic Healing 95.00
- *Meditation & Dhyan Yoga (for Spiritual Discipline) 95.00
- *A Complete Guide to Homeopathic Remedies 75.00
- *A Complete Guide to Biochemic Remedies 60.00
- *Common Diseases of Urinary System 75.00

- *Alopathic Guide for Common Disorder 125.00
- *E.N.T. & Dental Guide (in Press) 95.00
- *Wonders of Magnetotherapy 95.00
- *Family Homeopathic Guide 95.00
- *Health in Your Hands 95.00
- *Food for Good Health 95.00
- *Juice Therapy 95.00
- *Tips on Sex 75.00
- *How to Enjoy Sex (Question & Answers) 95.00

Dr. Renu Gupta
- *Hair Care (Prevention of Dandruff & Baldness) 75.00
- *Skin Care 75.00
- *Complete Beautician Course (Start Beauty Parlor at Home) 95.00
- *Common Diseases of Women 75.00

Dr. Rajiv Sharma
- *First Aid (in Press) 95.00
- *Causes, Cure and Prevention of Children's Diseases 75.00

Dr. Pushpa Khurana
- *Be Young and Healthy for 100 Years 60.00
- *The Awesome Challenge of AIDS ... 40.00

Dr. Kanta Gupta
- *Be Your Own Doctor 60.00

M. Kumaria
- *How to Keep Fit 20.00

Acharya Satyanand
- *Surya Chikitsa 95.00

Dr. R.N. Gupta
- *Joys of Parenthood 40.00

Dr. Nishtha
- *Diseases of Respiratory Tract (Nose, Throat, Chest & Lungs) 75.00
- *Backache (Spondylitis, Cerical, Arthrtis... Rheumatism) 95.00

Usha Rai Verma
- *Ladies Health Guide (With Make-up Guide) 75.00

Manoj Kumar
- *Diamond Body Building Course 95.00

G.C. Goyal
- *Vitamins for Natural Healing 95.00

Dr. Vishnu Jain
- *Heart to Heart (with Heart Specialist) 95.00

Asha Pran
- *Beauty Guide (With Make-up Guide) 75.00

Acharya Vipul Rao
- *Ayurvedic Treatment for Common Diseases 95.00
- *Herbal Treatment for Common Diseases 95.00

Dr. Sajiv Adlakha
- *Stuttering & Your Child (Question-Answer) 60.00

Dr. B.R. Kishore
- *Vatsyayana Kamasutra 95.00
- *The Manual of Sex & Tantra 60.00

Order books by V.P.P. Postage Rs. 10/- per book extra. Postage free on order of three or more books, Send Rs. 20/- in advance.

Diamond Pocket Books (P) Ltd.
X-30, Okhla Industrial Area, Phase-II, New Delhi-110020, Phones : 6841033, 6822803, 6822804, Fax : (0091) -011-6925020

Acupressure and Acupuncture Therapies

Dr. Satish Goel

Diamond Pocket Books (P) Ltd.
X-30, Okhla Industrial Area, Phase-2
New Delhi-110 020

ISBN : 81-7182-025-5

©**Author**

Publisher	: Diamond Pocket Books
	X-30, Okhla Industrial Area, Phase-II
	New Delhi-110020
Phone	: 011-51611861-865, 2638341
Fax	: 011-51611866, 26386124
E-mail	: mverma@nde.vsnl.net.in
Website	: www.diamondpocketbooks.com
Edition	: 2003
Price	: Rs. 95/-
Printer	: Aadarsh Printers, Shahdara, Delhi-32

Acupressure and Acupuncture Therapies   by   *Dr. Satish Goel*

Preface

Oriental therapeutic practices are as mysterious as the Orient itself but as miraculous as the rope-trick! However, these are not part of any magic or sleight-of-hand, for they are based on sound and logical reasoning. With the revival of the Chinese customs and ways of living-so far shrouded in the veil of mystery-acupressure and acupuncture therapies caught the world's attention. Many modern innovations were done to these, yet the efficacy of simple needle puncture or thumb-finger pressure could not be matched. It appears really amazing how pressing the point on the elbow could help cure the heart ailments.

These methods of therapy have undergone quite slevere and gruelling tests but they ever emerged victorious despite the 'tester' ignorance about their secret of success. The modern mind might not understand the process but the marvel of the end can't be gainsaid.

Although there are many books on these therapies yet either they are so big to drown the lay reader in the incomprehensible jargon and the typical Chinese terminology or too common place to make the reader gain some knowledge about these ancient therapies. Considering these factors this book has been planned in such a way that it should awaken the interest of the reader in these marvellous techniques of treatment. The present work has been divided in two books: One book covers acupressure and the other acupuncture. Since both of these therapies have almost identical concept and then the acupressure part covers the therapy from more practical angle. The emphasis on this part is more on the technique side—how and when to apply pressure, and in what measure etc. The theoretical part of the basic concept behind these therapies has been dealt elaborately in the second part of the work covering acupuncture. It has been done to avoid repetition yet present the work before the reader in its totality. That is why there are more charts and illustrative diagrams in the first book and the second part has more tables and linear representation of the essential conceptual points. Through this work our attempt is to present before the reader a sort of compendium on these therapies.

How far we have succeeded in achieving our aim is to be decided by our discerning readers but we have made a genuine attempt. The author expresses his gratitude for Narendra Bhai of Diamond Publications who provided all help and freedom to him to compile this work.

—Dr. Satish Goel.

Contents

	Acupressure & Acupuncture : The Therapies Par Excellence	11
	BOOK ONE : ACUPRESSURE THERAPY	**19**
1.	The Principles of Acupressure Technique	21
	The Causes of Ailments/Disorders ; the Principle of the cure; The Reflex Points : The Mirror of Ailments; Leakage of Bio electricity : Referral Pain Points: Various objects To Apply Pressure: The Time & Duration of the Pressure: Some Guiding Principles for Applying Pressure: The Three Metals' Potion	
II.	The Pressure (Reflex) Points And Their Corresponding Body Organs.	60
	Ailments/Disorders and Their cure By Pressing The Corresponding Reflex Points Some Prominent Points & The Diseases/Ailments They Help cure.	
III.	Acupressure and the Treatment of Our Body System	76
IV.	Glossary of Acupressure Terms Charts/Line Drawings/Illustrative	102
	BOOK TWO : ACUPUNCTURE THERAPY	**105**
I.	Acupuncture: A Miraculous Therapy	107
II.	Acupuncture: Origin, History & Concept	110
III.	Acupuncture Philosophy	114
	Toist Meditation; Health versus YIN and YANG; YIN and YANG and Physiological condsideration: Organs versus YIN and Yang.	
IV	The Governing Laws of Acupuncture Treatment	124
	Five elements, Law; Climate & Health; Emotions Versus five elements; The Mother-Son Law; Rhythm Round the Clock; The Mid-Day-Midnight Law; The Husband-wife Law.	

V. **Qi. Organs, Meridians & Acupuncture Points**   135
Qi:Blood;Body-fluids;The Organs; The Meridians; Acupuncture Points; Causes of Disease; The Basis of All Disease; Acupuncture Method of Marking The Diagnosis; The Treatments; Hering's Law of Cure; The eight Principles

VI. **Formulation of The Treatment**   159
Selection of the Points: Local & Distal Points; The Especial Effect Points; The Influential Points; The Xi-cleft Points; The 'MU' and 'SHO' Points; The eight Basic Diagnostic Principles; Junction Points; Modern Medicine; Auricular Points; Scalp, Nose, Head, Foot, Wrist & Ankle Acupuncture; Iridology; Applied Kinesiology; Through & Through Acupuncture

VII. **The Acupuncture Needles**
Sterillization of Needles; How to Insert the Needles; Other Techniques

VIII. **The Scientific Basis of Acupuncture Therapy**   17:
The Neural Theory; Circulatory Theory; The Gate control Theory; The Motor-Gate Theory; Augmentation of Immunity; Neurotransmitters; Endorphin Theory

IX. **The Methods of Moxibustion, Cupping & Massage**   187

X. **Introduction of the Latest Technology in Acupuncture Treatment**   196
Electro-Acupuncture, Laser Treatment; Cymatics; Applied Kinesiology; Magnetotherapy; Sonopuncture; Acquapuncture; Microwave; Homeopuncture; Ginseng; Enolite

XI. **Some Typical case Histories**   205

XII. **The Possible Dangers & Pit falls in Acupuncture Treatment**   211

XIII. **Glossary of the Acupuncture Terms**   215

"May I have breath in my nostrils, voice in my mouth, sight in my eyes, hearing in my ears; hair that has not turned grey; teeth that are not discoloured; and much strength in my arms.

May I have power in my thighs, swiftness in my legs, steadfastness in my feet.

May all my limbs remain unimpaired and my soul (atma) ever unconquered."

—RIGVEDA.

Acupressure & Acupuncture: The Therapies Par Excellence

According to the Indian Scriptures birth in the human form is the fruition of many lives penance and dedicated efforts. The ancient Hindus believed that there were about 8.4 million species available for life to come into existence. Since human existence is believed to be the ultimate culmination of the soul's efforts to come in the best creation of Lord Almighty, even the Gods are described to be trying for getting this form. It is, bcause, this form is the existence in which the soul can redeem its earlier failings and earn merit. And to be in this form in the robust pink of health is the dream of every human being. Hence the popular saying: "the foremost pleasure is to have a healthy body" ("Pahla Sukh ho nirmal kayaa"). It is due to the belief that says that the human existence is the only form of life which can maintain good health by one's own efforts-unlike the other forms which donot have enough intelligence to ensure it. A dog, a horse or even a lion would need a lot of care by other to ensure good health. But not a human body which is endowed with a mind capable of looking after its health. This human body is the most marvellous system ever created in the universe. It is capable of not only protecting its vitality but also maintaining itself in a good trim. It is only when we overtire itself or torture it beyond the limits that it shows the signs of various ailments. It is confirmed by the latest medical researches that thus far the human heart is the best pump system ever created; as it is capable of withstanding more than 400 times the pressure it is designed for. This fact is enough to prove the amount of load we thurst on it when it fails. In fact all the ailments are the results of the excesses we subject our body to.

With the appearance of these ailment syndromes the body prepares to cure itself. It is to help it cure the various foreign bodies like the viruses, germs etc., that we take help of the various systems of medicines. There are scores of them and unfortunately the most popular medical therapy is also the most damaging one to it, viz- the allopathy system of medicine. Since it is still in the formation process it involves lots of damaging after effects to the body having cured one ailment. Thus while it may cure cold it would leave the conditions in the body conducive to the growth of asthmatic disorder. The modern researches in this system seem to be demarcating its limits or exposing the weakness of it. A medicine found to be quite effective to cure one ailment gets banned after a decade or so owing to its leashing out the carcinomous effect in the body. When the medicines chloroquin was invented it was believed to be the ultimate to cure malaria. But now this medicine is banned in most of the countries owing to its in effectiveness to check not only the menance of malaria but also because it leaves many lever troubles in its wake. The malaria virus has grown totally immune to it.

In fact all those therapy systems that resort to foreign material have the similar damaging effect on the human body. However, there are a few system that enhance the resistance of the body against various ailments without resorting to any outside help. The systems of acupuncture and acupressure come in this category. Merely by applying pressure at a certain specific point on the body by means of the hand pressing or needle pressures or punctures they endeavour to rejuvenate the body and make it as powerful as to eject out the harmful elements from the body on its own.

Although both of these techniques are believed to have originated from the ancient Chinese therapeutic practices, they were not exactly unknown to India. Our ancients did not do exactly as their Chinese counterparts did, but they were quite aware that there existed some fine points on the human anatomy which governed the motor nerves of the particular limbs. For example the point exactly between the eyes or the tip of nose or the exact well of the temples had great significance for them along with the tip of a particular finger that touched them. That is why in the traditional Hindu houses, marking the forehead with a paricular finger or thumb has remained fixed from times immemorial. Even otherwise, it is a common experience that pressing the temple at the time of severe headache brings in temporary relief. But it has long been known, both in China and outside that it is not always necessary to put the pressures by fingers or by needle to obtain a beneficial result. Now the modern physiotherapy machines offer anatomical guides as to where the body should be pressed or massaged to gain the greatest relief for various disabilties which the physiotherapist treats. According to the physiotherapic terms these are called the motor points and they amazingly correspond to those points which are used in acupuncture and acupressure.

Before going into the details of the techniques we better know what the terms acupunture and acupressure stand for. This word 'acu' is derived from Latin language which means a very minute point. Hence these techniques stand for the therapeutic methods aimed to achieve cure by applying pressure or puncturing the skin at an 'acute' point. Taking advantage of the modern development in scientific fields now the pressure is also applied with electric stimulation or by electrodes. However notwithstanding these developments, one of the simplest, safest and yet effective methods of stimulating the site is performed with fingers which press the particular points of the body to ease pains, tensions, fatigue and other symptoms of various diseases. The advantages of such a method of treatment are self evident. The possibilities of home use, optimum repetitions of therapy and greater safety become clear. But it must be made clear at this juncture that these techniques can't be used on every diseases. However, it can be of great benefit in those ailments in which its nature has designed it to treat. And they can surely treat diseases most effectively provided one knows the technique well.

So, in brief these therapeutic system can be defined as treating the diseases by applying pointed pressure or puncturing the skin at a particular point. In acupuncture a special type of needle is used to puncture various points on the human body to cure certain ailments. These points are also known as sites. In acupressure the pressure on the sites is exerted by means of thumb and fingers. The intensity of pressure is determined by experience.

As a matter of fact, these sites are merely the points which vary in the depths from the skin surface also. So it is obvious that sites that appear from one quarter inch to several inches below the surface will require different pressure techniques. It is also obvious that the sites closest to the surface can respond to pressure and massage more easily than the deep ones.

Another point to note in these techniques is that these points are not merely a point but a circle of about a centimeter in diameter. Hence one has to be very guarded to press only the particular point as we all know the body symmetry of each person varies. There can't be any standard measure for assessing the length of the hand of all persons. Hence a unit of measurment such as an inch or a diameter can cause great inaccuracies in locating the right point. The Chinese standardised this measure by selecting a part of the body that was closely proportional to the individual's general anatomy. The distance is between two points on the middle point of the middle finger when the finger is totally bent. You stretch your finger totally and bend it from the two points it is bendable at. The creases of the middle of the knuckle form one "T' sun", the unit for the Chinese. But, as the reader would note, this unit formation is also quite awkward to utilize. Hence, now-a-days the breadth of an individual finger is deemed to be this unit. The unit "T'sun" can be derived from this unit by remembering that two "T'sun" equal to three finger breadth and three "T'sun" to four finger breadth, approximately.

In the technique of acupressure the pressure should be applied directly over it and any massaging of the site should be achieved by rotating the finger over the site while maintaining the pressure unabatedly. Even the layman must have experienced relief by slightly rubbing or caressing the injured part. It is because of the mild pressure exerted against the acupuncture or acupressure sites in the region of the injury. By exerting pressure and imparting rotational massage over the principlal sites after the first general rubbing, even more relief could be experienced. The pressure may also very from person to person because the strength a person can persist also varies drastically. And one must be cautious in selecting these sites as they could be very sensitive points overlying the nervers. When a tingling feeling of electricity passes down the course of the nerve which has an acupuncture site, it gets stimulated for getting the beneficial results. The same principle explains the efficacy of the shock-treatment also. We must have heard many on account on which a semi paralysed man is described to have acquired his total body strength when he suffered an electric shock. What happen in such cases is the fact that accidentally the stress-point of a particular nerve might have been pressed to revive the deadened nerves. However, if firm stimulation results in any unpleasant pain, less pressure should be used. In case at certain points where putting pressure by finger might appear impossible, the knuckles should be used to apply the desired pressure.

The Chinese style of numbering these points, however, is very confusing because they call these points over the particular limb by the internal organs they govern. The reader would be quite puzzled to find a point on the elbow named as the heart point, won't he? To avoid this confusion we generally prefer to call the points on their limbs by their limb name and not by the names of the organs whose nerves centres they control.

Owing to this confusion, by the beginning of this century (20th century) these therapeutic techniques had become almost extinct barring their practice by certain Chinese and Japanese physicians who too, could not make much impact. It was only in 1949 when Mao assumed power in China that he, in his attempt, to revitalise the Chinese roots, established the techniques, efficacy again. Since the Chinese government was at the back of their revival, acupuncture and acupressure techniques received a great boost, The Chinese people began to employ these technique at large scale to treat their ailments. With further researches to clear the confusion etc. about the reflex point selection, soon these techniques became popular. But Mao's these efforts kept their popularity with that country. It had to wait for about a quarter of century to acquire popularity all over the world. It spread to the west in a very dramatic way. In 1971, the then American president Nixon visited China for the first official US president's visit to the country after it became communist. Mr. Nixon's entourage had a lot of people also including a prominent journalist named James Ruston. It so happened that during the visit, Mr. Ruston developed appendix problem. Since his appendix had become swollen accompained by excruciating pain, he was to be operated open immediately for the cure of the problem. But even after the operation the pain persisted in his abdominal region. Since he was getting restless and the various sedatives administered to him failed to provide any relief, the Chinese medical experts were consulted who suggested using their indigenous medical therapics to cure the malady. After much confabulation, Nixon allowed Ruston, his good friend, to be treated by the Chinese acu- especialists. When these especialists applied their techniques Ruston was cured in no time. This case established the credibility of the techniques and they began to become popular in America almost overnight. In 1973, a team of the US doctors and medical experts visited China to assess the efficacies of these techniques. The leader of the team, Dr. White, was quite impressed and on returning home he wrote in his report: "Although I fail to find the reason of these techniques astounding success, I can vouchsafe their efficacy without even a shred of doubt."

Not only by pressing the certain points on the hand, feet or head, even by pressing certain fixed points on the ear zone the relief can be assured for the internal organs of the body. That the ear zone is inseparably attached to various body organs is mentioned in the old Chinese classical tomes of medicine. "Yellow emperor's classic of internal medicine." Pulling ears of the person to cure his or her headache or twisting the person's earlobe to revive his or her consiousness is the old remedy still adhered to in China. Even in India such treatments are not uncommon. In 1950 the famous neuro-surgeon of France Dr. Poll Nozier studied this kind of therapy deeply and gave it a form of a regular treatment. Dr. Nozier called it ocular therapy. Following the revival of these ancient techniques much study on ear-acupressure treatment has been done in China, leading to the discovery of more than 200 reflex points on the ear, although not all of them are accorded that much importance now. It is not surprising to find a similar treatment practised in India from times immemorial. It is believed that peircing the ear-lobes of young girls protects them from asthmatic disorders. Similar piercing the fleshy portion of nose, besides assuring fertility of the female beings is also believed to be a good stimulant to regulate the menstual cycle. Although this hypothesis is based upon the experience of the ages, yet it can be said without any doubt that had these piercings been not effective to ensure good health, this cumbersome and painful custom would have not survived for such a long period.

Now these techniques have acquired a global recognition. Most of the international stars, belle-dancers top heroines like Marbu Maunoe are recorded to have praised these techniques efficiency in superlative terms. The gold medalist in the Montreal Olympics, Dwight Jone's these words are worth quoting: "the help that we received to tone up our muscles and electricity them with unbelievable ability from the technique of accupressure is what no other method or technique could give our physiques to."

These wondrous techniques are not only helpful in curing the various ailments, they could be ideal in the preventive treatment also. By pressing certain points you could keep the various disease and ailments at bay. The ancient Chinese records indicate that in the olden times, a doctor in China was given fees regularly till he or she was able to keep the persons in good health. The moment the person of a specified region fell sick he would stop giving any fees to the doctor. During that person's illness the concerned doctor was made to provide medicines and other necessary items essential for the sick for regaining his health free of cost. In fact the doctor had to bear all the medical expenses of the sick person, for it was considered a doctor or physician's bounded duty to keep the people of the region in good health. In case the sick person died, the failing doctor was forced to hang a lighted lantern outside his home to symbolise his patient's death. It was a big social stigma and no doctor would like to see a lighted lantern outside his home. Of course death is a certainty but death by natural process of aging is a diferent matter. Death can't be prevented but life can be made to survive to its full age by following the preventive tratment. Famous thinker and author, Dr. Jhonson says: "To preserve health is a moral and religious duty, for health is the basis of all social virtues—we can no longer be useful when not well." The famous Sanskrit saying: "Shareeraamaadyam khalu dharmasaadhanam" also points to this fact.

It is actually in this sphere of preventive treatment that these techniques: acupressure and acupuncture score over other method of treatments. Like Ayurveda the main aim of these techniques is to keep a human body healthy for the full span and not to first cure illness or disorder.

Another great plus point with these techniques is their resorting to no outside help for the treatment. They require nothing to be injected or put in the body to make it fight the disease or develop resistance to evict the foregin matter in the form of viruses or germs. Only by giving pressure by hand or the needle they activate the body's resistance to fight out the trouble and keep itself healthy. That is why these treatments have no side or after effects either.

It is on account of their these qualities that they are increasingly becoming popular. Now besides the individual organisations accompanied by the goverment help in many countries, even the United Nations Organisation is paying more attention to these techniques. The W.H.O is now opening a seperate cell for the research and development in these techniques.

Before further elaborating on these techniques principles and method of working, let us first understand the difference between these two techniques.

The Difference Between Acupressure & Acupuncture

As hinted earlier these are the words coined with the help of Latin language. The main operative word is 'acu' which in Latin means a pointed object like a needle. So acu + pressure means applying pressure pointedly and acupuncture means a mild incision by a needle. Basically these two techniques are similar. In acupressure the pressure is applied by hand and in acupuncture special needles are used to apply pointed pressure. Mostly all the reflex points are similar. For acupuncture we use very thin needles made of special material. Henceforth we shall be elaborating on their method and treatment in seperate section.

No doubt that both of these technique have their similar origin and almost similar concept but there is some distuiction in their basic concept despite the end analysis being the same. First we shall be discussing acupressure technique with brief analysis of its difference with the other technique, that is, acupuncture. Then in the other part of the book we shall be elaborating on the acupuncture technique alone.

Book One:
Acupressure Therapy

The Principles of Acupressure Technique

Acupressure and treatment system does not regard human body as composed of two distinct units: the emotional or the physical but treats the whole body as one integrated whole. This principle is fundamental in this kind of treatment. Whether the disorder in the body has been caused due to emotional disturbance or the physical ailment, it is treated in the same way for this school of treatment believe both emotional and physical entities of the body like one inseparable whole.

Another important principle of this system is based upon purely a scientific basis. According to it the nerve ending of all small-big blood vessels and that of the nervous system lie at the base of the hand and feet. Hence the hands and feet have the control points of the entire human system.

The second principle raises a very pertinent question as to which points control which part of the body and how they are to be linked and identified? How to pin point, which point corresponds to heart and which to mind?

In order to identify these points scientifically the entire human body was divided vertically and horizontally. (See the charts ahead). If the whole body, right from head to foot is divided into 10 vertical parts we

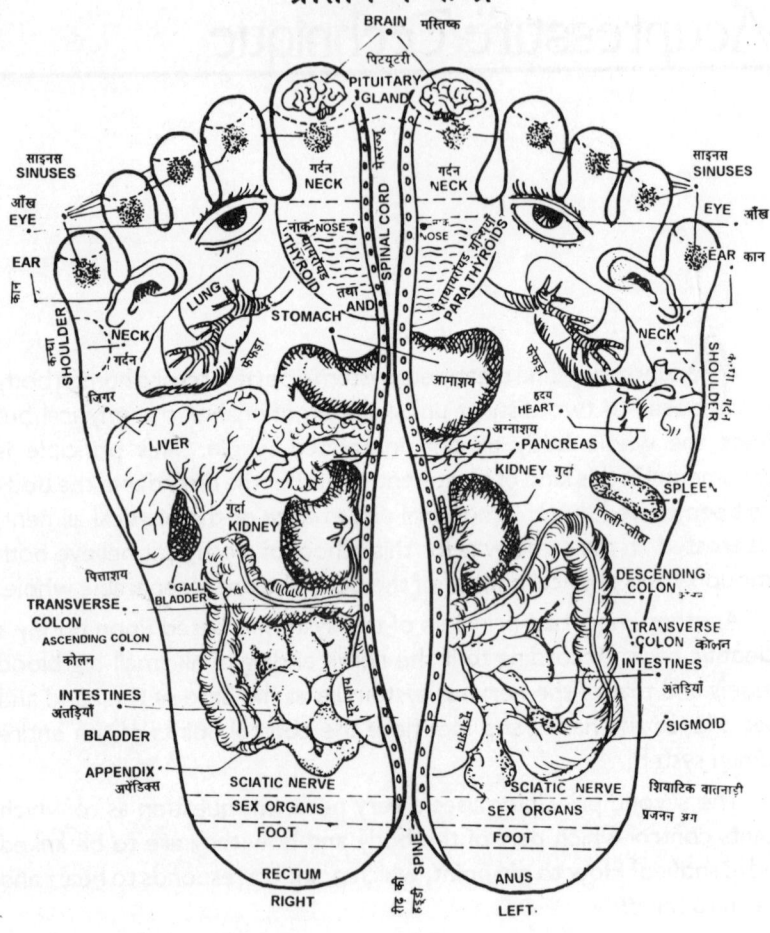

Fig. 1. Miraculous Mirrors of the Body-Reflex centres—Feets

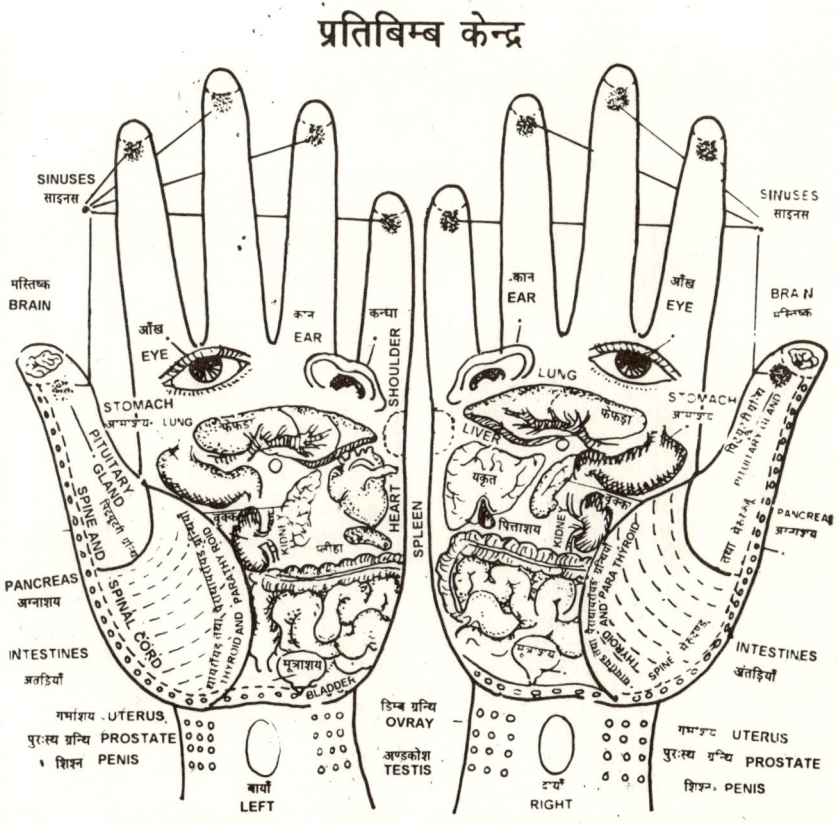

Fig. 2. *Miraculous Mirrors of the Body-Reflex centres—Hands*

would know which part of the body corresponds to which point on the foot. Similarly the body was also divided into three parts horizontally.

In fact these are the points that are known as reflex points. The

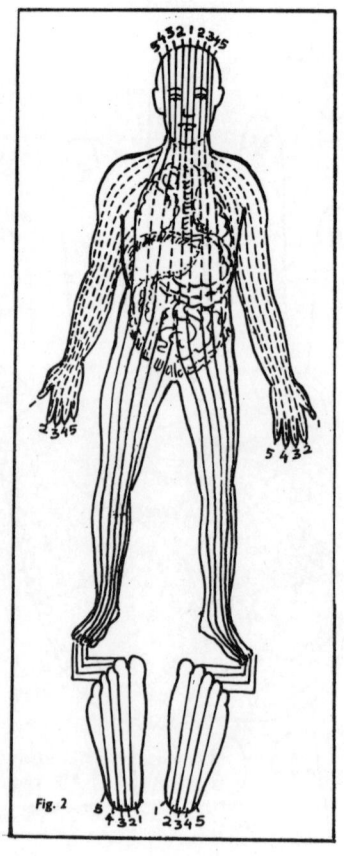

Fig. 2

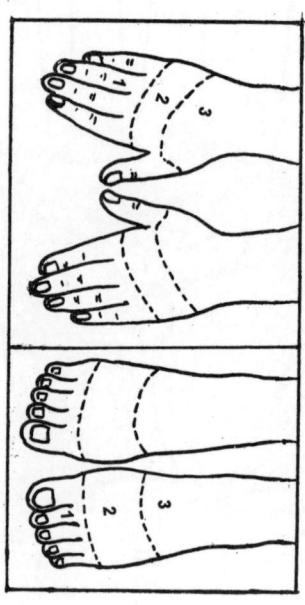

Fig. 3

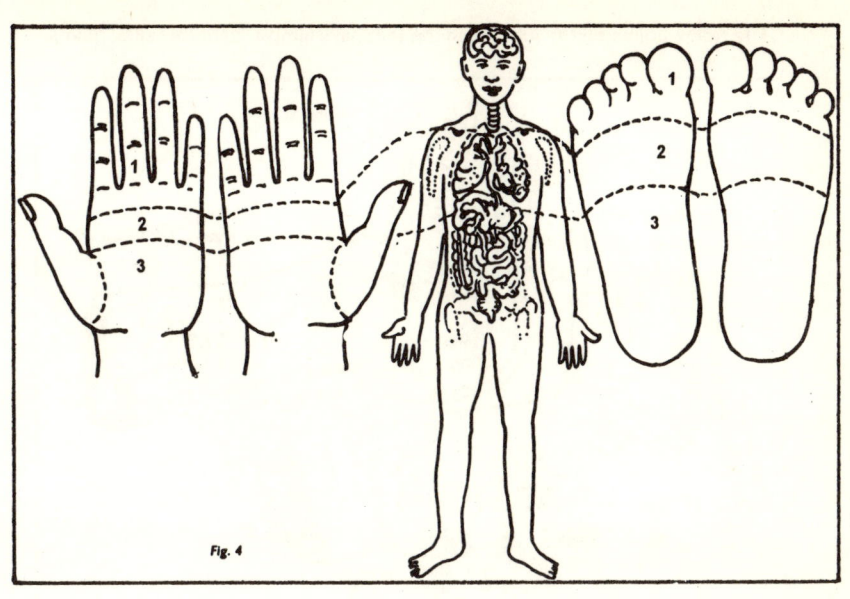

Fig. 4

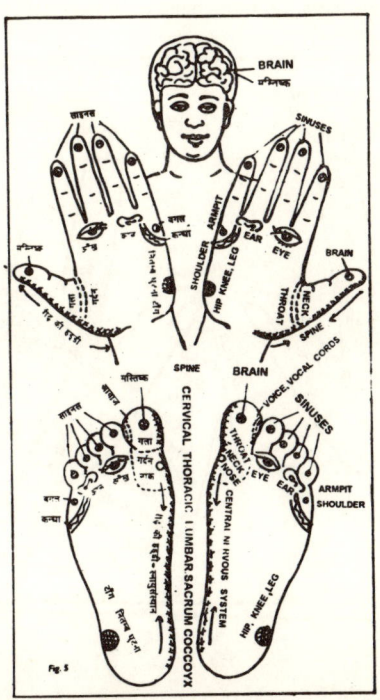

Fig. 5

The reflex points on the foot. Both the feet have almost identical reflex points.

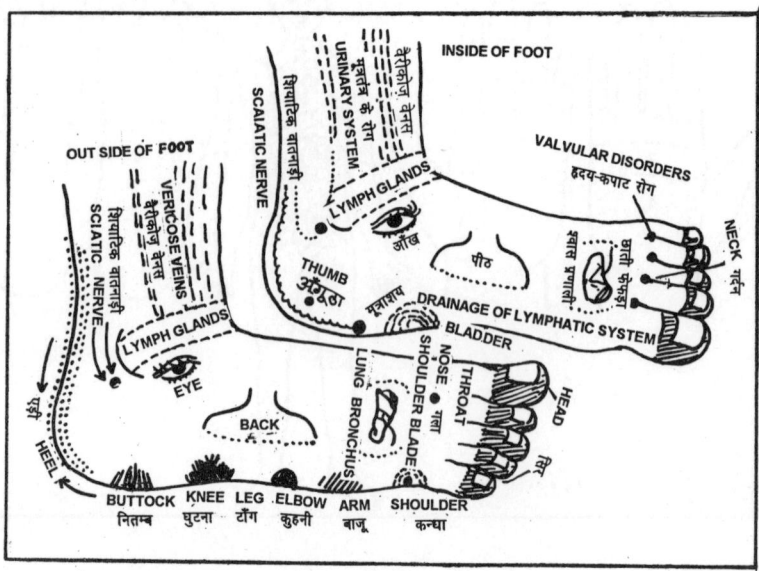

Fig. 6

The reflex points on the hand. Both the hand have identical points.

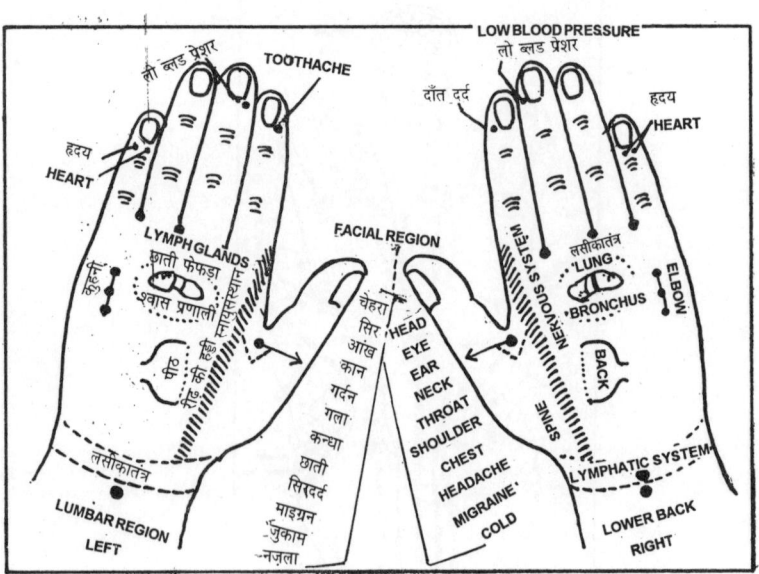

Fig. 7

horizontal division of the body are known as the transverse zones of the body. According to this transverse principle of body division first part represents head and the various reflex points at the neck region. That the top portion corresponds to feet and hand points. The second part corresponds to the reflex points above the diaphragm. The third section corresponds to the region normally below the waist. These divisions of the body greatly help in identifying which reflex points corresponds to which portion of the body.

The causes of Ailment/Disorder etc. of the body limbs according to Acupressure therapy:—

On the basis of their experience the protagonist of this therapy have identified the causes of the body ailments. We shall be discussing only those salient causes which have stood the test of research and time upon them:

(i) This school believes that when a particular organ of the body doesn't have the smooth flow of blood it becomes sick. This lack of proper blood supply also gives rise to various nervous disorder which either atrophies the nerves or makes their ending shrink, leading to the coldness or numbness of the affected organ. In certain cases they also become overheated. Both the conditions signify ailment or disorder of the limb. By resorting to the acupressure techniques the normal, smooth blood supply of the affected organ is restored.

(ii) According to another theory some blood vessels develop a sort of crystalline formation at their end which disturbs the smooth flow of blood. These crystals act as insulators which slacken the nerve system of the particular organ. Unless these crystals are removed by applying pressure or puncturing them, the ailment of the part doesn't get cured. This theory also endorses the view that various ailments to the body are the consequence of the faulty or impeded blood supply to that part.

(iii) As all branches of medicine believe the whole human body is kept in good trim by the smooth supply of blood. It is blood which nourishes all parts of the body and energises them to fight out the foreign material which accentuates the ailment in the body. By giving pressure at the right point further strength is provided to that part to get rid of the crystals/foreign matter etc. This pressure removes it and the smooth flow of blood takes the impurities to various 'scavengers' of the body like kidney/skin etc. to eventually eject it out of the system.

(iv) According to old Chinese School a body becomes sick when many of its centres (reflex point areas) develop unhomogenious tendencies, like their becoming unusually hot or cold, extra sensitive or numb, extremely oily or dry, discoloured or over coloured etc. In short when the body becomes a conglomeration of various unhomogeneous pockets it disturbs the nature's equilibrium in the body leading to various disorders.

(v) According to the well-established ancient belief, our whole body is made of five principle elements earth, water, fire, sky and air. The guiding force behind these five elements is our body's inherent bio-electricity or bio-energy. According to this technique's fundamental belief when this energy starts 'leaking' from certain points, they become sick. By giving pressure on these 'leaking holes' these are plugged to restore the body's health.

The Principle to cure the body of the ailments/disorder

Since this technique believe accumulation of the foreign material to be the Chief cause of body ailments, the application of the various pressures is meant to remove these foreign material and restore blood's normal supply. The apparent symptoms on the skin to prove their conducive effect are the following:

(i) The skin assumes a natural, healthy glow.

(ii) The application of pressures activates the blood flow to nourish the body organs.

(iii) It brings flexibility in the muscular tissues.

(iv) It helps to remove the bone defects also.

(v) This technique revitalise the nervous system.

(vi) Acupressure helps to regulate the secretion of the endocrine glands.

(vii) Acupressure technique can also activate the functions of the internal organs.

(viii) It reactivates the body, internal resistance against the assaults of outside germs or virus.

Despite all these readings of the apparent parameters it is still not clear how a pressure application on a point on the hand can help to cure an ailment. Or, how a mild pressure on the sole can recharge the heart with a renewed strength? Nevertheless, it can be said that these are, according to present level of their comprehension, almost miraculous ways of keeping the body in the pink of health.

It is better to realise at this outset that these techniques have no in-compatibility with any other line of treatment. No matter if a patient is adhering to allopathic style of treatment he or she can still take the pressure or the puncture. In certain ailments it is not advisable either to completely forgo the earlier treatment. For example in heart troubles, diabetes, mental disorders etc. one should continue to take the medicines irrespective of one's now trying acupressure or acupuncture style of treatment. Even otherwise the patient shouldn't reduce the dose of the medicine without consulting the regular physician. These technique are compatible with other kind of treatments because there is no side-effects or after-effects of acupressure treatment whatsoever.

However, it is eminently advisable to clearly identify the patient's reflex points concerning the ailment he or she is suffering before resorting to the pressure or puncture therapy. Generally it is easier to identify the reflex points at the feet than at the hands. Moreover, pressure applied through feet give better results. The hand reflex points generally become no easily identifiable owing to hands being busy doing some work all the time which hardens these points and hence pressure on them becomes less effective. Another advantage of using the foot-reflex points is their availability in a widely marked area unlike the hand points in which the reflex points are not so clearly demarcated owing to the paucity of space. However, those who walk mostly bare footed donot have these points so clearly marked. In their case hand points should be given preference. The hand and foot reflexologies shall be dealt with in separate chapters ahead.

Reflex-Points: The Mirror of the Ailments

Before resorting to the 'Acu' therapies it is always better to study the symptoms of the disease the patient is apparently suffering from. Some times the patient himself know what kind of disease he is suffering from. Then the physician should concentrate those very points. Sometimes even the patient may be quite confused about his problem. There have been frequent cases wherein the patient was treated for the stomach disorder but the root of the disease lies in the heart region. A typical case of this type is the problem of acidity. Mostly this is deemed to be the stomach/liver related problem but nine out of ten times it signified the heart ailment case on further verification.

Acu-techniques scrutiny of the reflex point is quite capable of finding the basic cause of their trouble. Many a time various clinic tests fail to identify the root cause of the problem. But an expert acupressurist can identify it almost in no time. Hence these reflex points are said to be the mirror of the body ailments. It is always better to have the full objective diagnosis done before resorting to this kind of treatment. Even the most exhaustive diagnosis can help in identifying the most difficult to diagnose ailment like cancer or even the AIDS.

Seeing the Charts given earlier can throw much light on the parts to be treated by pressing the relevant reflex points. By mere pressure from hand can reveal the true nature of the ailments. One precaution, needs to be always taken while studying the reflex points. Their position is not identical in all hands and feet. Like body structure differs from person to person, so is the position of these reflex points. Some persons might be having long feet or hands or their palm and foot may be quite broader than the average. Accordingly the position of these reflex points would also change a bit.

Pressure should be given by means of the physician's thumb, fingers, wooden objects or plastic pieces (shown ahead). We shall be giving greater details about applying the right type of pressure when we will discuss the technical part of these theories.

Fig. 8

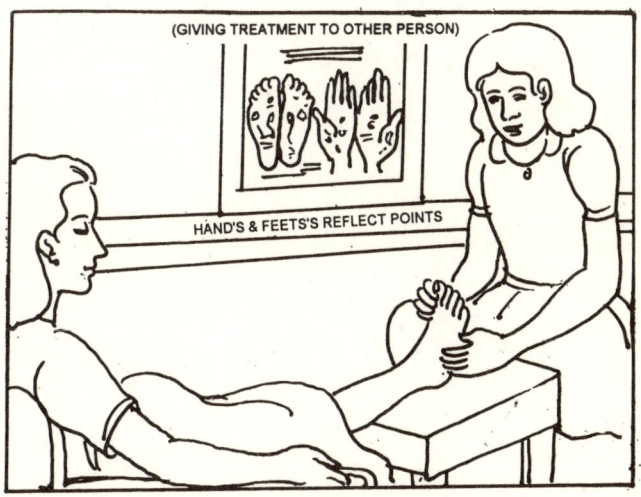

Fig. 9

The pressure applied should be optimum-neither very hard nor very mild. It should be enough to make the person feel it comfortably. If even the optimum pressure makes the person uncomfortable, it is a sure sign of the limb corresponding to that pressure point being defective.

To start with all reflex points ought to be given even pressure by hand. If the patient feels unbearble pain at a particular point or points these parts may be marked separately on the first chart attached with this book. Note down these points and start treating them one by one to identify the root cause of the trouble: The absence of any pain on applying pressure is a sure indication of those parts corresponding with those points as working perfectly. Pain on pressure means deposites of the crystals of the foreign material which needs to be removed by this technique to cure the trouble.

Endocrine System And the Corresponding Reflex Points at the Hands and Feet.

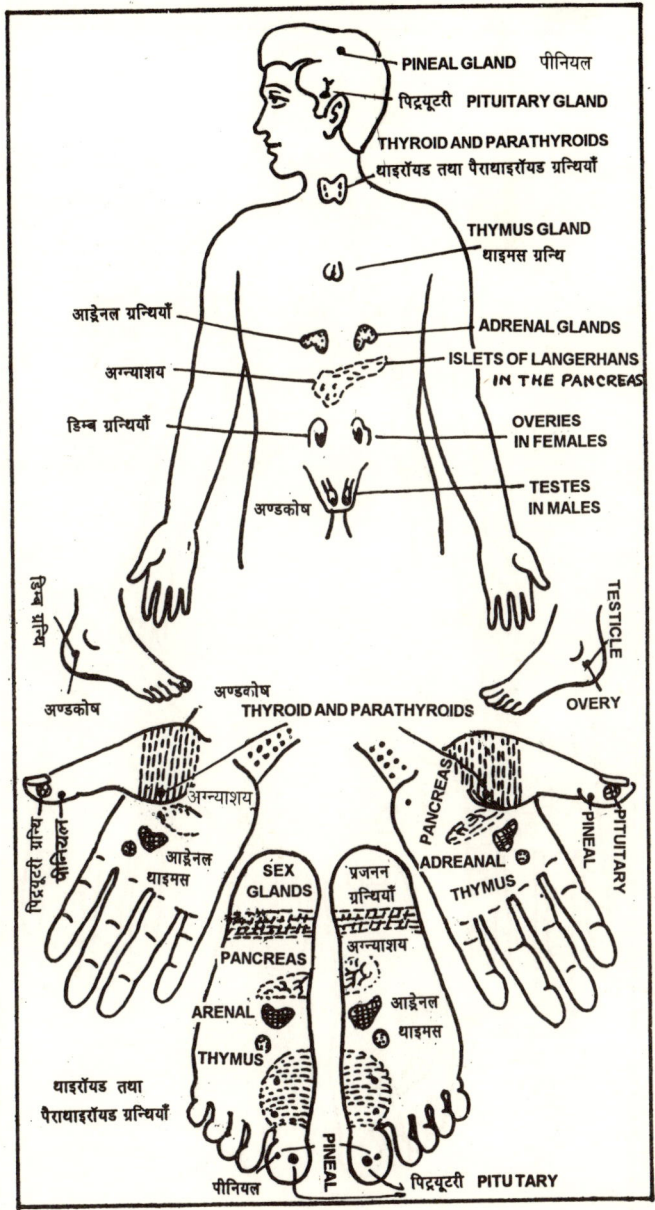

Fig. 10

Heart & Spleen And Corresponding Reflex Points at the Hands & Feet.

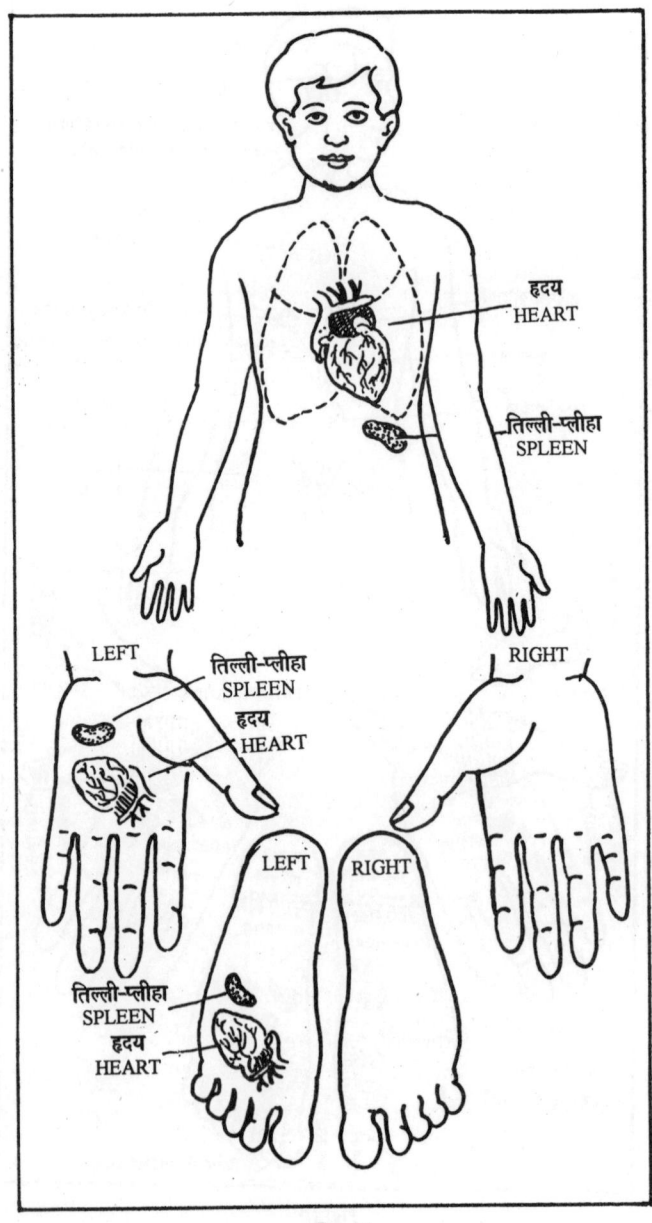

Fig. 11

Respiratory System And the Corresponding Reflex Points At the Hands & Feet.

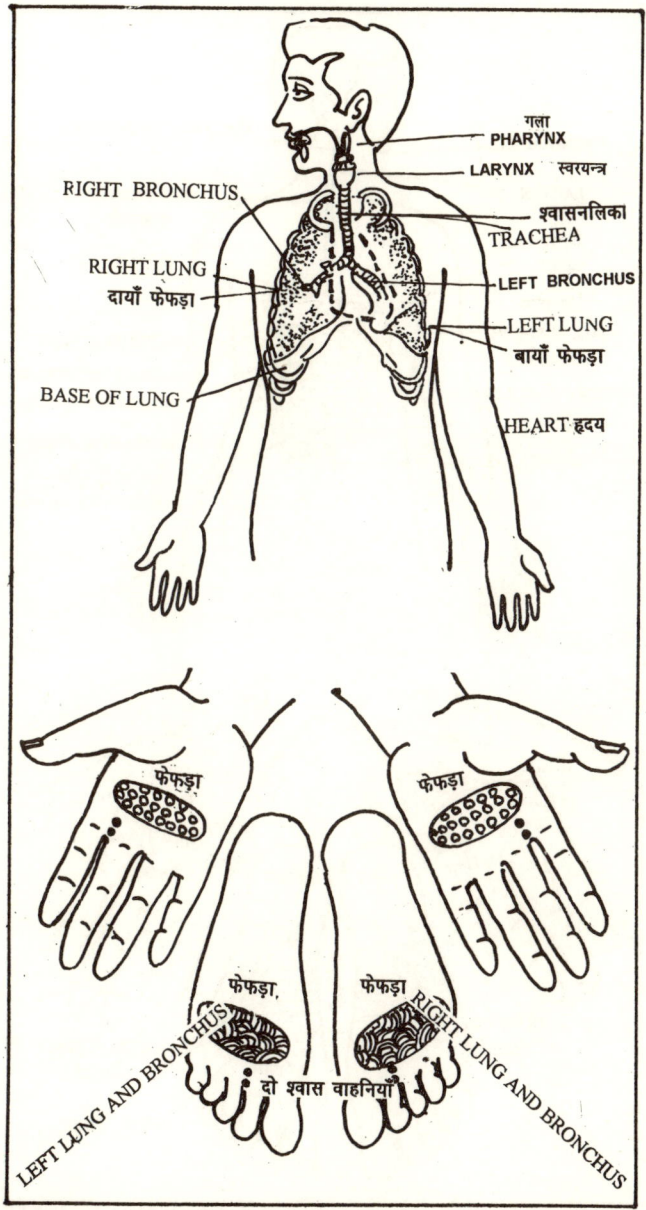

Fig. 12

Digestive System And the Corresponding Reflex Points At the Hands & Feet.

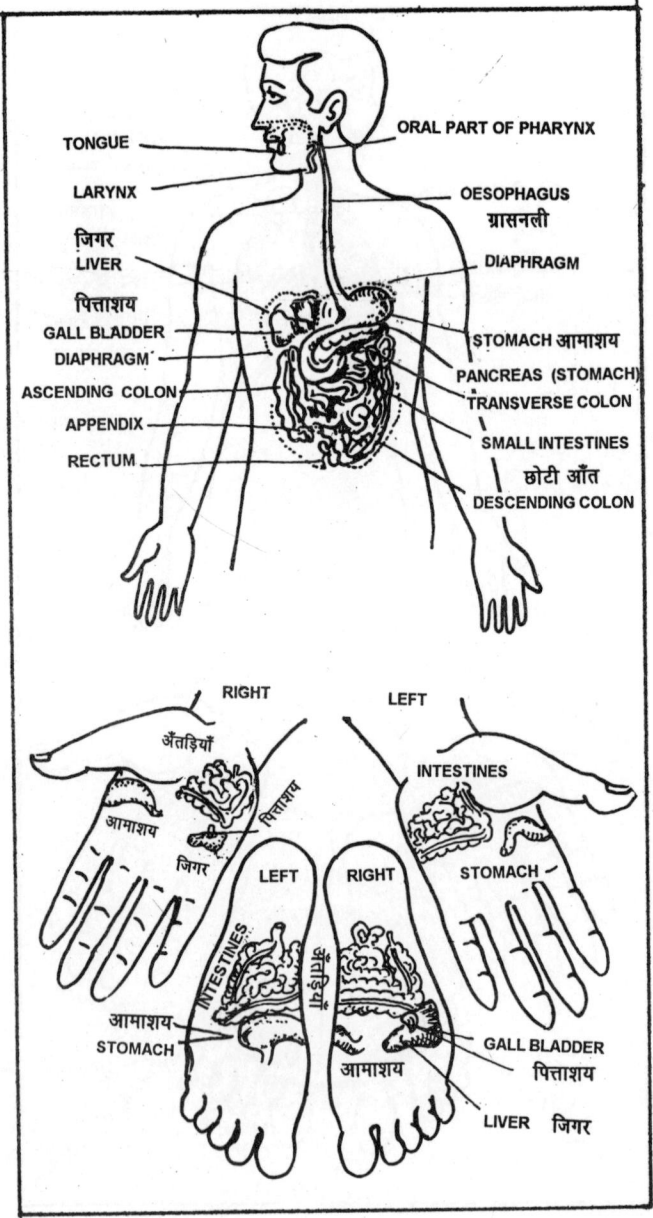

Fig. 13

Urinary System And The Corresponding Reflex Points at the Hands & Feet.

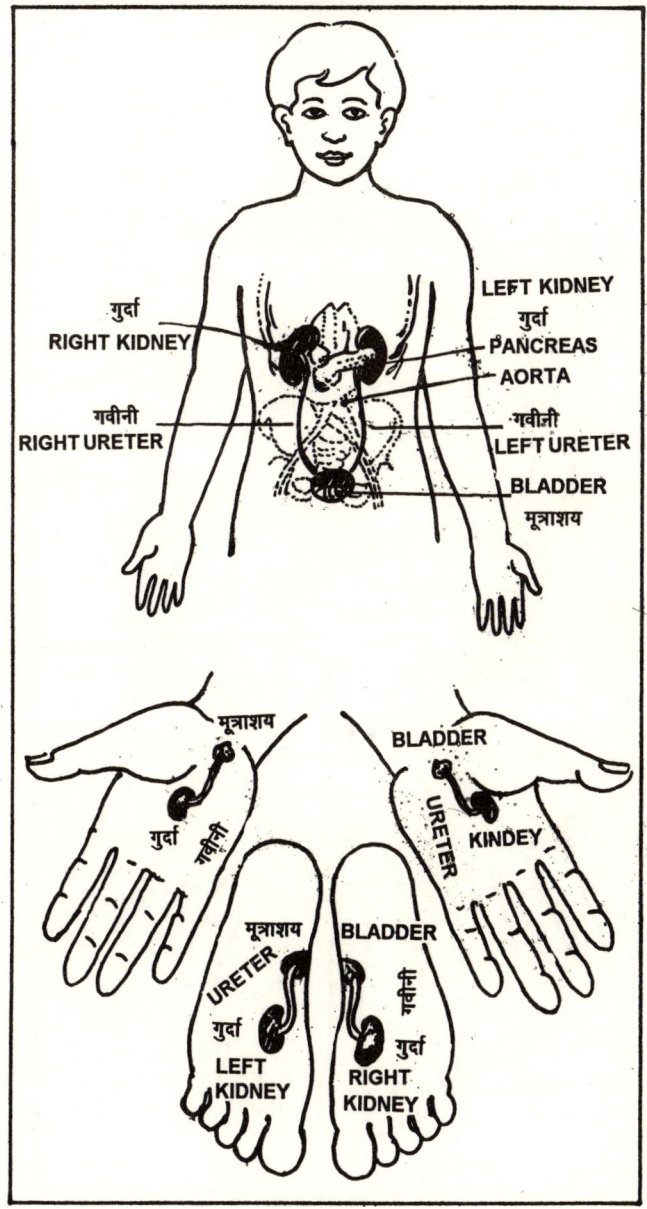

Fig. 14

The Male & Female (Human) Reproductive Organs and the Corresponding Reflex Points at the Hands & Feet.

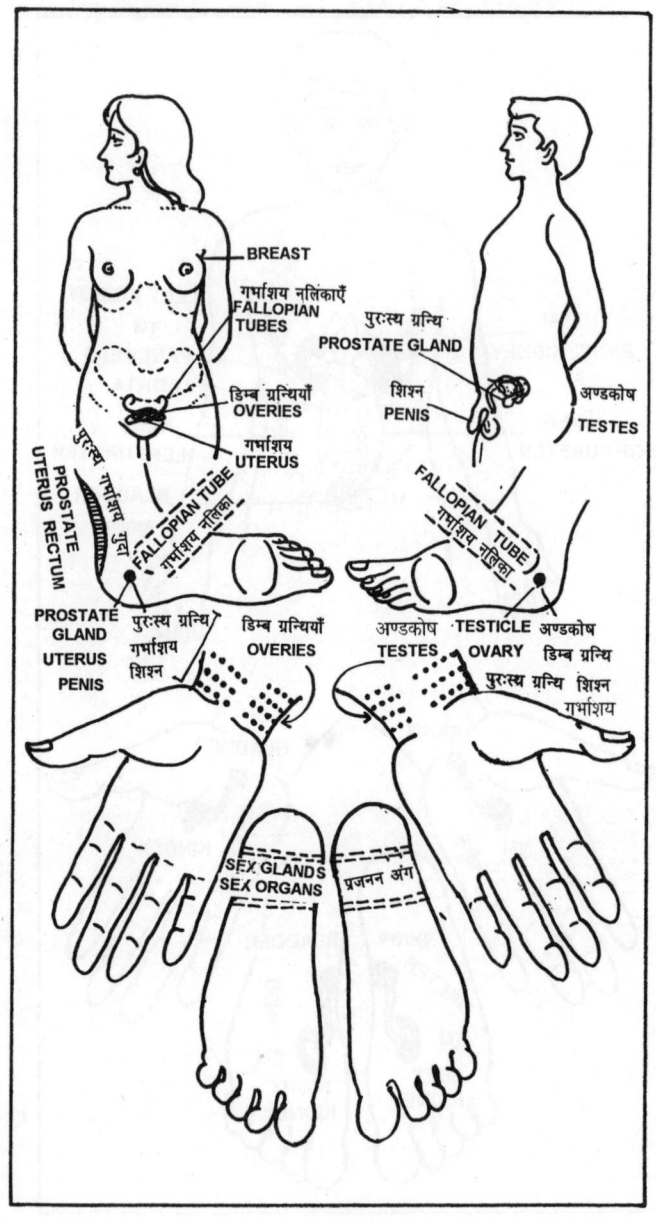

Fig. 15

The Right way of Applying Pressure at various reflex points.

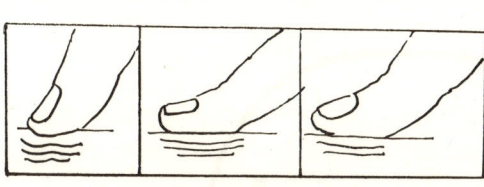

Fig. 16. The Right Way   Fig. 17. The Wrong Way

As shown in the above charts, the right way of applying pressure is not applying the pressure vertically but in a slanted way.

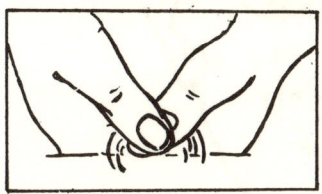

Fig. 18
For applying concentrated pressure use both the thumbs.

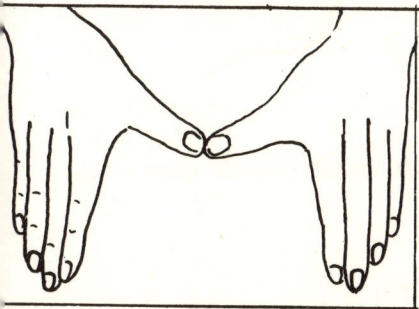

Fig. 19
The Right way of applying pressure at the back.

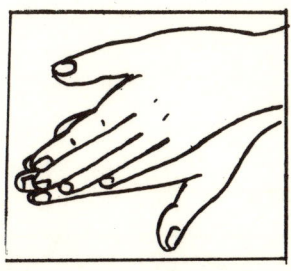

Fig. 20
The Right way of applying pressure on the reflex points located at the stomach (soft) regions.

The Male & Female (Human) Reproductive Organs and the Corresponding Reflex Points at the Hands & Feet.

The Reflex Points at the face.

Giving pressure with the thumb and finger at the points shown

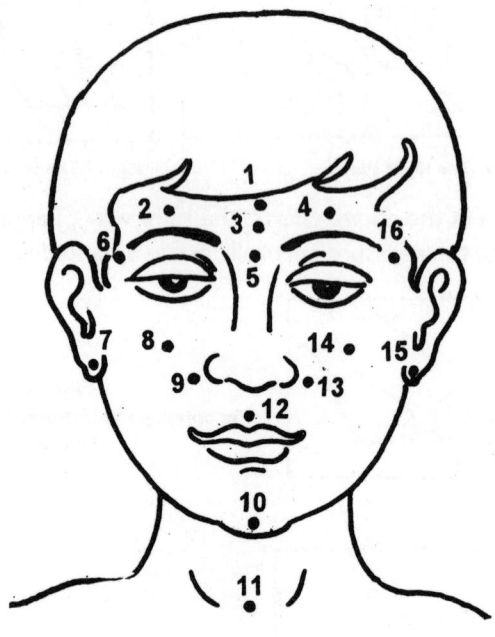

Fig. 21

above for about five to seven seconds would provide relief in the following ailments and disorders:

1, Menstrual troubles

2, 4, 8, 9, 13, and 14 catarrh-head cold.

3. Pelvis troubles

5, Headache, giddiness

6, 16, Severe Headache

7, 15, Sleep disturbance, palsy/paralysis

10. Complaints related to menopause.

11. Throat cough, dyspepsia and Asthama

12. Tooth ache.

B.

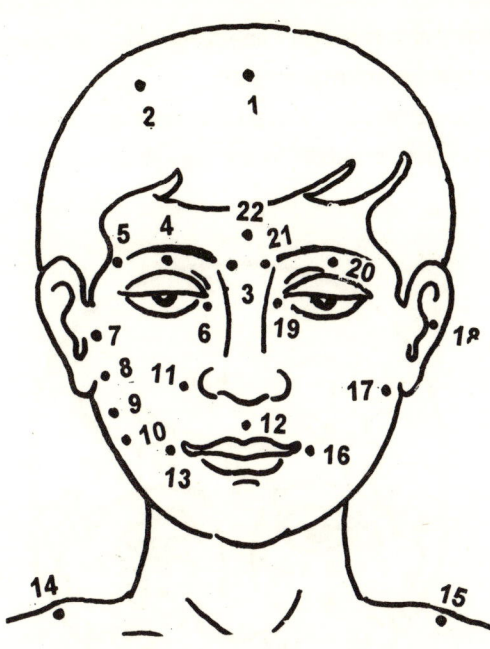

Fig. 22

The pressure should be applied mildly. One should never casually apply any pressure on the relex points. Apply pressure for five to seven seconds at the above shown points to get relief from the following troubles.

1. Piles, urinary bladder, Involuntary urination especially during sleep.

2. Double-vision-diplopia

3. 21. Mental disorders, cold-catarrh and insomnia.

4. 20. Sciatica-related problems, head, liver and stomach problems.

5. Eye troubles (exactly at this point on the left hand side)

6. 14, 15 and 19. Problems connected with eyes.

7. Humming voice echoing in the ears.

8. 9. Palsy-paralysis, mental tension.

9. 17. Toothache.

11. Obstruction felt in the nose, nasal discharge (exactly at this point on the left also)
12. Palsy-paralysis, recurrent sneezing, unconsciousness, epilepsy.
13. 16. Toothache, mental tension
18. High blood pressure, frozen shoulder and bodyache.
22. Eye-problems, troubles in the legs, stomach disorders.

C.

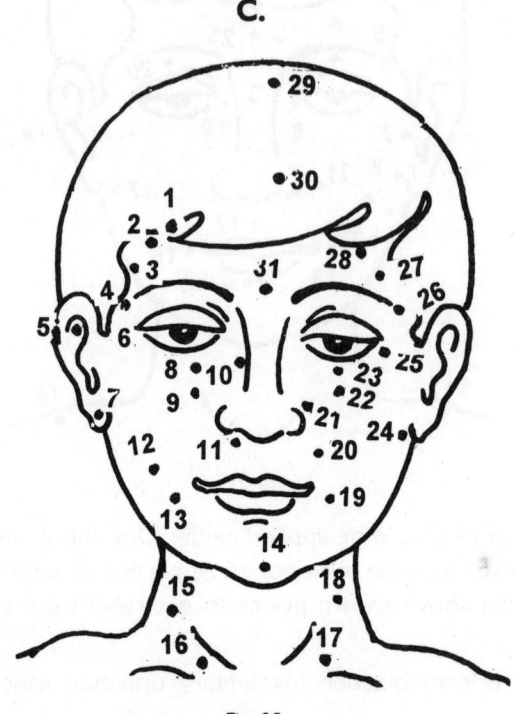

Fig. 23

Apply pressure for five to seven seconds at the above shown points. to get relief from the following troubles.

1. To revive memory and cure dementia.
2. To cure sciatica nerve related problems.
3. 25. Gastric problems.
4. Liver ailments.
5. Troubles related to blood circulation.
6. 24. Goiter problems.

7. Palsy-paralysis.
8. Kidney problems
9.14 and 22. Constipation
11. Pancrea related complaints
12.13. Problems related to the right lung.
15.18. Sex-stimulation related problems.
16.17. Abdominal problems.
19.20. Problems related to the left lung.
23. Kidney troubles
26. Spleen-related problems.
27. Heart ailments
28. Sciatica nerve related problems.
29. Shooting Headache.
30. Problems related to reproductive organs.
31. General Headache.

Reflex Points At the Ear

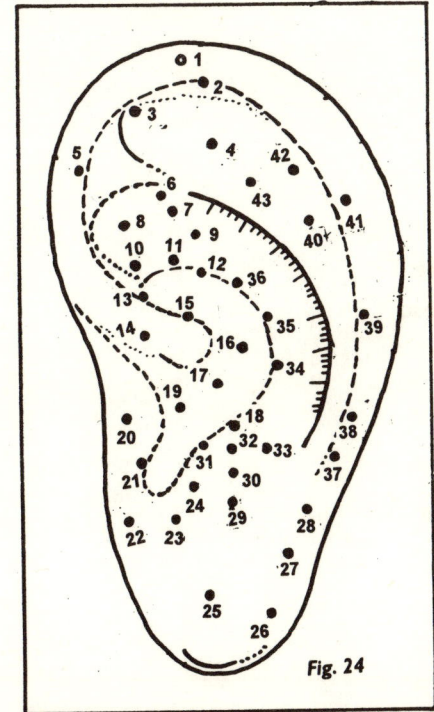

Fig. 24

These pressure points relate to the problems/ diseases given below. The reflex points corresponding to liver, stomach and appendix trouble exist only on the right ear while the corresponding points for the spleen problems exist only on the left ear. Applying pressure for five to seven sconds bring relief to the following troubles.

1. Tonsils
2. Appendix
3. Heel
4. Knee joints
5. High blood pressure
6. Asthma
7. Hip joints
8. Sciatic nerve
9. Buttocks.
10. Urinary Bladder
11. Ureter
12. Kidney
13. Deudonum
14. Rectum
15. Small Intestines
16. Bronchus region
17. Lungs
18. Lungs
19. High Blood Pressure
20. Inside portion of nose
21. Eyes
22. Eyes
23. Ovaries
24. Eyes
25. Inside portion of ear
26. Upper Jaw
27. Lower Jaw
28. Lungs
29. Testicles

30. Asthama
31. Cerebullum region
32. Toothache
33. Liver
34. Spleen
35. (i) Pancreas
    (ii) Gallblader
36. Neck
37. Shoulder joint
38. Shoulders
39. Abdomen
40. Elbow
41. Knee joint
42. Hip joint

Leakage of the Bio-electricity :

Human body is not only a unique machine but a store-house of infinite energy too. This energy, called bio-electricity in the 'acu-parlance' gets dissipated everday owing to age and other factors. This dissipation is on account of its leakage. This leakage accentuates the process of aging and hence the body gets afflicted with a variety of diseases. There is only one reflex point in the entire body-on the right

Fig. 25

forearm about midway between the wrist and elbow (see the chart). This reflex point covers about one square inch area. If we start giving regular pressure on it just for a minute's duration every morning we can always plug this leakage of the bio-electricity and ensure a happier, healtheir and longer life. This point is not difficult to locate. Apply pressure at this point regularly for about a week and see the change in your life. One week would be sufficient time for you to judge it's beneficial effect. Then you can continue this practice not only for staying healthy but also for preventing the diseases afflicting your body.

The Reflex Point To Immediately Revive consciousness of an unconscious person.

This is an almost miraculous point. If a person has lost consciousness due to shock, exhaustion or any other reason, gently apply pressure on the last two fingers of both the hands with a mild kneading style. The person's consciousness would be immediately revived. The moment he or she is conscious, make him or her drink a little of water and ask the person to keep lying for about a couple of minutes more. Then he would be normal. This is a tried and tested technique and invariably found very effective. Follow the method as shown in the accompanying chart. Massage these points from top to bottom while applying gentle pressure with your thumb and finger.

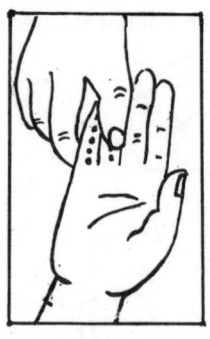

Fig. 26

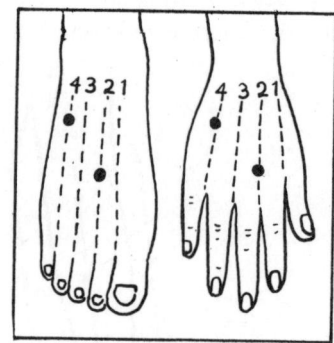

Fig.27

Referral Pain Points:

The speciality of this technique lies in removing the pain of the part without even touching it. Giving counter pressure at the corresponding point the pain can be easily removed. This technique is known as referral pain point technique. According to this principle of pain removal the corresponding reflex point on the opposite limb (hand-feet etc.) is determined (see the chart.). Then giving pressure on that counter point the pain in the affected limb is removed.

Various Objects To Apply Pressure

Besides thumb and fingers some other objects have also been devised to apply pressure at the precise reflex points. These gadgets

Fig. 28

are made of rubber solid plastic etc. The no one object is a kind of rolling pin. This object is used to apply pressure on soles and other points. Owing to its versatile use it is also called 'Jimmi'. The other object is a rubber ball like thing with protrusion. It is also called Acupressure magic massager owing to its very efficacious use. When these objects are not being used to apply pressure and you are using only your thumb and fingers the right way of applying pressure is shown in Fig 29.

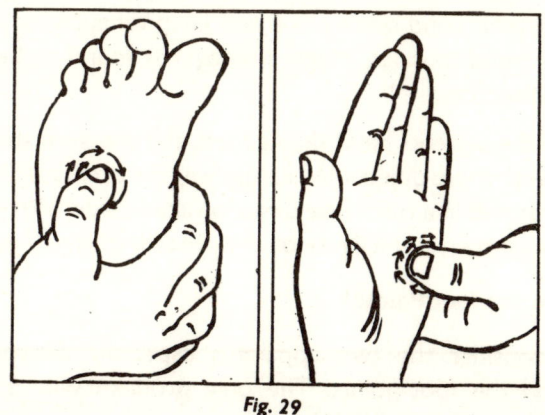

Fig. 29

As is shown in the figure while applying pressure the thumb should be moved in clockwise direction for activating the reflex points more effectively.

Fig. 30

The pressure with the magic massager could be applied in two ways: either simultaneous pressure in both the hands by placing the magic massager in between or separately. In the first way, place the massager in both the hands and press it for five to seven seconds at the required reflex points. While giving pressure the massager should also be gently rotated in the hands. When giving pressure at the reflex point one by one, at one hand hold the massager and move it gently by pressing it with your hand. This kind of pressure technique is especially effective for those patients who are afflicted with pavasis or palsy - as is normally. the cases are. They should keep on holding the magic massager in their hand one by one and keep on applying pressure to revive their hand muscles. Magic massager is found to be especially effective in their case.

In case the patients hand skin is hard, the pressure should always be applied with these objects. While applying the pressure these objects should be rotated in a clockwise direction like you do with your thumb and finger-as shown in the figure on the preceding page (figure No.29).

Pressure on the foot Points

Now consider the two apparatus especially designed to give pressure on the foot-points. The only problem with these is the

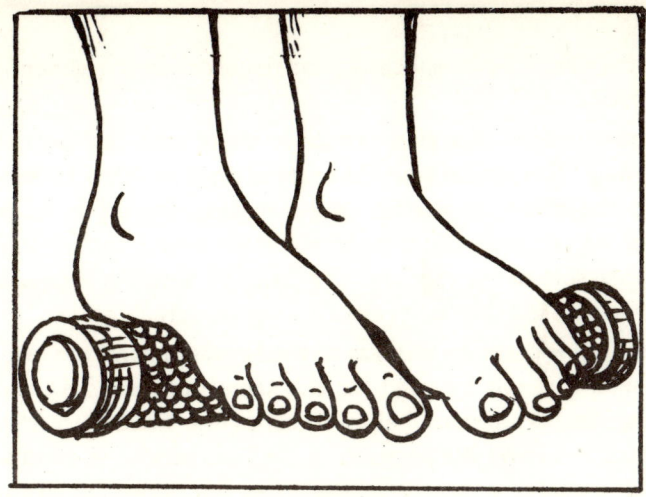

Fig. 31

pressure given by them is not pin-pointed.

The first object is a kind of rolling pin with tiny protrusions. It is specially designed in such a way that each point on the foot may receive the pressure when the patient is asked to press it by his foot or he or

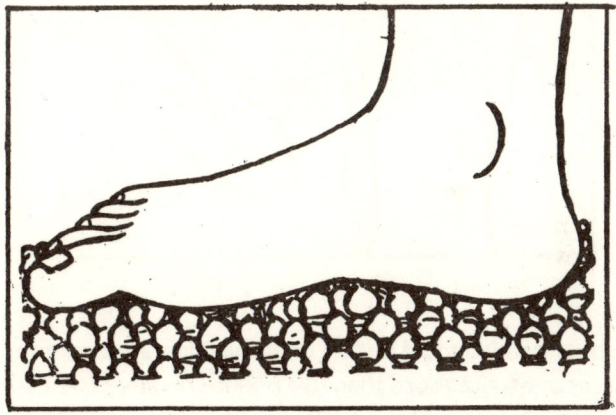

Fig. 32

she may stand on it. The ideal way is to make the patient sit on a comfortable sofa or chair and press the rolling pin with small protrusions by his foot one by one. He or she may also stand on it in case an intense pressure at each point is required. This rolling pin should be used in a variety of way for early cure. Rolling it on the heel by holding it in the hand is also a good way of giving extra pressure on the required reflex points on the heel. This is especially good to cure stomach ailments and reduce obesity.

The other object is a kind of rubber sheet with tiny protrusion spread all over. The patient should just stand on it for 10 to 15 minutes every day. This sheet can also be used in making slippers or shoes for the patient. After the slipper is made put sheet over it and get it glued on the upper sole of the slippers. The patient's wearing it casually at home would give the desired pressure automatically.

Besides giving pressure this way to the fingers of hand and feet, the rubber bands can also be used for the same purpose. This sort of pressure application is found helpful in curing the ailments connected with the face and mind like paralysis of the face, headache, toothache, eye and ear troubles, gout and the like. How the rubber bands should be tied at the fingers and toes is shown below.

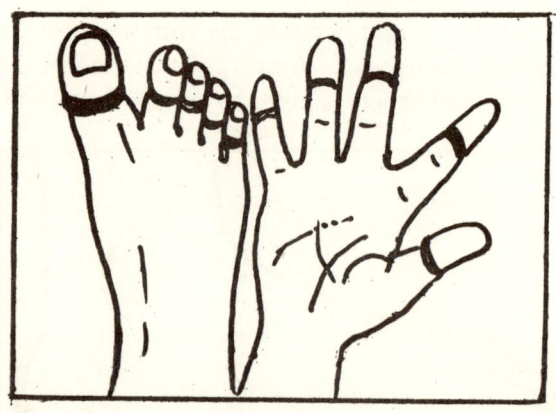

Fig. 33

The rubber bands should be tied over the fingers and toes for about one to five seconds, not more than five minutes in any case. Make sure that the colour of the tip of the fingers or toes does not start turning blue, indicating the stopped supply of the blood to these portions. Remove the rubber bands before the tips start turning blue. Having removed the rubber band massage the end points of the toes and finger gently in order to restore the normal supply of blood.

Instead of the rubber bands the clips which are used to hold the clothes when they are dried could also be used. It is better to use to plastic clips instead of the metal clips as the former sometimes creates the wound on the end parts of the fingers. How these fingers are to be clipped is shown below.

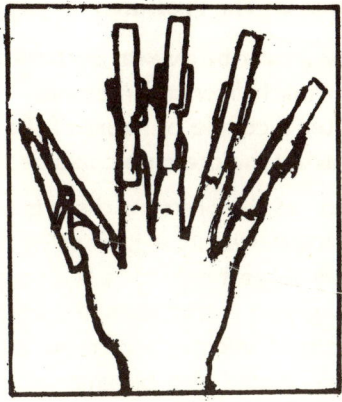

Fig. 34

Although the above mentioned methods-using clips and rubber bands are useful yet most effective ones are the ones that use jimmy or the rubber pointed rolling pins. It is observed that initially people have their concerned parts swollen or the reflex points in the hands and feet start aching. It is because the crystals (foreign material) are forced to leave the points they were stationed at, causing somewhat vaccum in which the accumulated air creates counter pressure to give the feeling of pain or swelling. This is a natural consequence and should not cause any unwanted worry. The best course is to stop giving pressures at those points for a day or two. Then the pressures could be applied and there would not be any swelling or feeling of pain.

How Much Pressure Is To Be Given:

This is very vital to ascertain before giving the pressure. Normally the pressure should be as much as to reach the reflex points below the skin. It should be neither very intense nor very mild. Initially the pressure applied should be minimum. The moment swelling comes up or the reflex point starts aching, it should mean that the pressure is reaching the desired reflex point. Then after, giving a gap of a day or two the same amount of pressure should be applied. The provision should also be made for the texture of the skin and natural tenacity of the part the pressure being applied at. The points on the knees, ankles do require somewhat intense pressure to activate the reflex points. Some parts which are fleshy, like the heel etc. should bear more intense pressure.

The Time And Duration Of The Pressure:

Normally the pressure can be given at any time but there are certain points- like close to stomach, liver and intestines—where the pressure should be exerted after a couple of hours of the person's taking his meals. After light breakfast the pressure could be applied immediately.

About the duration of the pressure there is a wide difference of opinion. While some acupressurists suggest giving the pressure for one to nine minutes, others suggest only for a few seconds. However, the author's considered opinion is that normal duration of the pressure should be between 2 to 7 minutes and in no case for more than 9 minutes. This pressure should also be given after some gaps if the patients feel uncomfortable. To children one to five minutes continuous pressure should be more than sufficient. However, the frequency could be about three to four times a day. In case of adults the duration should be 5 to 9 minutes and the frequency should be about 5 to 6 times a day.

Like in everything, excess is bad in acupressure treatment. Giving more pressure than required is as counter-productive as giving less pressure. The accupressurists would know by his experience the optimum amount of pressure required or the optimum duration of the pressure. As for the time of giving the pressure, the ideal time is morning when the stomach is empty. Avoiding the time immediately after the patient's having his or her meal or immediately after his or her doing physical strenuous job would be better. Initially the pressure session should be ideally of two minutes after a gap for 10 to 15 minutes. The frequency could be three to four time, depending clearly upon the response from the reflex points and the feeling of well being of the patients. The patient must feel more cheerful after each session, not withstanding the mild feeling of pain. If the patient feels drowsy or monose, the acupressurist should reconsider the reflex points for giving the pressure as apparently the result is not encouraging. In the case of kidney or heart ailment the gap between the application of pressure ought to be more than the normal. Then the time, duration and frequency of the pressure application should be enhanced according to the observation of the desired response.

Some Guiding Principles for Applying the Pressure

(i) As far as possible the place selected for giving the pressure should be airy and clean.

(ii) The patient must keep his or her body in a totally relaxed way before receiving the pressure. The patient should not feel nervous and tense. It is the duty of the acupressurist to see that the patient feels normal and relaxed. Soft background music is found to be quite conducive to make the patient feel relaxed and composed.

(iii) The patient should apply a little of talcum power or some soft cream or perfumed oil on the parts selected for the pressure application. The helps in applying pressure at the right reflex point. Normally application of dry powder is found to be better because the application of oil or cream makes the skin rather slippery which prevents the pin-point application of the pressure. However, this depends upon the choice of the acupressurist or the aesthetic liking of the patient. Some physicians prefer oil or cream especially in those parts which have become rather rough, like the sole of the feet or the mounts at the base of the fingers.

(iv) Before applying the pressure the acupressurist must ensure that his own nails are not over grown. Over grown nails give unwanted pain on the desired pressure points. The nails of the acupressurist should be well cut and his hands should also be clean.

(v) Although acupressure is an effective treatment to cure all sorts of diseases and disorders, yet in case of the heart/kidney or liver ailments it is always advisable to consult the family physician of the patient. It is chiefly for ensuring no untoward psychological effect on the patient as also to assess the mental and physical condition of the patient likely to be treated through acupressure technique.

(vi) While applying pressure to treat the pregnant ladies, care should be taken to avoid those points which have any relation with the woman's reproductive organs. In such case any pressure on the woman's stomach or breast region may have an adverse effect.

(vii) Similar precaution is to be taken while treating a patient having any fractured bone in the body. In those regions direct pressure should not be applied.

(viii) Acupressure treatment is ineffective to treat the contagious diseases. Such patients should be treated by the normal physicians and not by acupressurists.

(ix) The acupressurist must never forget that the human body is one integral entity. Many a time the real cause of the trouble is manifest through clear symptoms. So while applying pressure on the concerned parts the acupressurist should also apply pressure at the relevant points in the palm or sole of the portion in order to avoid disturbing the 'harmony' of the body.

(x) The acupressurist must advice his patient that following a strict dietary regimen is a precondition to ensure speedy recovery. Excessive intake of sugar, fats, alcohol can always supply the desired effect of the acupressure treatment. It is always advisable to plug the holes through which the bio-energy might escape before controlling its effect on the desired points.

(xi) There are some diseases or disorders in which total rest is recommended-like the sciatic trouble or the problem connected with spine. In such cases the acupressurist must also stop the treatment temporarily to allow natural recovery.

(xii) Of course this pressure on the desired points can be given at any time or place-even while the patient watching a movie or travelling-but it is better if the pressure is applied when the patient is stationary. Sitting at home is the ideal condition.

(xiii) It must be understood that acupressure treatment not only ensures cure to various ailment but it is also a very good preventive treatment as well. Even when you are well, taking pressure at the well appointed reflex points occasionally would also ensure your keeping yourself free of any trouble. These pressures the healthy person can himself exert on the few selected points (like the one at the middle of the forearm) to keep all physical trouble at bay.

(xiv) Acupressure not only treats your body but also your mind. Taking pressure at the desired points would not only keep you cheerful and free of worries but would help you in concentrating your mind and fully activating your mental faculties.

(xv) For self-treatment the person is not required to have the full medical knowledge of his entire body. The knowledge of the right points and right technique to apply pressure would serve the purpose admirably.

(xvi) It is advisable that while treating any disorder or ailment the acupressurist must apply mild pressure regularly on those points that correspond to the nervous system of the patient. The pressure point at the thumb (top phalanx) and the base of the big toe are the ideal sites to apply regular pressure besides applying pressure on the points corresponding to the disordered part. [Pressure points on the hands and feet which correspond to nervous system and spine region of the body.]

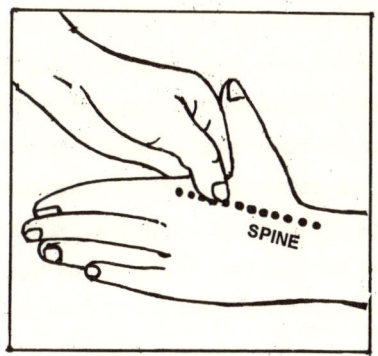

Fig. 35

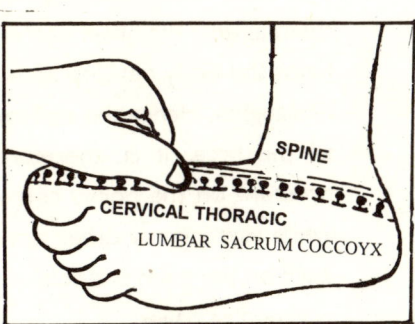

Fig. 36

Other two points are shown in the above diagrams.

(xviii) Almost all acupressurist emphasise on the 'solar plexus' (Naabhi Chakra) or diaphragm's retaining their normal position. It is these two regions of the body that maintain the total equilibrium of the body. If these two are displaced the body cannot be healthy. Hence all the seasoned acupressurists aver that while treating any

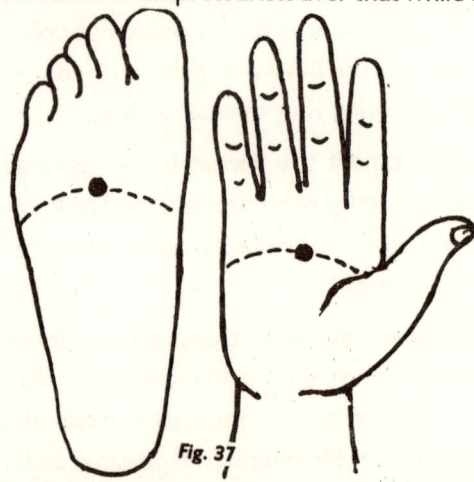

Fig. 37

part of the body the points corresponding to these two regions should be regularly given pressure. The two points corresponding to the 'solar plexus' and diaphragm are shown above.

(xix) Human body's lymphatic system secretes a kind of fluid called the tissue fluid which not only nourish the body organs and protects them against the onset of the various virus and bacterias but also helps the body develop its natural resistive power against these onslaughts. Hence this system of the body must be kept fortified all the time. It is, therefore, advisable to exert simultanous pressure on the points corresponding to the lymphatic system while treating any other ailment or disorder. These points also exist on the palm and sole as shown in the figure 6 and 7 on the preceeding pages.

(xx) As has been repeatedly stressed, acupressure treatment has no side effect whatever. Moreover, it is also compatible with any other style of treatment. It ensures only benefit and no loss or damage of any kind.

The Three Metal's Potable Drink (Tridhaatu peya)

Acupressure is almost a miraculous way of curing the diseases and disorders. In order to cure certain chronic ailment, if this treatment is accompanied by this special potion made from the concoction of the three metals, residual water-left after boiling this treatment becomes more efficacious and cures the ailments at a faster pace.

It is said that in the feudal times the kings and princes used to eat food and drink water in utensils made of silver and gold. They would eat various jams and jellies (Murabba) having the garnishing of the silver and gold foils. Even now the Ayurveda school of medicine uses a variety of Bhasmas and Avaleha having prescribed amount of gold and silver. These metals-rather their use in the kitchen—not only signify the affluence but they are very conducive to keep the body in good trim provided they are made so that the body is able to absorb them.

Each of these precious metals have their properties which show their conducive effect on the human body. Their effects, in brief are listed below.

(a) Gold: The absorption of this metal by the body is very helpful in checking and curing all diseases connected with the respiratory disorder—like asthma, short of breath, bronchal trouble, lung-ailment and heart troubles. Its intake in the prescribed quantity is also helpful to cure even certain mental and nervous disorders.

(b) Silver: The prescribed intake of silver is especially helpful in curing the diseases connected with digestive disorders. It strengthens stomach, liver, spleen, prevents raw mucus formation and generally helps body to digest the food easily.

(c) Copper: This is especially helpful in curing the body-joint disorders like arthritis gout, polio, leprosy, blood pressure related troubles, mental tension and even palsy or paralysis.

These three metals, potion is good for all—whether the drinker be a child or a grown up person. Those who have this potion regularly while undertaking the acupressure treatment recover more quickly than the ones who resort to only acupressure treatment.

The Method of Preparing This Potion:

(i) Take a gold ornament or any object of gold of about 10 to 20 grams. weight. While taking the gold ornament for this purpose, see that it has no gem or stone embedded or having too many joints.

(ii) Take about 20 to 50 gms. of pure silver piece having nothing embedded into it. You could also use some silver ware of the desired weight.

(iii) Take about 40 to 50 gms. of pure copper coins or any utensil or object made of pure copper. Avoid taking the copper wires used in electrical wiring as they are not found conducive to making this potion. You could have pure piece of copper from the goldsmiths. It is easily available with them and doesn't cost much either.

Every morning clean the three metal pieces throughly. Now put about three to four cups of clean water in a stainless steel pan and put all the objects into it. Don't use silver or aluminium pans for this purpose. Allow the water to boil on the low fire till the water is reduced to just a cupful. Now remove all the metal pieces and strain water carefully through a clean white cloth of finer variety like the muslin cloth. Allow this water to cool a bit Now this three metals potion is ready for your drinking it. In case the patient's ailment is of long standing, boil the water as much as only 1/2 cupfull remains. Then it would have enhanced potency. In the evening you can prepare this potion afresh. This potion should be drunk fresh. It should not be used for the next day. Even keeping it in the fridge would make it ineffective. While hosing the gold, silver and copper piece make sure that you are using the metal piece in their purest and not in the adulterated form.

Caution: When drinking this metals stop eating all sour things including lemon or curds. This is a very potent potion. In case you are not able to get pure pieces of the three metals, it is advisable to have the potion made of Anwala (fruit of Embtio Mynobalan).

The way of preparing Anwala potion is almost similar. Take fresh Anwala fruits (you can take old piece also but ensure that they are clean and not eaten by the insects). While putting these Anwala fruits in three-four cups of clean water, put about half a spoonful ground ginger paste also into it. Now allow this water to boil till only one cupful of water remains Now strain, cool and drink it after adding half a spoonful of honey also. It should be taken when it is lukewarm. This potion is also very good for the body. It immediately restores the body vitality. Persons of all age groups can take it alongwith their acupressure treatment to derive speedy benefit. It is not necessary to have these tonics immediately before or after the acupressure sessions. They should be ideally taken early in the morning and late in the evening.

Although acupressure is not a supportive but an independent style of treatment, yet resorting to external regimen by the patient concerning his diet and other habits is very helpful in this style of treatment.

The Pressure (Reflex) Points and Their Corresponding Body Organs

. **Location of The Reflex Points**

   1. Elbow Point 1:— Located at the depression of the end of the fold which appears when the elbow is bent 90° and raised to the horizontal position.

   2. Elbow Point 2:— Located in the elbow fold, on the radial side of the biceps. The point is on the elbow crease at the outside (lateral) portion of the tendon.

   3. Elbow Point 3:— Located by bending the elbow part away and

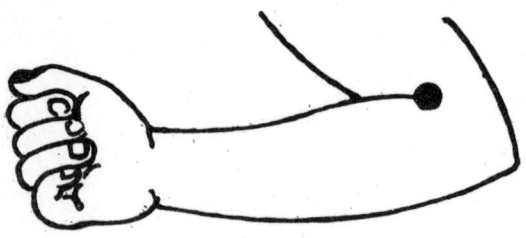

Fig. 38

locating the biceps tendon, which is the thick bend you feel in the middle of the front of the elbow. The point lies under the elbow crease at the inside (medial) portion of the tendon.

4. Elbow Point 4:— Located at the indentation near the inside elbow fold next to the tendon on the inside of the upper arm; the end of the crease is where the elbow point is located.

5. Elbow Point 5:— Located by bending the elbow and feeling for the depression two finger breadths above the point of the elbow on the backside. The point is located at the centre of the depression.

6. Back Point 1:— Exact location is between second and third lumbar vertebrae, just behind navel. To make their location easy, remember that these points are located on each side of the spinal column, each point lying about two finger breadths to the side of the middle of the spinal column. Points are located at the same level as the bottom of the rib cage.

7. Back Point 2:— Located by bending neck slightly and noting prominent vertebral bone protruding at the base of the neck. Counting it as one, count down five vertebral spines (spines to the backbone). In between the fifth and sixth spine and two fingerbreadths to each side of the centre of the backbone lies the points.

8. Back Point 3:— Located beneath the tip of the tail bone, about a finger breadth below the dividing line of the buttocks.

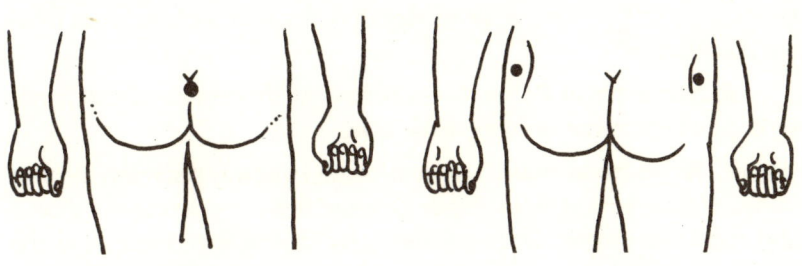

Fig. 39   Fig. 40

9. Back Point 4:— Located by standing slightly on tip toes and noting the depression formed at the sides of the buttocks. The point is located in the centre of the depression or ring.

10. Back Point 5:— Located at the midpoint of the crease the lower end of the buttocks makes with the thigh. If using acupressure

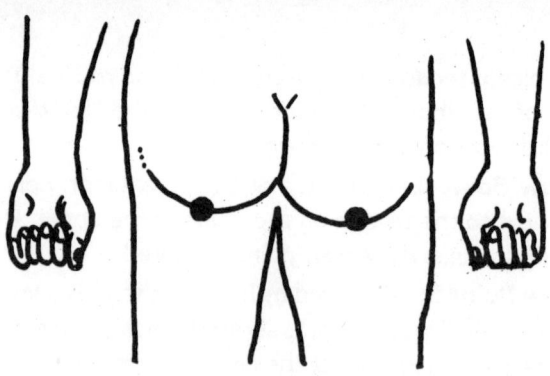

Fig. 41

technique then apply greater pressure as this part is very tender. The basic guideline in using this technique is: unless the site is unusually tender, deep strong pressure, rotating the finger when useful, is required.

11. Wrist-hand Point 1:— Located on the thumb side of the wrist just above the projection of bone—just above the thumb side of the wrist. It can be found by placing the hands together with middle and first finger forming 'V' and both the hands are touching each other in over hand-touch style.

12. Wrist-hand Point 2:— Located on the back of the wrist at about the middle of the wrist at the flexion crease.

13. Wrist-hand Point 3:— Located on the first crease of the wrist towards small finger side when the fingers are fully stretched. Its exact location could be found at seven eighth of the width of the wrist from the thumb side.

14. Wrist-hand Point 4:— Located at the centre of the hand-wrist junction crease on the palmar side.

15. Wrist-hand Point 5:— It is located midway between the two bones of thumbs and index finger. One can find it by closing the thumb and the index finger. One can find it by closing the thumb and the forefinger together and noticing the little mound that forms at their junction on the back of the hand. The point lies under the peak of the little mound. Alternatively, it can also be found by bending the thumb of the other hand over the web between the thumb and the index finger. It lies under the end of the thumb.

16. Wrist-hand Point 6:— Located under the thumb side of the index finger. One finger-breadth below the base of the finger at the mid point of the side of the hand.

17. Wrist-hand Point 7:— It is located in the web between the little finger and the ring finger on the backside. The wrist-hand point 7 should be pressed at a 45° angle toward the hand, the point being approached from the top of the hand.

18. Wrist-hand Point 8:— Located on the side of the hand one finger-breadth above the base of the little finger.

19. Wrist-hand Point 9:— Located under the side of the hand two finger-breadths above wrist point 8.

20. Wrist-hand Point 10:— Located on the backside of the forearm three finger-breadths from the middle of the wrist crease.

21. Wrist-hand Point 11:— Located on the palm side of the forearm three finger-breadhts from the middle of the wrist crease. Wrist-hand point 12 is located at the centre of the palm.

22. Knee Point 1:— When you bend your knees almost 90° from the thigh, you can find its location at the depression at the lower outside edge of the knee-cap.

23. Knee Point 2:— It is located in the muscle that runs on the outside of the thigh, two inches up from the knee-cap. Make the person sit on a chair and bend his leg at a 90° angle. Measure two inches up from the top of the knee cap. The point is slightly outside of the leg.

24. Knee Point 3:— You can locate it by bending the knee and finding the crease formed on the medial or inner aspect. The point is at the end of the crease.

25. Knee Point 4:— Located on the back portion of the knee exactly at the mid-point of the crease.

26. Knee Point 5:— Located at the top of the shinbone, on the inside of the leg. To make its location easier, place three fingers exactly below the protruded side-portion of the knee. To be precise, it is located at a level three finger-breadths below the lower level of the knee cap at the intersection of an imaginary line travelling vertically along the middlle of the side of the leg.

27. Knee Point 6:— Make the patient sit and bend his leg at a 90° angle. Catch the centre of his knee-cap with the centre of your palm. The tip of your thumb will touch knee point 6, two inches above the knee-cap. In fact it is located at a level three finger-breadths above the upper border of the knee-cap where an imaginary line travelling vertically up the middle of the inside of the thigh crosses that level.

28. Knee Point 7:— Located in front of and below the head of the fibula, which is the rounded knob located near the middle of the outside aspect of the leg at a level about two finger-breadths below the lower level of the knee cap. The point itself is located in the depressed area in front of and below the fibula head.

29. Ankle-foot Point 1:— Located in the centre of the ankle crease as one flexes his ankle.

30. Ankle-foot Point 2:— Located directly in front of the lowest level of the medial malleolus or the middle ankle bone (the rounded bone protruding from the ankle on the inner aspect).

31. Ankle-foot Point 3:— Located one finger tip below the medial malleolus or the middle ankle bone (the rounded bone protruding from the ankle on the inner aspect, or the 'Gutta'—as it is called in Hindi).

32. Ankle-foot Point 4:— Located in the depression in the back of the medial malleolus (at the 'Gutta').

33. Ankle-foot Point 5:— Located in the depression in the back of the lateral malleolus.

Of these ankle-foot points, point 3 has a greater use in the area of foot and ankle injuries, but ankle-foot point 4 which lies opposite two ankle foot point 5 can be grasped ankle-foot point 5 (index finger on one and thumb on the other) and this area is not a tender area.

34. Ankle-foot Point 6:— Located four finger-breadths above the medial malleolus or the inner rounded ankle bone at the middle of the inside aspect of the leg. Another easy way of locating this point is to flex the person's foot and put his four fingers on the inside of his leg with little finger resting on top of the anklebone and the other fingers going up the leg. The point exists where the four finger lies, behind the shinbone.

35. Shoulder Point 1:— It is located on the outside of the shoulder bone. Have the person raise his bent elbow to an angle of 90° from the body. The indentation is easier to identify. It is located at the mid-point of the top of the outside arm just below the end of the shoulder bone.

36. Shoulder Point 2:— Located at the mid-point of the outside of the arm (upper arm) where the tip of the (upside down appearing) triangular deltoid muscle is.

37. Shoulder Point 3:— Located on the back of the shoulder above the armpit, in the soft tissue just below the bony top of the shoulder.

38. Shoulder Point 4:— Located on an imaginary line drawn from the tip of the shoulder to a point lying over the middle of the base of the back of the neck. The point is one third along that line from the shoulder.

39. Shoulder Point 5:— Located on an imaginary line drawn from the tip of the shoulder to a point lying over the middle of the base of the back of the neck. The point is on the mid point of that line.

40. Shoulder Point 6:— Located on an imaginary line drawn from the tip of the shoulder to a point lying over the middle of the base of the neck. The point is one-third along that line from the neck.

41. Neck Point 1:— Located just above the strenal notch or just above the breast bone where the soft tissue of the front of the neck begins. The site is directly under tip of index finger.

42. Neck Point 2:— This point is located by bending the neck slightly and noting prominent bone at the base of the neck. Point is located just below this prominent vertebral spine in the space in between it and the next lower vertebral or backbone spine.

43. Neck Point 3:— This point is located just below the first cervical vertebral located on each side of the spine at the natural level of the hair line, each point being one finger-breadth to the side of the spine.

44. Penis Point:— Located in the mid-point of the base of the penis at its junction with the scrotum.

45. Face Point 1:— Located on the centre of the forehead midway between the eyebrows.

46. Face Point 2:— Located on each side of the forehead at the middle edge of the eyebrows.

47. Face Point 3:— Located on each side of the forehead at the outer edge of the eyebrows.

48. Face Point 4:— Located on each side of the forehead one finger-breadth lateral to the eyebrow in the temple are a.

49. Face Point 5:— Located on side of the face by opening the mouth wide and feeling the depression formed in front of the ears at the top of the ear lobe level. Apply pressure when mouth is closed.

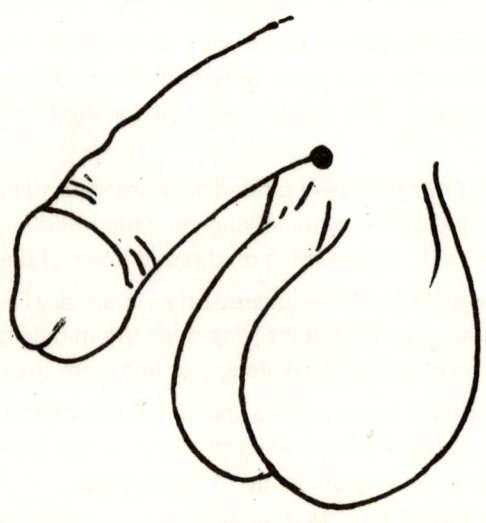

Fig. 42

50. Face Point 6:— Located under the pupil of each eye just below the lower border of the eye-socket.

51. Face Point 7:— Located just to the side of the base of the nose on each side.

52. Face Point 8:— Located on each side of the face just above the point that the angle of the jaw makes.

53. Face Point 9:— Located over the centre of the nose just above the tip.

54. Face Point 10:— Located midway between the bottom of the nose and the top of the upper lip.

55. Face Point 11:— Behind the ear lobe just in front of the rounded mastoid bone.

56. Abdomen Point 1:— Located by placing the fingers of the left hand together and straight, then placing the tip of the index finger by the umbilicus just below the web between the ring finger and little finger lies the point.

57. Abdomen Point 3:— Located two breadths below the umbilicus.

58. Abdomen Point 4:— Located in the middle of the abdomen, one and a half inches below the navel four finger breadths below the umbilicus.

59. Leg Point 1:— Located four finger-breadth below the lower level of the knee cap and about one finger-breadth to the outside of the skin bone in the soft tissue there.

60. Leg Point 2:— At the lower tip of the calf muscle in the vertical midline of the back of the leg. It is located roughly in the centre of the leg just at the centre of the swollen portion of the shin.

61. Chest Point 1:— Measure two inches from the nipple (in the direction of the arm). Count up three ribs. The point is between the first and second ribs from the top, one inch below the middle of clavicle the collarbone.

62. Chest Point 2:— Located between sixth and seventh ribs, directly under the nipple. Other way of finding them is by detecting two ribs below the nipple on about a vertical line travelling through the middle of the natural position of the nipple (in a woman lying on her back with the breast positioned so that it is symmetrical with the nipple in the middle).

B. Ailments and Their Cure By Pressing The Corresponding Reflex Points

Listed below are some common ailments which can be cured by following acupressure treatment. However, it is advisable to seek guidance of an expert acupressurist in using these methods to cure the following ailments. If the right point is pressed the cure could be hundred percent.

1. Asthma, Cough and Hiccoughs:— Asthma is a disorder of the respiratory system characterised by severe paroxyms of difficult breathing. The onset of an attack is sudden, though the patient starts feeling uneasy, drowsy and irritable a little before the difficulty of breathing starts. Respiration becomes difficult and the breath comes with a wheezing and sometimes whistling sound. The general belief is that asthma is a chronic disease and that once gotten continues to dog its victim till the day he dies. The allopathic doctors believe that it is due to allergy in most cases. Whatever be the 'genre' of this disease, these techniques assure almost a miraculous cure from these respiratory disorders. But these conditions should be treated only under the guidance of some acupressurist. However, after a diagnosis and with the physician's consent—or in an emergency while waiting for a physician to arrive—pressure, massage or puncture over these sites may be beneficial and conducive to speedy relief.

Press 'Chest Point 1' on the both sides and massage it. Additionally, 'Elbow Point 2' and 'Wrist-hand Point 1' may also be pressed and massaged unilaterally or bilaterally. Other Points that may be pressed are 'Neck Point 2'. 'Back Point 6' is especially useful for cough if pressed bilaterally. For hiccoughs 'Back Point 6' should be pressed. Press it firmly and you will be surprised how often it works and gives the desired result. 'Wrist-hand Point 5' is also useful for asthma. For any individual who hopes to get relief from pressure points, there are numerous points to cure these respiratory disorders. You can apply pressure on these points by an experienced acupressurist and know by trial and error which points gives you maximum relief. 'Back Point 8' is also good to cure coughing and asthma.

2. Back Ailments:— Back ailments or backache may be due to many reasons. Disorders which cause it should be tackled first. Gout, constipation, a wrong posture and menstrual disorders of women can cause these troubles. Even the sports-people often complain about these troubles. Although golf playing is good for the aged persons, the back is invariably their target. The most important point to treat this is 'Back Point 1'. This is a trigger Point. These trigger points are points that are tender but are not acupuncture sites. A set of trigger points are 'Back Point 1' and provides the cure. It may not be overly effective for everyone but is an important point for low back pain. Sciatic-nerve's disorder are set right by pressing the 'Back Point 4' which is about three quarters of an inch in the back of the hip joint and obviously lies deep under the skin, and to stimulate it requires a fair degree of pressure and massage. The particular point is especially beneficial for sciatica, but is also very useful bilaterally for low back pain. Another deep point is 'Back Point 5', which can be used bilaterally. Again, unless the site is unusually tender deep strong pressure, rotating the finger when useful is required. 'Knee Point 4', 'Leg Point 2' and 'Ankle-foot Point 5' are also effective points in low back pain, even though they are extremity points. They should be used bilaterally. Pressing these points are good to cure sciatica, muscle spasm and tired legs. For tired legs pressing 'Leg Point 2' brings the desired results.

3. Bedwetting:—Voluntary urination during sleep is a common ailment with children and in medical parlance is known as enuresis. When it is involuntary it is also known as nocteria. Acupressure technique offers easy cure for this problem. The child's small-finger should be pressed for several minutes at his or her bed-time. The child should be asked to void his or her bladder at that time. Awaken the child again about midnight and again ask him or her to empty his bladder and again press the finger for several minutes. Repeat the procedure nightly until the child doesn't bedwet for an entire week.

4. Chest-pain:— Chest-pain can also surface due to a variety of reasons. It can be a symptom of the most serious illness with a fatal attack of heart disease, the rupture of a big blood vessel and even a simple of gas attack. Pressing 'Chest Point 2' is a good remedy for rib-pain or intercostal neuralgia. Use the point bilaterally with pressure and massage if the sufferer feels relief. Sometimes the sufferer himself begins to suppress his heart region. Pressing Wrist-hand Point 3 is very effective. 'Wrist-hand Point 10' also can be used in chest-pain including angina if permitted by your physician.

5. Excessive Sweating or Polyhydrosis:— Pressing Wrist-hand Point 12 can bring the desired relief. It should be pressed hard bilaterally to prevent sweating, especially of the type associated with nervousness and the menopause. Do it for 5 or 10 minutes either before an anticipated sweat or to stop it once it has started. 'Wrist-hand Point 5' can also be punctured or pressed. The two points may be pressed simultaneously, with the middle finger on 'Wrist-hand Point 12', and the thumb on 'Wrist-hand Point 5'. Push straight down on each point simultaneously for 10 to 15 seconds for quick relief.

6. Fainting:— Fainting is a common feature among certain persons who are basically of nervous temperament. Fainting means the blood supply to the brain is obstructed, albeit temporarily, which causes the person to lose his or her consciousness. 'Face Point 10' and 'Face Point 3' should be used to rouse a person in a faint. They could be pressed unilaterally and bilaterally. 'Face Point 10' also can be used alone or in conjuction with 'Face Point 9' to stifle a sneeze. As mentioned earlier, this point, 'Face Point 10' is located in the centre of the hollow just below the nose, on the upper lip.

Alternatively, removing the shoes and pressing hard on 'Ankle-foot Point 8' also may be used to revive a faint person's consciousness. It may be done bilaterally for best results.

7. Gout, Arthritis and Related Problems:— Gout is a disease of the joints and is a form of rheumatism. It is actually a constitutional disorder connected with excess of uric acid in the blood manifesting, itself by inflammation of joints with deposition of urate of soda and also by morbid changes in various important organs. Modern medicine believes gout or arthritis to be hereditary since it has been found in 50 to 80 percent of the cases that the patients, parents or grand parents suffered from the disease. The disease affects the sedantry persons more than those who lead active life, but it is not always true. On the other hand inadequate exercise, a luxurious manner of living, habitual over-indulgence in rich foods and especially in alcohol are the precipitating factors in the onset of the disease. But ironically, some teetotallers and vegetarians are also found to be victims of gout and arthritis. Arthritis has many forms and people suffer from it to various degrees. For the most part arthritis becomes worse as one ages, and the youth are not particularly involved with it unless they abuse themselves as some atheletes do, especially major league baseball pitchers and the like. Pressure can help the sufferer of arthiritis whether traumatic, rheumatoid or osteo. But the individual with severe impairment should not rely on pressure acupuncture or even needle acupuncture alone but should use it as adjunct therapy to more orthodox treatment as prescribed by his physician.

The ideal treatment for this is pressing 'Elbow Point 2', 'Elbow Point 3', Leg Point 1' and 'Leg Point 2' and Back Point 2 and 3'. Press these points and find for yourself which pressure brings in the maximum relief. Press these points with one thumb, avoiding any sudden pressure, for 7 to 10 seconds three times. Once maximum relief has been obtained, occasional pressure will keep the part in otimum repair and possibly reduce its susceptibility to reinjury.

8. Headaches Including Migraine:— Migraine is a recurring disorder in which headache—sometimes mild and relatively bearable by often severe and disabling—may be accompanied by a wide variety of symptoms which indicate temporary disturbance of brain function, particularly of those parts of the brain which are concerned with seeing speech and feeling. 'Face Point 4' is the commonly used temple area that becomes almost automatic to the headache sufferer. Other points are 'Face Point 1' 'Face Point 3' and often encountered 'Wrist-Hand 5'.

Pressure more than massage is beneficial in these cases but massage can be tried. Those sites are bilateral and should be used bilaterally. Migraine and headaches, once they get hold of an individual, go with extreme reluctance. Therefore, it must be emphasized to institute the treatment quickly. If the headaches are severe enough much effort must be taken to obtain relief. Help by a friend to press the wrist-hand sites while you press the face points is useful. Although medicines prescribed by a doctor may be necessary, yet in many such cases pressure acupuncture can be of enormous help either as the prime treatment or as an adjunct.

9. Impotence:— Impotence is the inability to perform the sexual act. It may be partial or complete, temporary or permanent. The affliction is not very uncommon and can be best categorised into organic and psychological. Organic impotence may be caused by lesions of the external genitalia, e.g., a tight foreskin, disturbances of the endocrine glands such as diminished activity of the gonads, thyroid gland, or pituitary gland; diseases of the central nervous system such as locomotor ataxia (disordered movement of the limbs in walking); any severe disturbance of health as diabetes, addiction to alcohol and the like. Among the psychological factors which give rise to impotence are ignorance, fear, weakness of sexual desire or abnormality of such desire.

In the case of organic impotence, the only way to treat is to deal with the disease which has caused it. If it is due to tightness of the foreskin, surgical help can be taken to free the glan penis or the folds of the prepuce. But most cases of imptence are, forunately be it said, of psychological origin. At the back of the mind of the person who complains inability to perform sexual act is a feeling of guilt which may have been engendered because of his having been addicted to masturbation in his adolescence or having fallen from his moral standard by indulging in incestuous or otherwise prohibited sexual relationships or some similar causes.

In such cases also, pressure and massage can be beneficial. It can be of greater value if the person afflicted remains calm and his partner uses restraint in criticising or showing contempt even by facial expressions. Pressing the 'Penis Ponit' is the key point. Pressure against it with rotatory massage can be used by either partner. Besides this Point, pressing 'Back Point 2', 'Knee Point 3', 'Knee Point 6', Ankle-foot Point 67', 'Abdomen Point 6', and 'Abdomen Point 4' are all useful points and should be tried. Remember to use those points bilaterally which are bilateral. Pressure and massage can both be used. Apply strong pressure except where a point may be particularly sensitive, like the 'Penis-Point'. Ten or even fifteen minutes should be devoted to the acupuncture sites. At that point an attempt at the conventional type of love play or stimulation should be made. But always bear in your mind that acupressure is not a form of love- play; it is a therapeutic effort to restore the proper balance in the nervous system so that an erection can take place. Pressure on these indicated points is not in itself a form of sex. It is used so that the conventional forms of sex which are not working at the time will start to work.

10. Insomnia and Anxiety:— In a way both the problems are inter-related or one can say that one tends to grow on what the other feeds to it. Sleep is a periodic resting condition of the body, especially of the nervous system and there is a natural rotaion of sleeping and waking every twenty four hours. But the modern medical science has not been able to explain—much less understand—the mechanics of this phenomenon. But it is a natural thing for a person to sleep and no body can do without it for long. Insomnia or sleeplessness, is a condition that often casuses annoyance, and depriving the person of natural rest produces interference with the full activity during the day time. When it becomes a habit, it may form a serious menace to health. And extreme anxiety also causes this stage often. Because you're anxious, you don't sleep well and because you are short on sleep your anxiety increases. It is a vicious circle and psychologically relief can only be expected when you break this circle. In acupuncture and acupressure therapy, there is much hope for the sufferers of this syndrome.

Although insomnia is a problem that confronts everyone from time to time. For some it is completely agonising experience, requiring heavy reliance on sedatives. Pressure on the acupuncture sites can be of benefit. The points are 'Wrist-hand Point 3', 'Wrist-hand Point 5', and the 'Face Point 4'. And since wrist- hand points lie in close proximity to each other both points can be pressed simultaneously. Use the thumb on the 'Wrist-hand Point 3'. Also the same wrist-hand site can be pressed on each side simultaneously. Apply hard pressuure for seven minutes, then relax. When you grow tired and weary of pressing the hand points, try 'Face Point 4' bilaterally which have already been discussed as the migraine point. Do it in a relaxed manner and forget that you are indulging in some therapeutic practice. Do it at your leisure or while reading a light book. If you do in a relaxed manner, you won't be able to count even ten sheeps before you fall asleep. 'Neck Point 3' also brings relief soon and if you press it bilaterally with massage plus the three preceding points, you won't need any tranquiliser for sleeping. And when you sleep well your anxiety will automatically be lessened and cured.

11. Obesity:— Obesity means being fat disproportionately. Obesity or corpulence is a condition of the body charactersized by over accumulation of fat under the skin and around certain integral organs. While the state of health differs from person to person, other things being equal, the normal observation is: the fatter the person, the slower he will be. It has been proved from experience that the obese have a greater chance of dying early than those of average weight. Obesity has two main cause for its existence. It could be a hereditary phenomenon, or due to the disturbance of some of the endocine glands, like the thyroid, pituitary and the sex glands. The more immediate cause is over-feeding and excess of indulgence in sexual delights, eating a lot of rich food and not doing any 'exercise to burn the body-fat'.

Using acupressure sites is a recent entry into this area and is presently the subject of research. With pressure there has been an initial success with some extremely difficult patients. Using the technique of acupressure has also brought quite favourable results. The key point to get rid of this trouble is 'Abdomen Point 1' on the left side, overlying the stomach. It must be pressed deeply. Massage is not required. 'Leg Point 1' can also be used on both legs, or on one leg. If using the two points is cumbersome, one also works well enough. In general, the way obesity points should be utilized is at the time one feels hungry. The most effective points should be pressed for several minutes. The ones that work best ought to be discovered for each individual by himself by trial and error or by constant experimentation.

As far as curbing the food intake or appetite is concerned, the ears are also beneficial in curbing it. Simply place the index fingers into the ears, pressing over the points. A fair amount of pressure ought to be used even if it is a little unpleasant. If you do it regualarly before your meals, you are bound to eat less than what you normally eat.

12. Menstrual Problems:— Menstruation is a periodic change occuring in human beings and higher apes, and consists chiefly in a flow of blood from the cavity of the womb, and is associated with various slight constitutional disturbance. The duration of the menstrual period varies from two to eight days and is a regular process in the majority cases. The interval between the two periods is generally 20 to 30 days. Menstruation ceases between the ages of 45 and 50. The final stoppage is known as menopause or the grand climacteric. But menstrual problems are a plague for many women whether it is the agony of premenstrual tension or the inconvenience of exccess or irregular flow. As an adjunct treatment to main medical treatment, these techniques render great help in curing it. The first point is 'Ankle-foot Point 6'. Additional points are 'Knee Point 5', and 'Abdomen Point 3'. Bilateral points needs to be pressed and massaged from both sides.

C. Some Prominent Points and The Diseases They Help Cure

1. Face Point 4:— For *red swollen eyes and dizziness* press these points with one-thumb gradually and hard 7 to 10 seconds, three times.

2. Face Point 7:— For *nasal obstruciton, running nose, facial tension* press hard and inward at a 45° angle with the index finger for 10 to 15 seconds, three times.

3. Face Point 10:— For *loss of consicousness, epilepsy* press hard and inward with index finger or a pointed object for 7 to 10 seconds, three times.

4. Elbow points 4:— Stimulation of Elbow Point 4 alone can be effective for heart palpitation. If this point is pressed with one thumb, hard, 7-10 seconds, three times, it also gives relief to *cough, elbow pain and wheezing sound with breathing or laboured breathing.*

5. Wrist Hand Point 3:— If pressed hard and inward for 5 to 7 seconds, three times, it helps in *reviving an unconscious patient, insomnia, irritability and constipation.*

6. Knee Point 2:— If pressed hard and inward one thumb for 7 to 10 seconds, three times, *stomach pains, diarrhea, arthritis* in the knee get much relief.

7. Knee Point 6:— For *itching, neurodermatitis hives and menstrual pain* press hard and inward.

8. Leg Point 1:— For *general well-being and tired legs* press hard and inward with two thumbs for 10-15 seconds, three times.

9. Abdomen Point 4:— For *menstrual cramps, frigidity* press this point inward gradually and deeply with palm of hand for 10-15 seconds, three times.

10. Abdomen Point 3:— *For stomach pains, diarrhea, wet dreams, constipation,* etc., press inward gradually and deeply with the palm of your hand for 10-15 seconds, three times.

11. Chest Point 2:— For *rib pain, poor lactation in nursing mothers* press these points softly inward with one thumb for 5-10 seconds, three times.

12. Back Point 1:— If these points are pressed with one thumb, avoiding sudden pressure, for 7-10 seconds, three times then *headaches and nasal obstruction* also get relief.

13. Leg Point 2:— Press softly and inward with one thumb for 10-15 seconds and get cured of *sciatica, muscle spasm and tired legs*.

14. Wrist-hand Point 5:— If pressed hard with one thumb towards the index finger for 10-15 seconds, three times, one gets relief from *diarrhea, rashes, toothache, facial tension*.

15. Shoulder Point 5:— For *lack of milk in nursing mothers* press firmly but gradually inward with one thumb for 10-15 seconds, three times.

16. Back Point 6:— For *poor circulation* press these points hard and inward with two thumbs for 5-7 seconds, three times.

17. Back Point 8:— For *breathing problems* press these points hard and inward with two thumbs for 5 to 7 seconds, three times.

18. Elbow Point 1:— For any problem *relating to arm*, press the point hard for 5 to 7 seconds, three times.

19. Ankle Point 5:— Press this point hard inward for 7 to 10 seconds, three times to get relief in *sciatica, dizziness and epilepsy cases*.

20. Knee Point 7:— For *any pain in the ankle or head press* hard inward for 7 to 10 seconds, thrice.

21. Ankle Foot Point 4:— For *kidney malfunction one should* press this point hard and inward with one thumb for 7 to 10 seconds.

22. Ankle Foot Point 6:— You get relief if there be any problem relating to ankle *pain, insomnia, overweight, digestive problems or menstrual pain or any female sexual problem,* by pressing this point hard inward with one thumb for 5 to 7 seconds, three times.

23. Face Point 5:— If you feel any ringing in the ears, press hard and inward with index finger for 7 to 10 seconds, three times.

Acupressure And the Treatment of Our Body System

In this chapter we shall be considering various systems of the body and their possible treatment by acupressure therapy; considering the points of pressure on hands and feet.

(a) **Diseases of the Eyes** : The acupressure points are located at the hands and feet where the fingers join the main part, as shown below. Pressing these points with a rubber or wooden part for sometimes would keep the eyes healthy and painless. How the pressure is to be given by these objects have been given, in details, in the earlier chapter

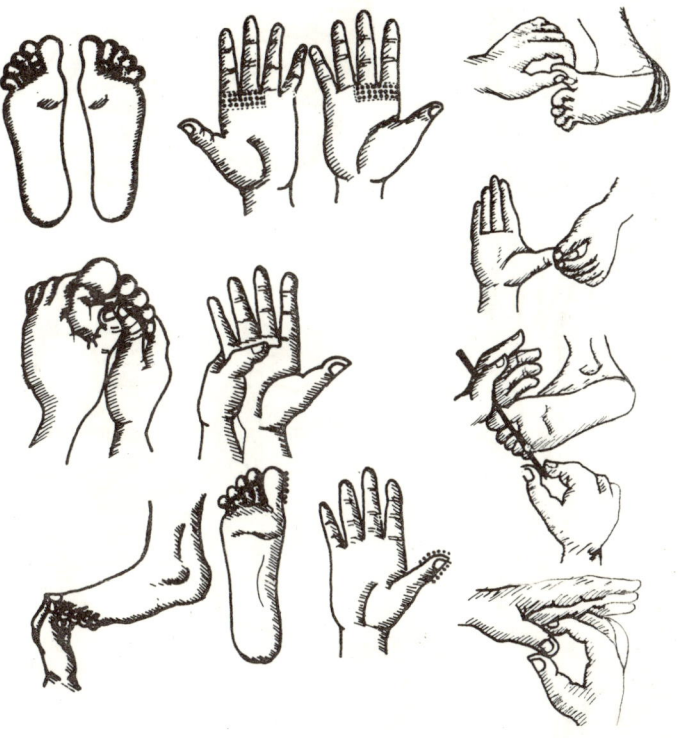

(b) **Diseases of The Ears** : These include deafness due to some accident or congenital besides the hole in the eardrum, oozing of the fluid from the ears etc. Sometimes some hard drugs given in excessive quantities like quinine to cure other disease cause these ailments. Of course, the deafness caused due to the congenital defect may not be easily curable but pressure applied on the following points for the given duration—30 sec. to 1 minute would make the ears again healthy. Moreover, the ears ailments have direct bearing upon the functioning of the kidneys and the related kidney points, shown elsewhere, should also be applied pressure at.

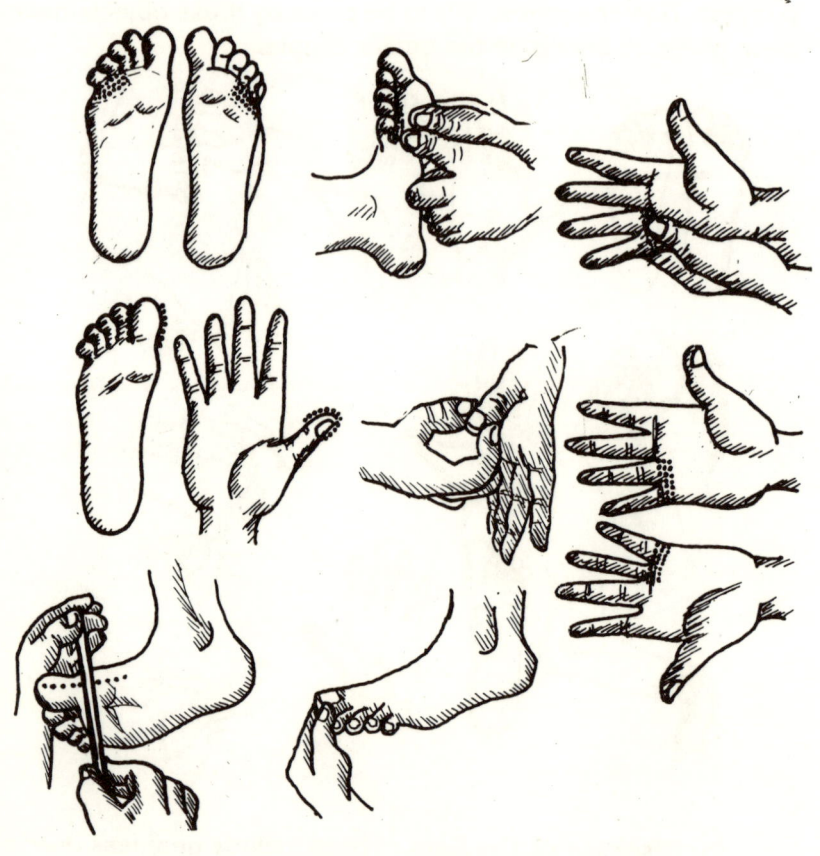

(c) **Chronic Head Colds, Acute Sinusitis, Epistaxis, Hay Fever** etc. In these cases the acupressure therapy works wonders. Even chronic ailments get cured in no time. The main pressure points and the supporting auxiliary points should be applied pressure at

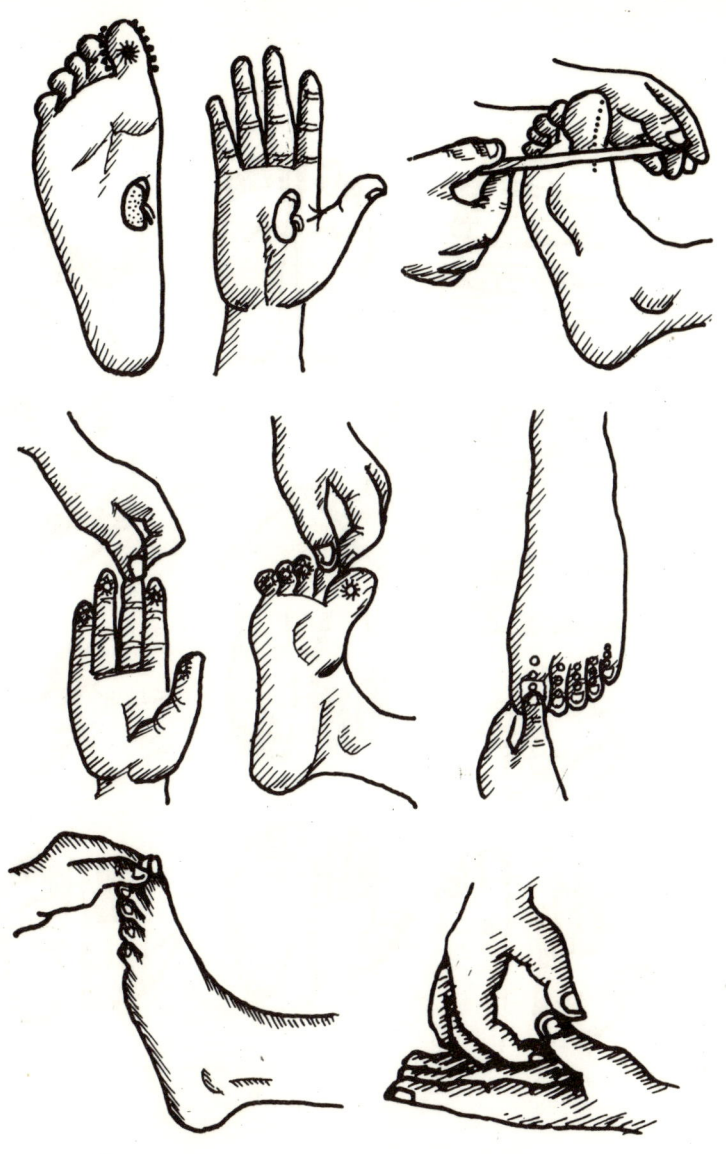

(d) **Diseases of Mouth & Throat :** The acupressure treatment is found very effective in the case of tonsillitis, anenoids, sore-throat, goitre, tooth-ache, gingivitis and dryness of mouth etc.

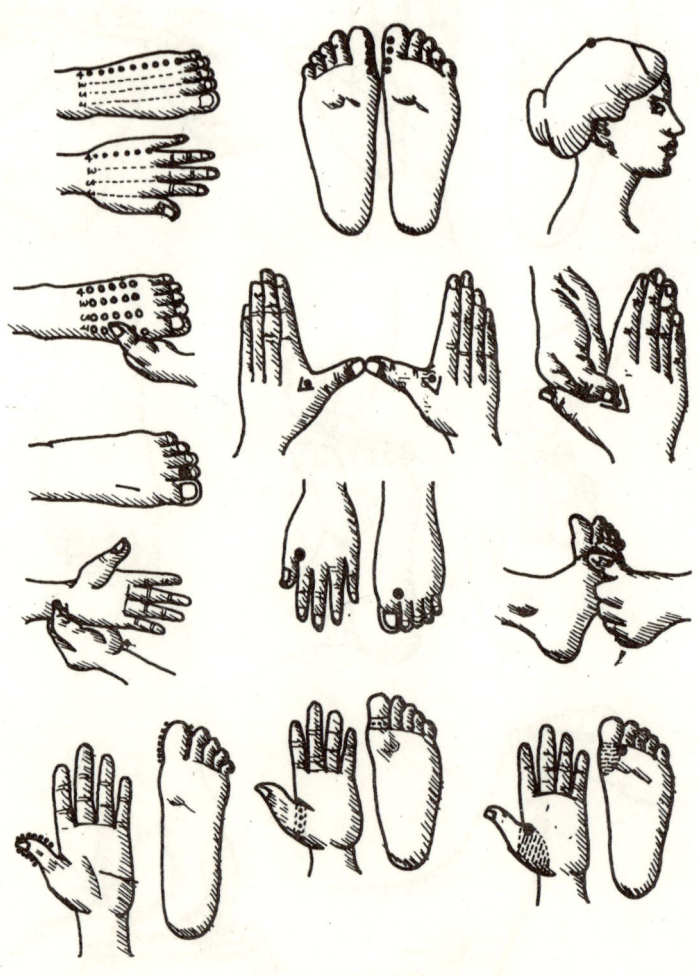

(e) Ailments connected with Cervical, Shoulder, Back, Leg, Heel And Foot Pain : In treating the problems of cervical spondolysis, shoulder pain, frozen shoulder, numbness in arms, tennis elbow, back, legs, heels and feet pains acupressure has been found especially effective.

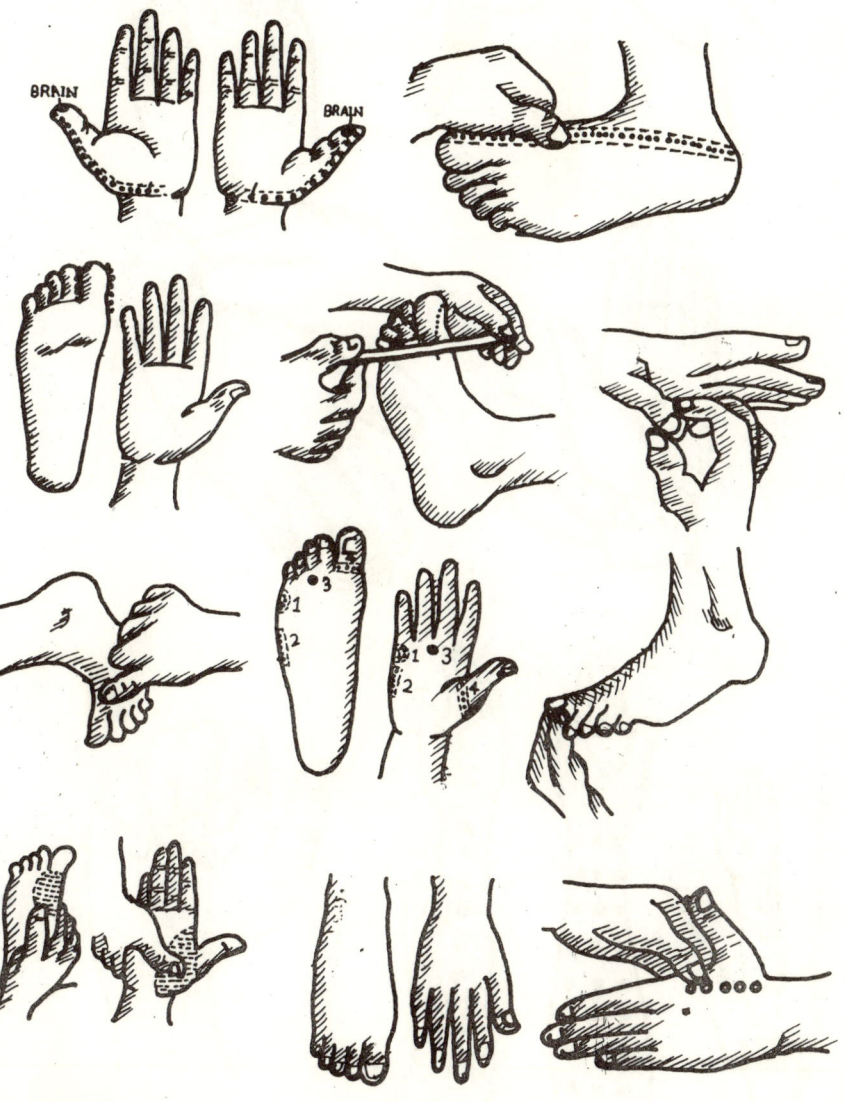

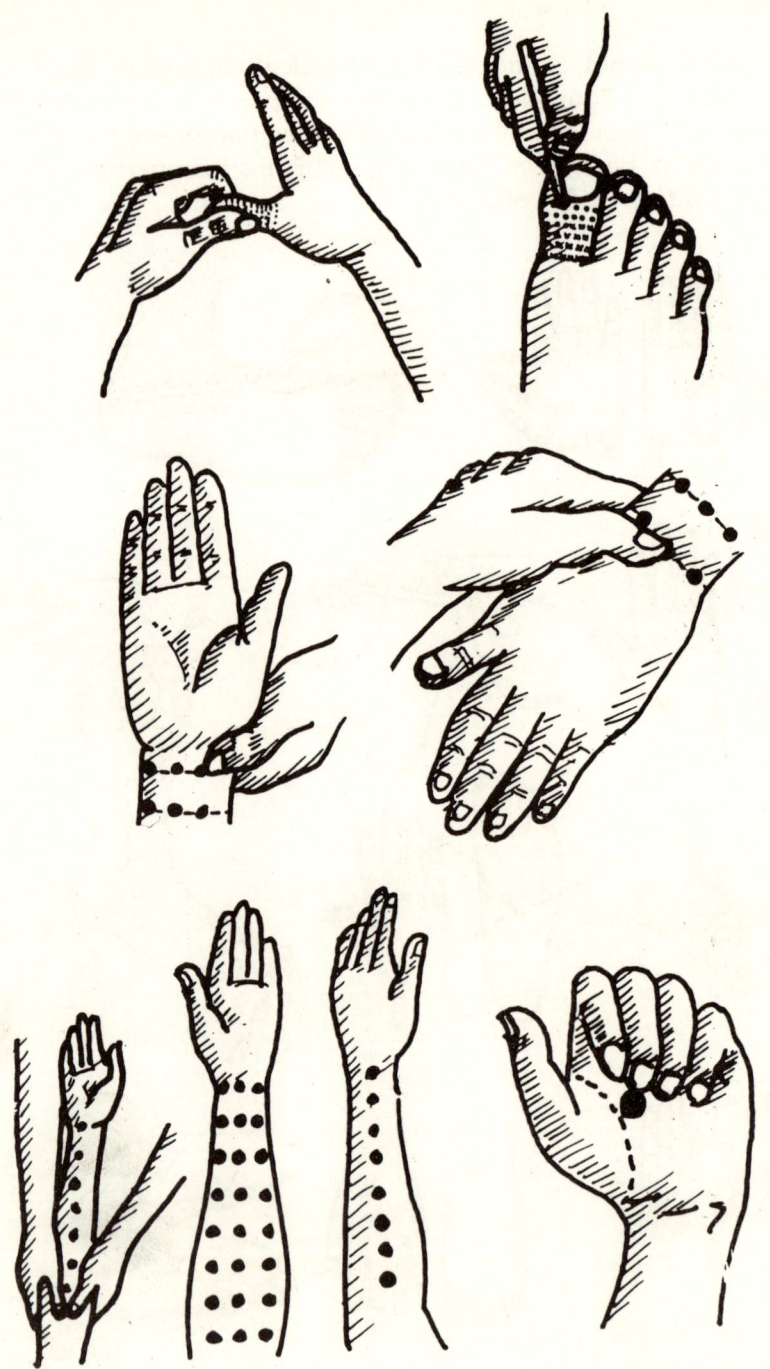

(f) Acupressure Treatment of the Ailments Connected with Back and Leg pains, Lumbago, Slipped-Proplased Disc.

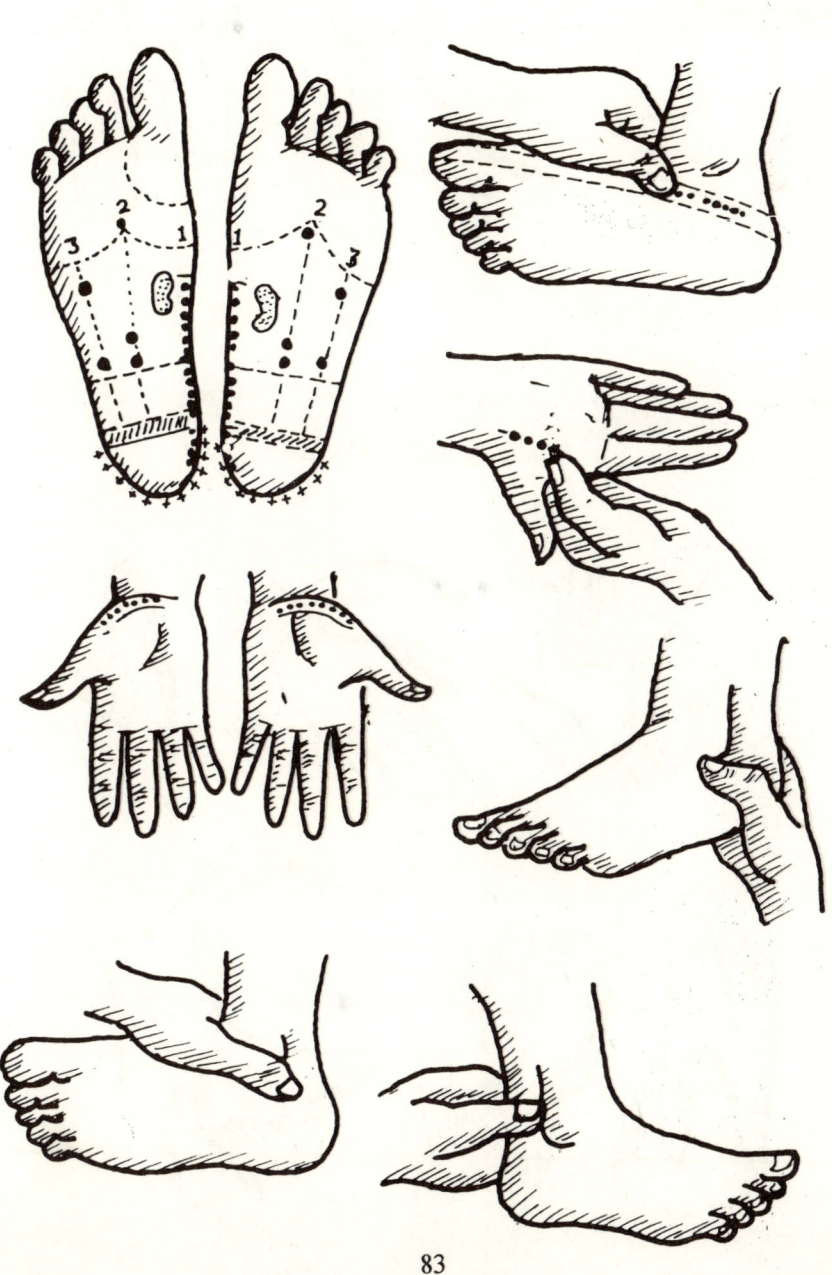

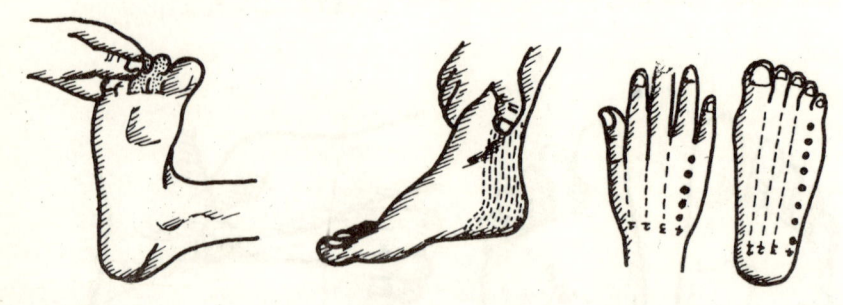

Auxiliary Reflex Centres

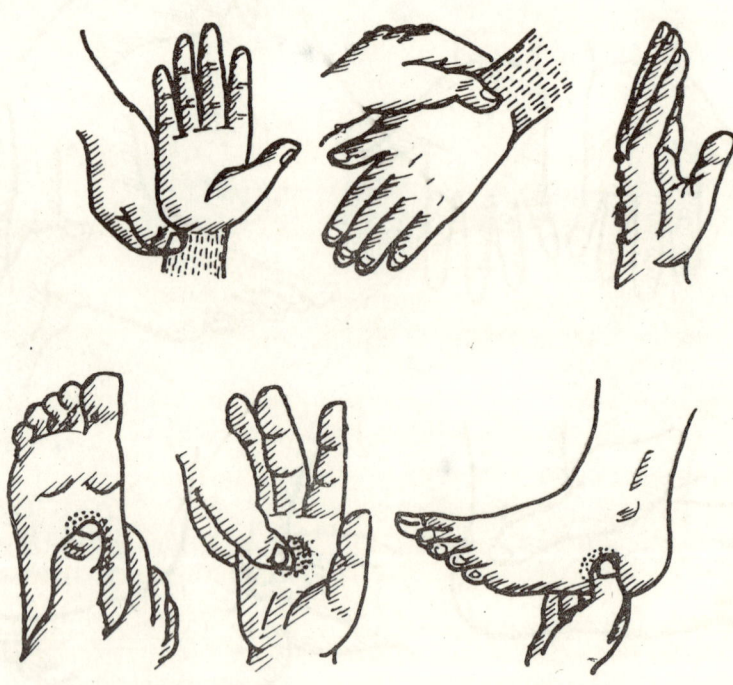

(g) Sciatica Related Pains : Sciatica is a nerve in the leg going from the thigh joint to the knee. Ayurvedic school treats gas as the main cause of this trouble. It shoots out very excruciating pain when the trouble develops. In olden times, tying a tight knot in the big toe of the leg having this pain was believed to be a very efficacious method to provide relief. In fact that too was a sort of giving pressure on the nerve.

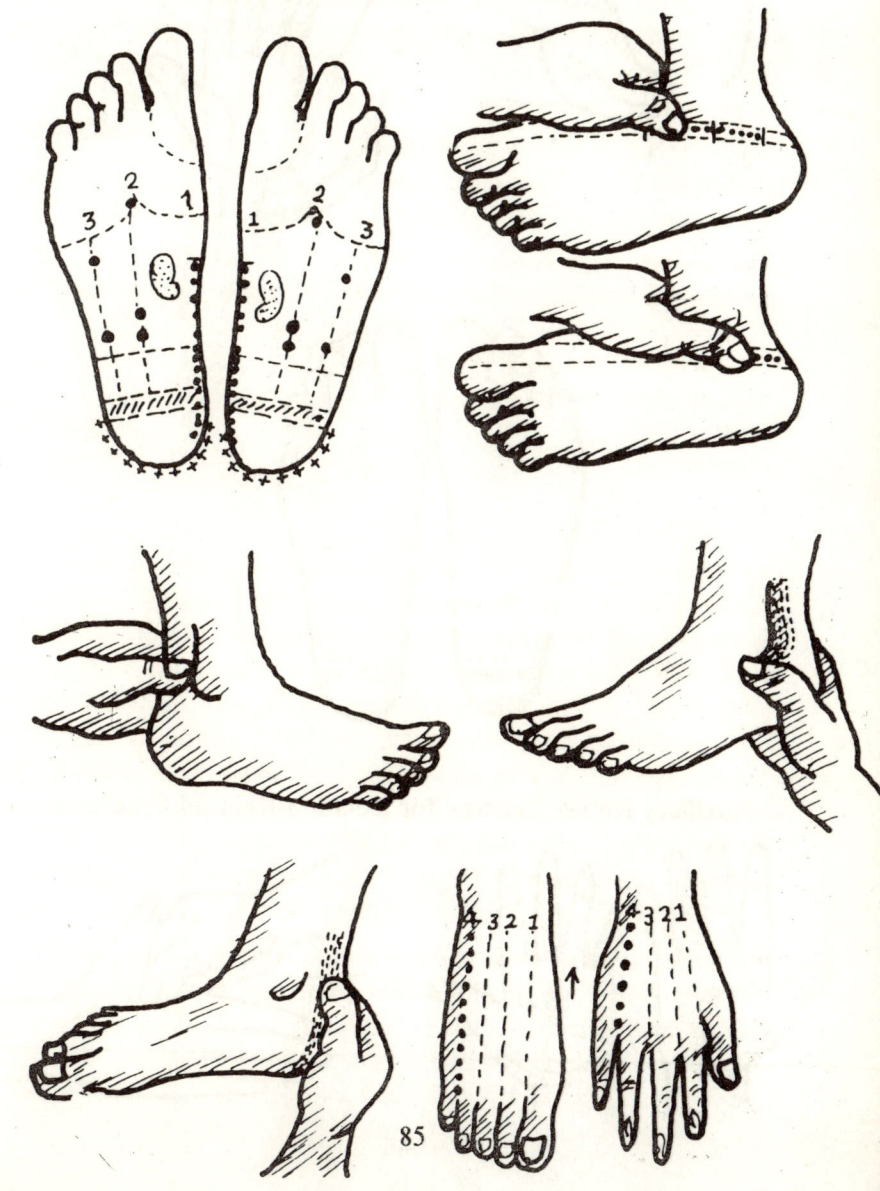

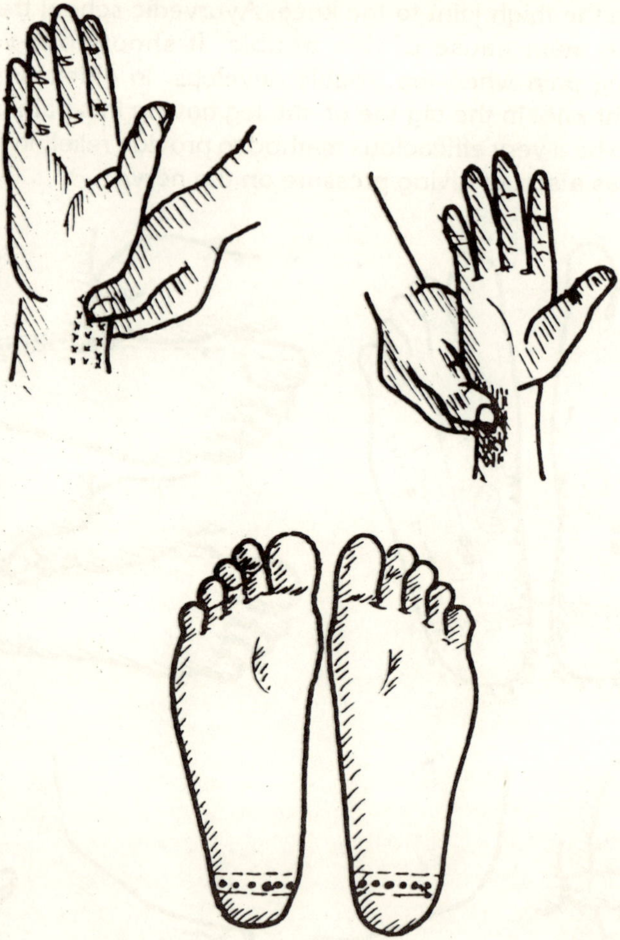

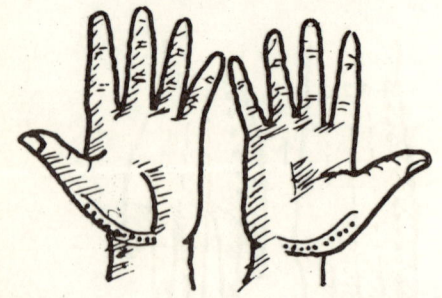

Auxiliary Reflex Centres for Sciatica-Related Problems

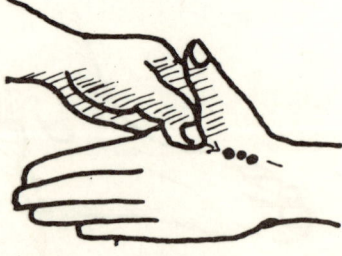

(h) Harmonal Problems Related to Glandular Disturbance: At times the secretion from the endocrinal glands cause change in the body chemistry which can be set right by acupressure treatment. The glands included in this sub-chapter are : Pituitary Gland, Thyroid Gland, Para-thyroid Glands, Thymus, Gland, Adrenal or Suprarenal Glands, Pancreas, Ovaries, Testes and Pineal Gland. While managing these glands this precaution should be taken the following way. If you want your glands to be activised further, movement should be left to right and the reverse way if you want overcharged glands to lessen their secretion. Massaging of the thumbs of the right and big toe of the left foot should be done. Besides that, the following parts of the body should be applied pressure at.

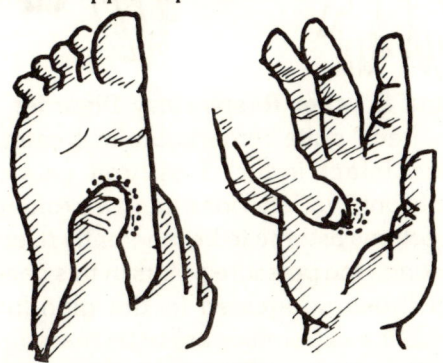

(i) Disorders of the Heart & Circulation : For curing these the following parts should be applied pressure at or massaged. These ailments include blood pressure related problems also. This treatment accompanied by strict dietary control and adequate exercises work wonders. Apart from it having the metal drink (described in the beginning) should also be adhered to regularly and religiously.

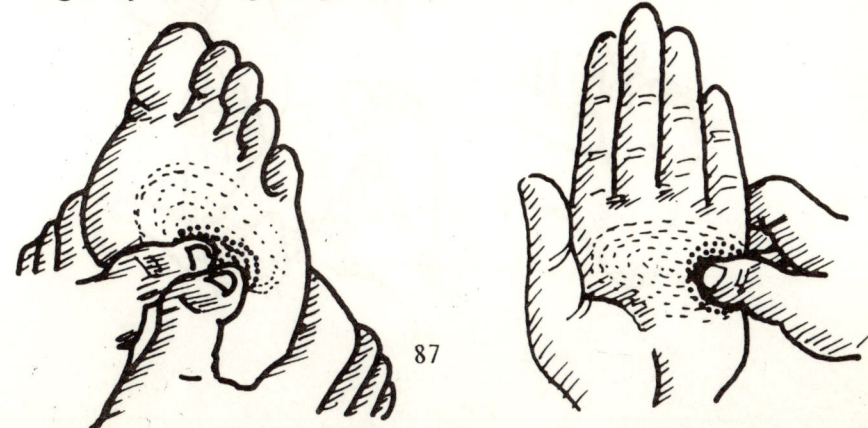

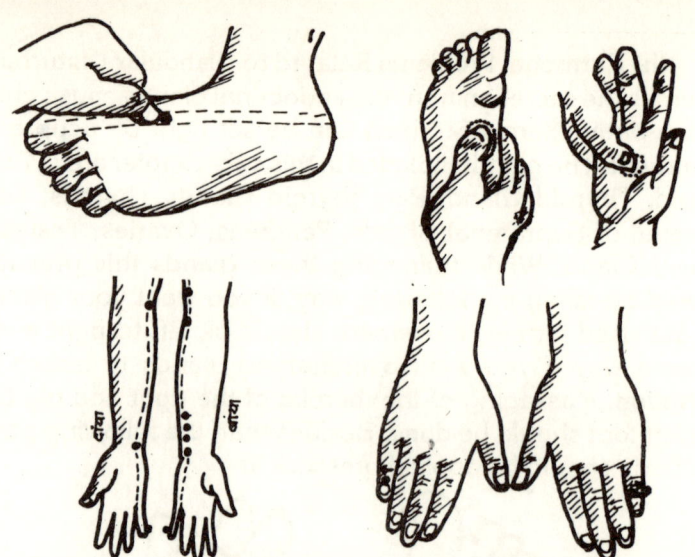

(j) **Asthma & other Respiratory Disorder :** Acupressure treatment has been quite remarkable in treating asthma and allied disorder. Infact induced asthma gets cured quickly although the chronic variety does need a prolonged treatment. Acupressure reckons asthma to be inherently related to glandular disturbance. Hence the pressure points in this case are not much different than those suggested in the glandular disorder's, treatment. In this the extremities are to be massaged and applied pressure at.

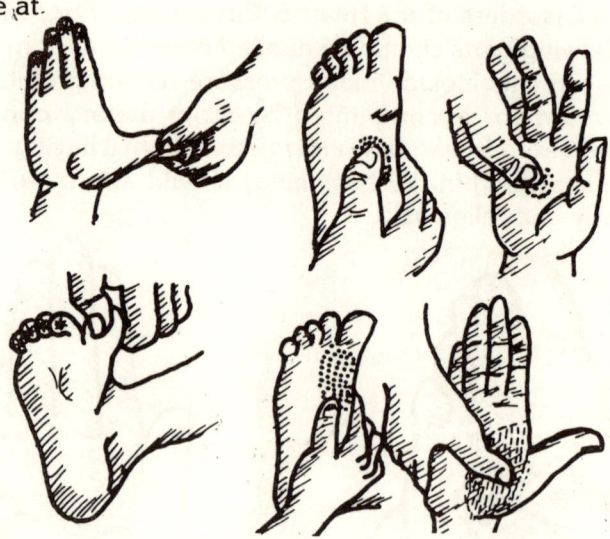

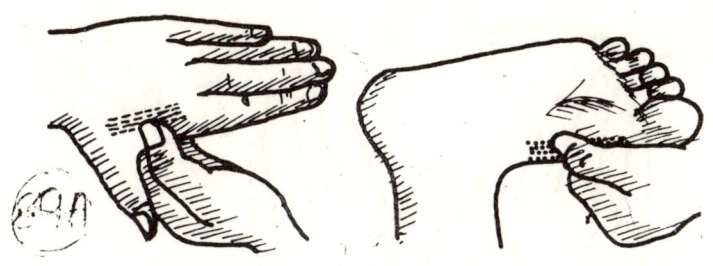

(k) Disorders of Digestion : Included in this section the ailments related to liver like jaundice, dispepsia, dysentery and the like. Apart from the hands and feet, the pressure points of the glands should also be applied pressure at.

For curing piles, fistula etc. the following points should be pressed.

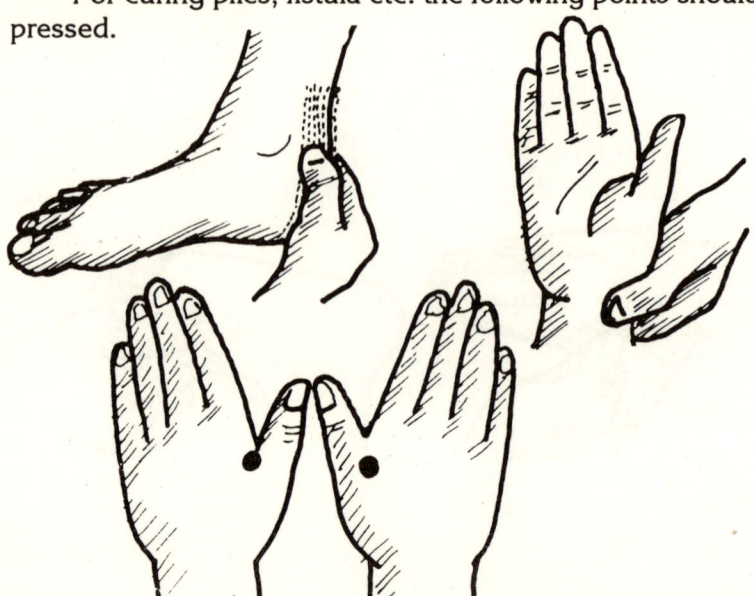

For solar plexus related disorder-the following points should be pressed and massaged. That your solar plexus is disturbed, is easily known by this following method. Lie down flat on empty stomach with your legs and body fully stretched. If you find both of your big toes not at even level, deem it that your solar plexus is disturbed. Since this is not easily detectable generally, people indulge in all sort of stomach treatment without knowing the real reason. So, whenever you feel your stomach is disturbed conduct the test given before.

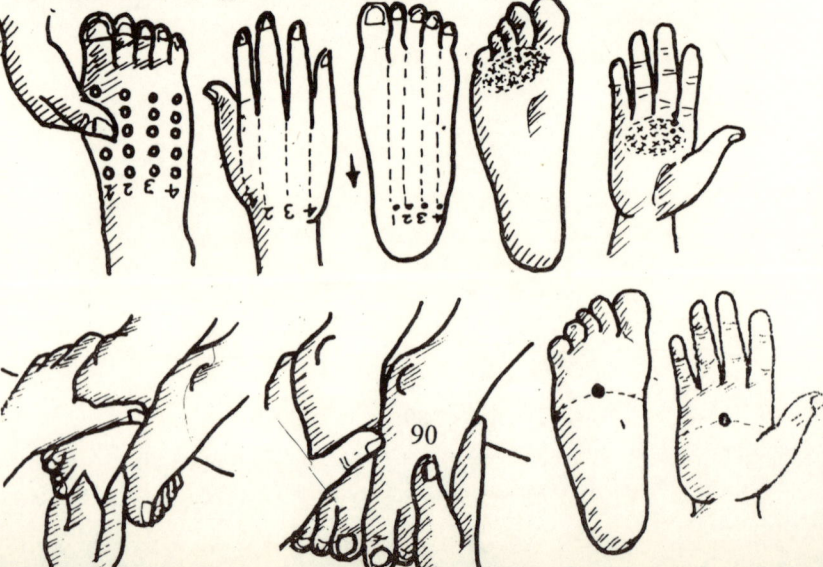

(l) Disease of the Kidney And Urinary System : The charts below show the relation of the kidneys with the hand and feet pressure points.

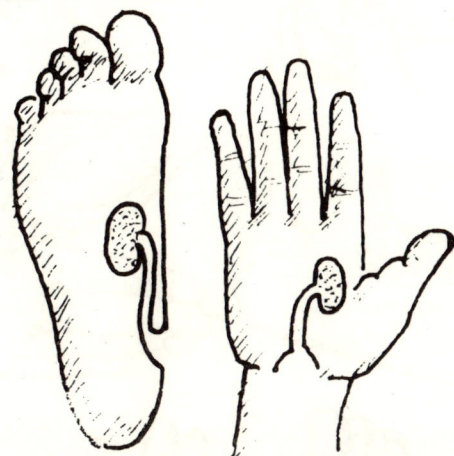

For treating various kidney and urinary tract related ailments, the pressure points given below should be pressed or massaged. As we have shown above the left and left leg/foot control the kidney function of that side. In fact the big toe is actually the main control tower.

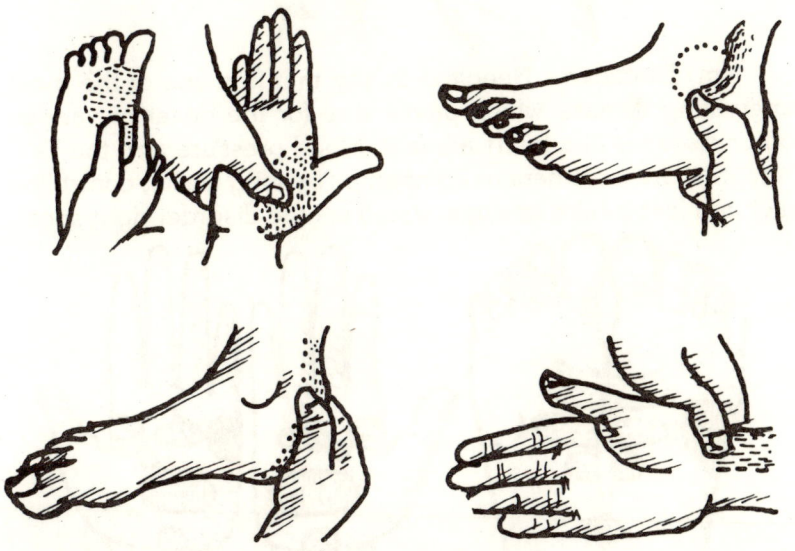

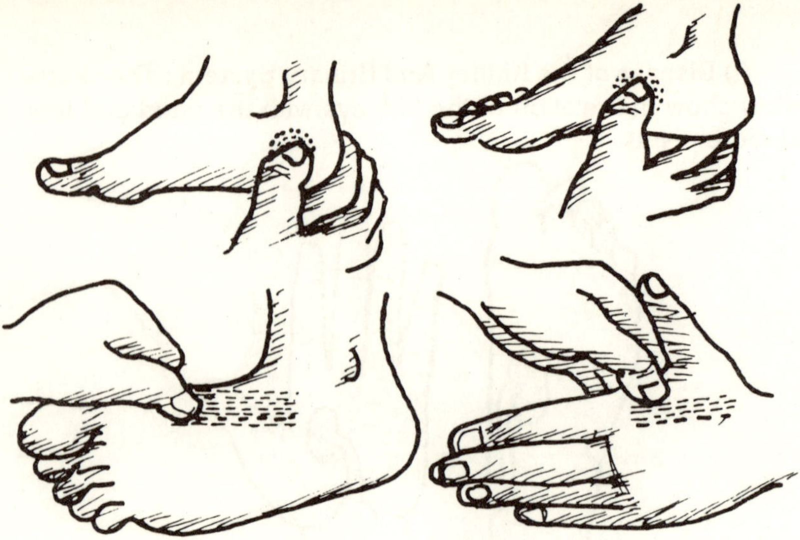

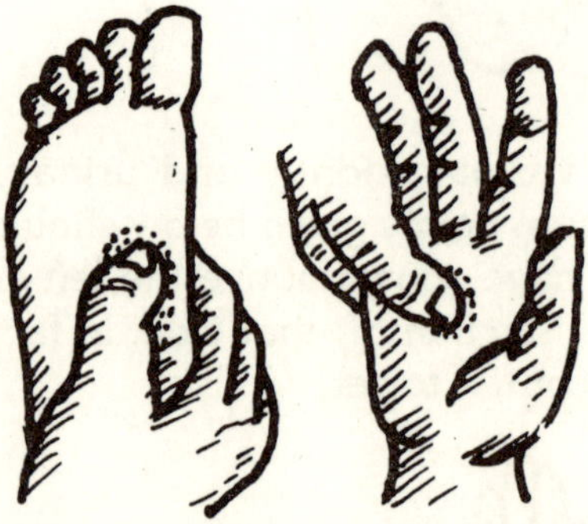

(m) **Diabetes** : Needless to say that it is one of the most enervating disease which paves way for the onset of various other diseases like heart-ailment, blood pressure and the like. Acupressure treatment accompanied by long walks, controlled diet and less intake of sugar would set the disorder right soon.

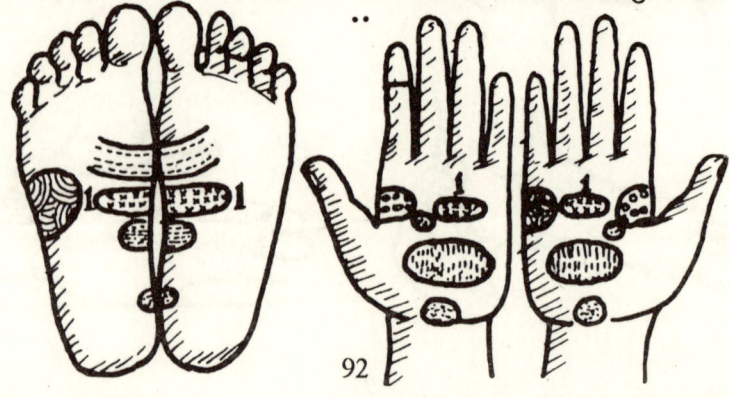

(n) Disorders of Joints and Muscles : Included in this category are arthritis, rheumatic arthristis, rheumatic fever, muscular rheumatist oesteoartritis, osteomalacia, gout, ankylosing spondylitis, Juvenile Chronic arthristis, bursitis and pain in the knees. The following points should be applied pressure at and massaged.

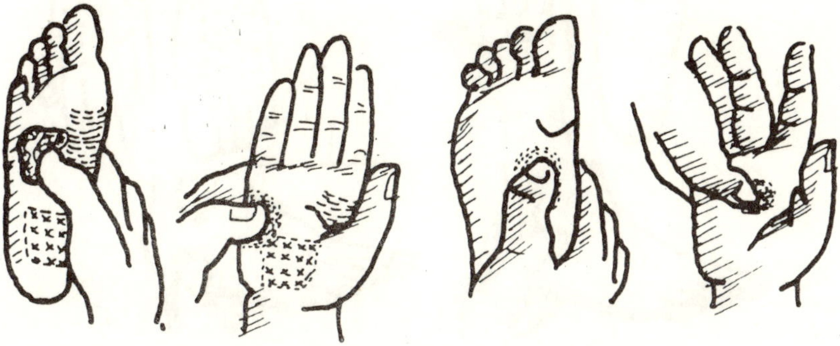

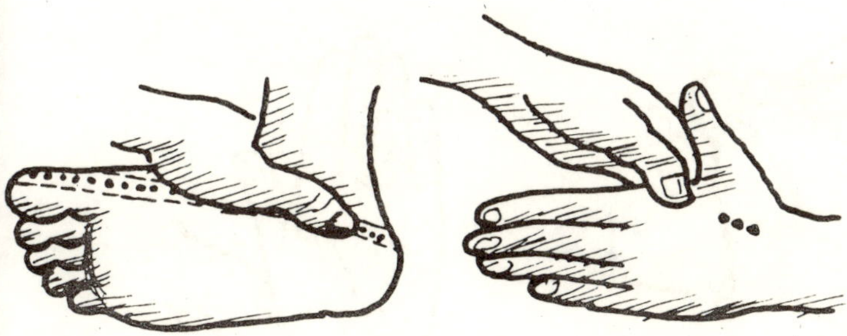

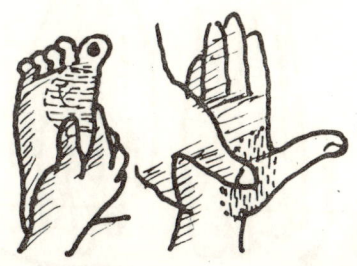

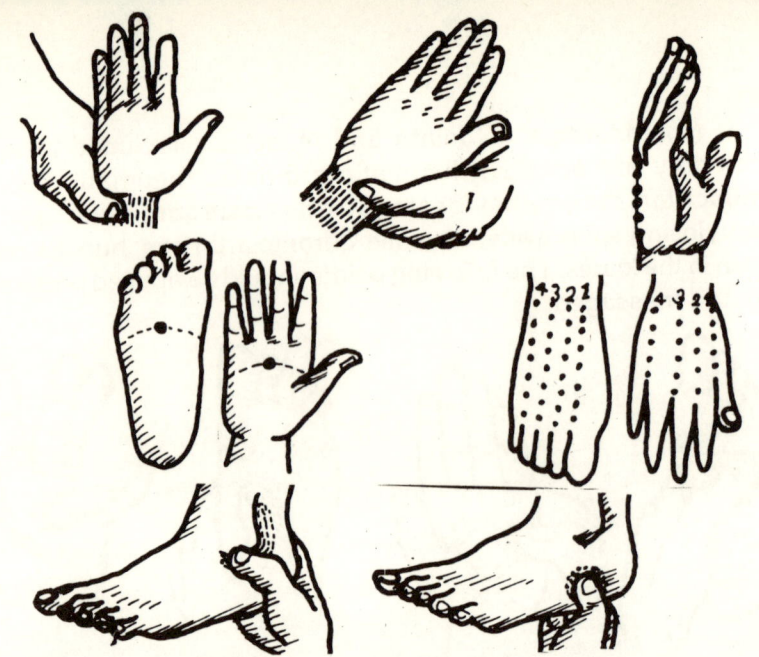

For joint pains the following points need to be pressed and massaged.

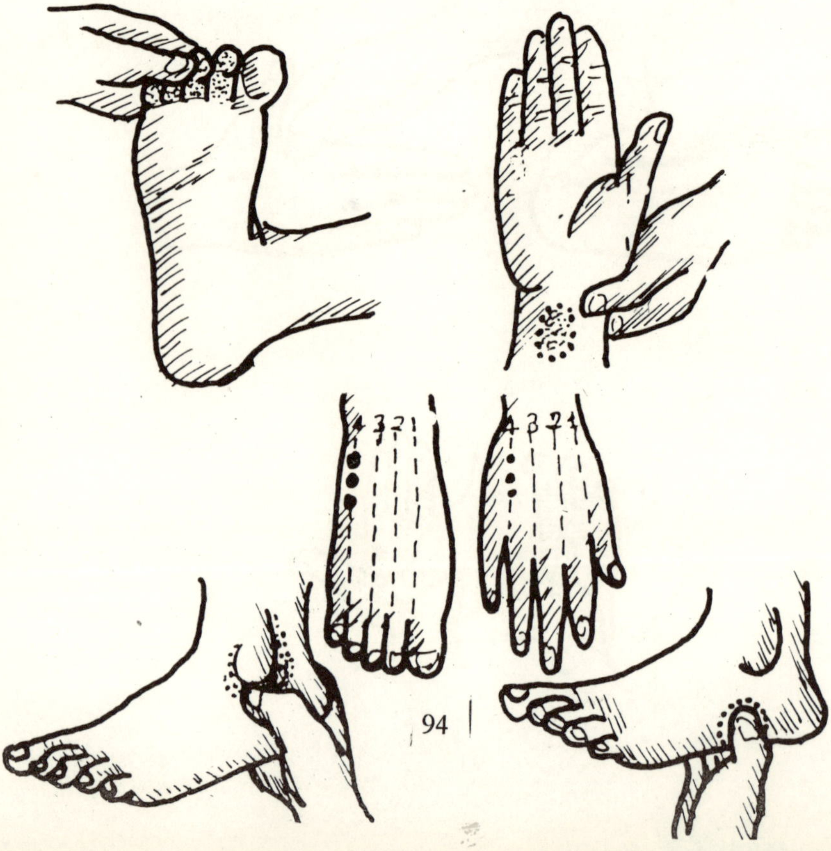

(o) Typical Female Disorders : Before treating any female disorder apply pressure at the big toes and thumb of the hand as shown below.

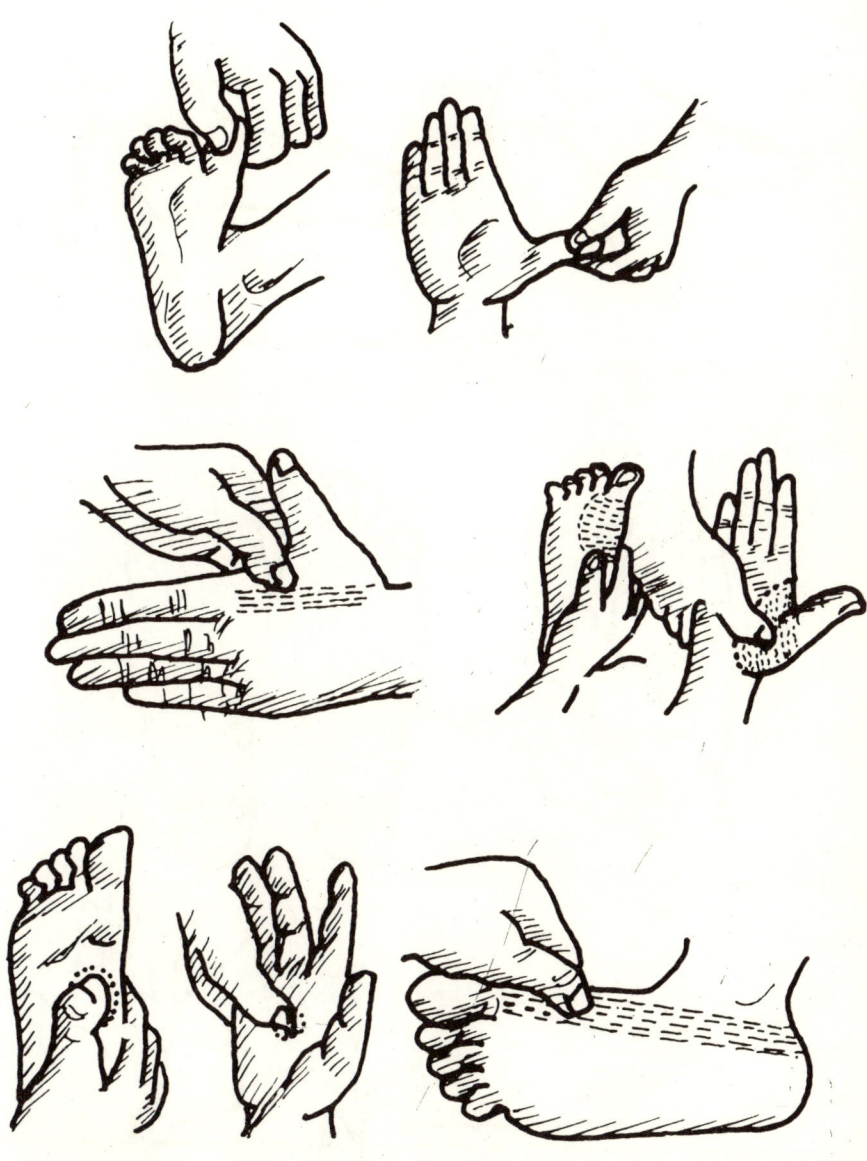

For uterus related problems the following points should be pressed and massaged.

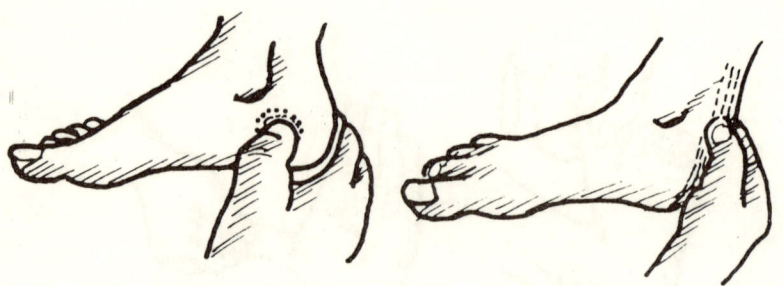

For ovaries related problems the following points should be pressed and massaged.

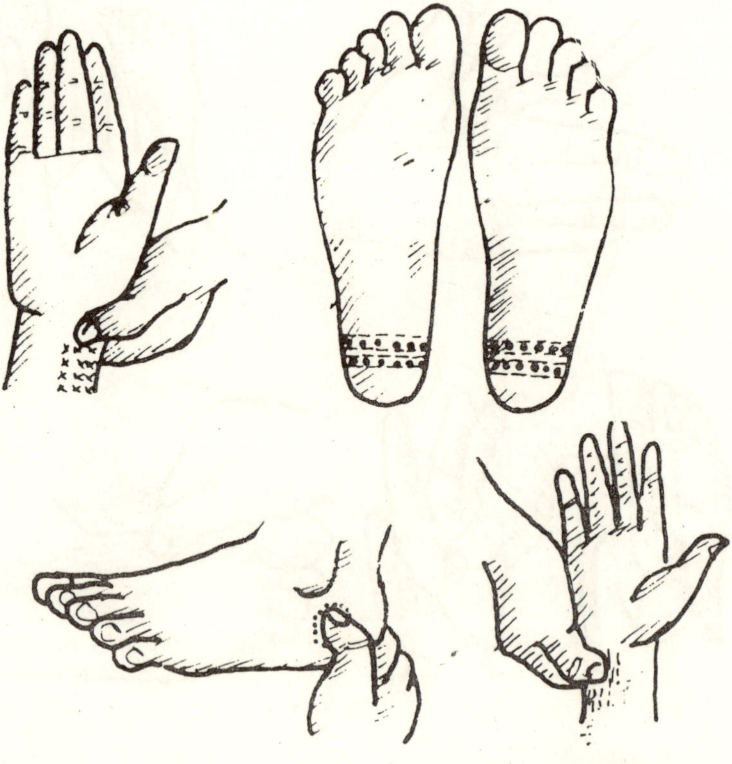

relationship the following points or regions should be pressed or massaged.

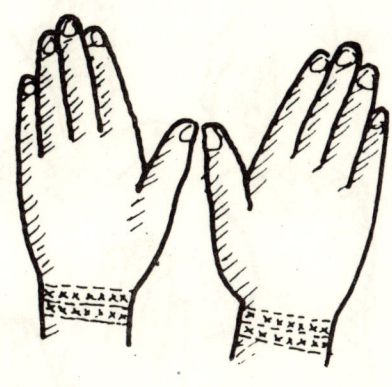

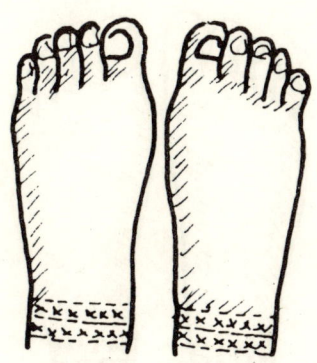

(p) Special Male Problems : This list includes impotence premature ejaculation, abnormal involuntary discharge of semen without orgasm, passing semen before and after urination sterility of men, loss of sexual desire, enlarged prostrate gland and the disease of the testes. First the pressure points and region should be located on hands and feet.

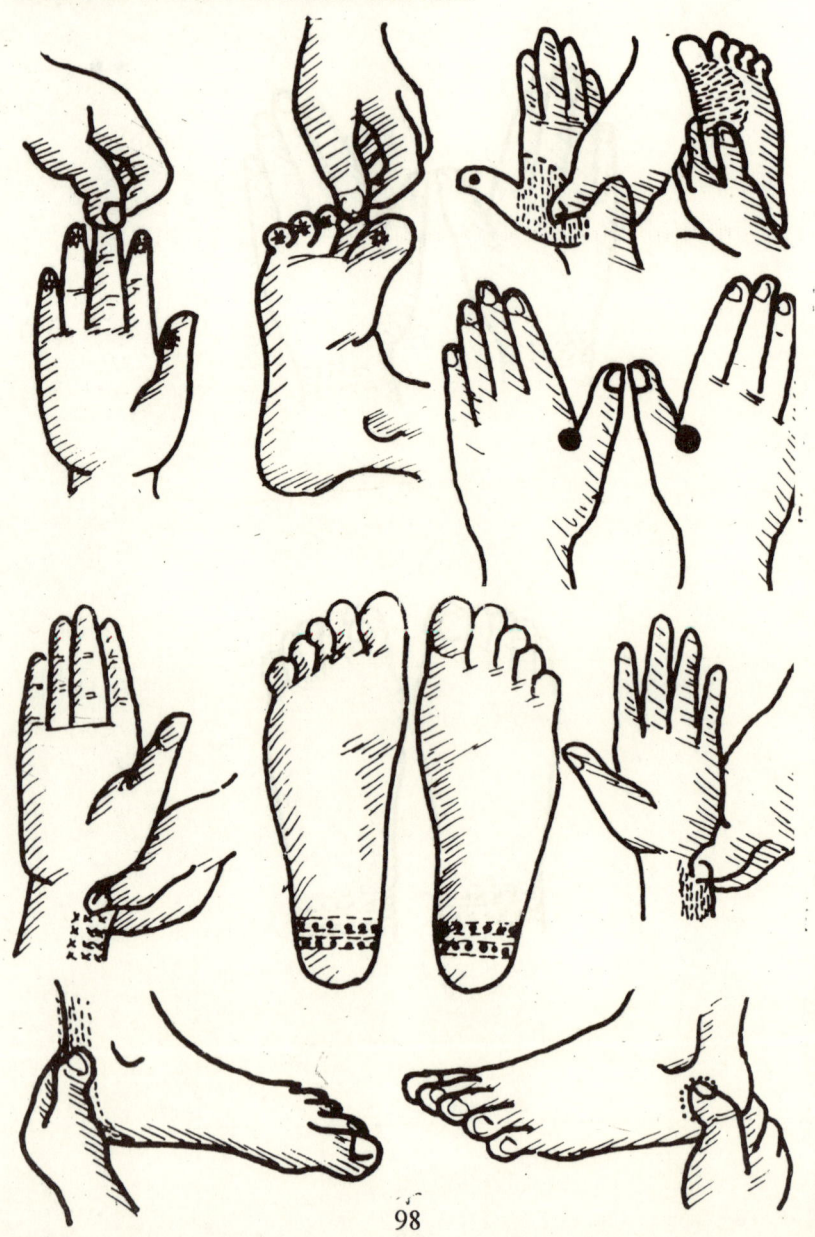

(q) Disorders of the Brain And Nervous System : These include paralysis, multiple scelerosis, muscular dystrophy, myopathy, cerebral palsy, parkinson's disease, Polio-poliomyelitis and epilepsy. The pressure points of the disease are shown below in the order given above. The first two charts show the location of the points or regions where pressure or massage should be given at.

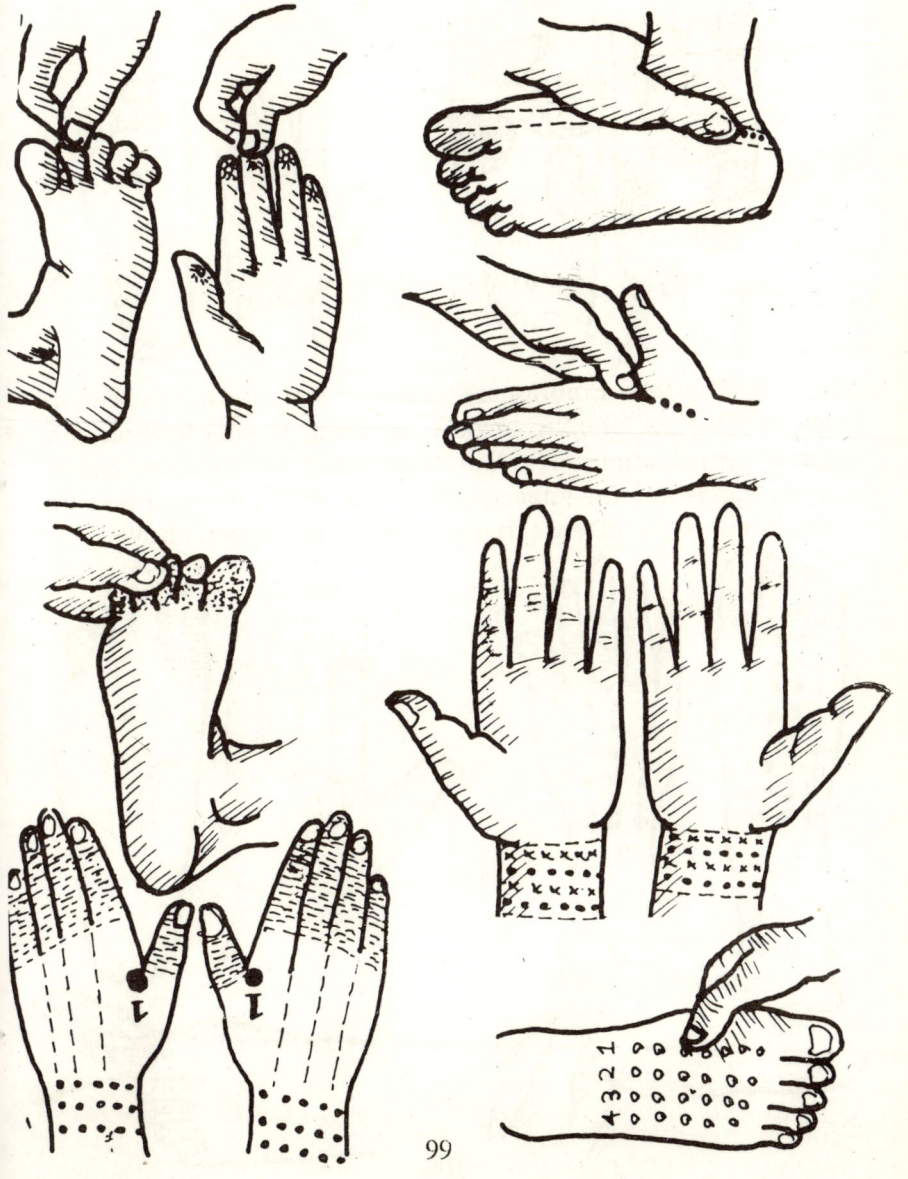

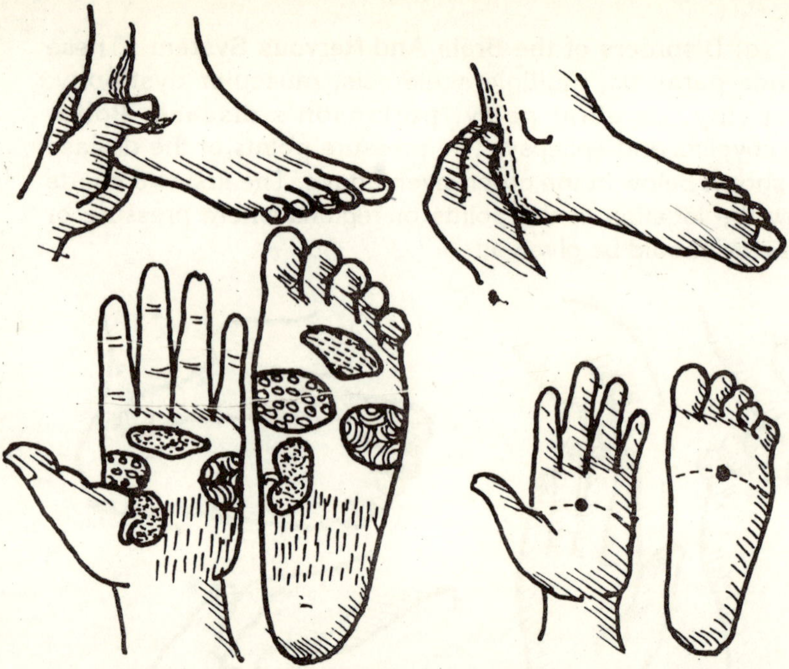

(r) Mental & Emotional Problems : Included in this section are depression, phobia, anxiety, hysteria, mental tension and allied complications. The first chart marks the pressure points and regions and the subsequent charts shows the acupressure treatment of the disease in the order as mentioned above.

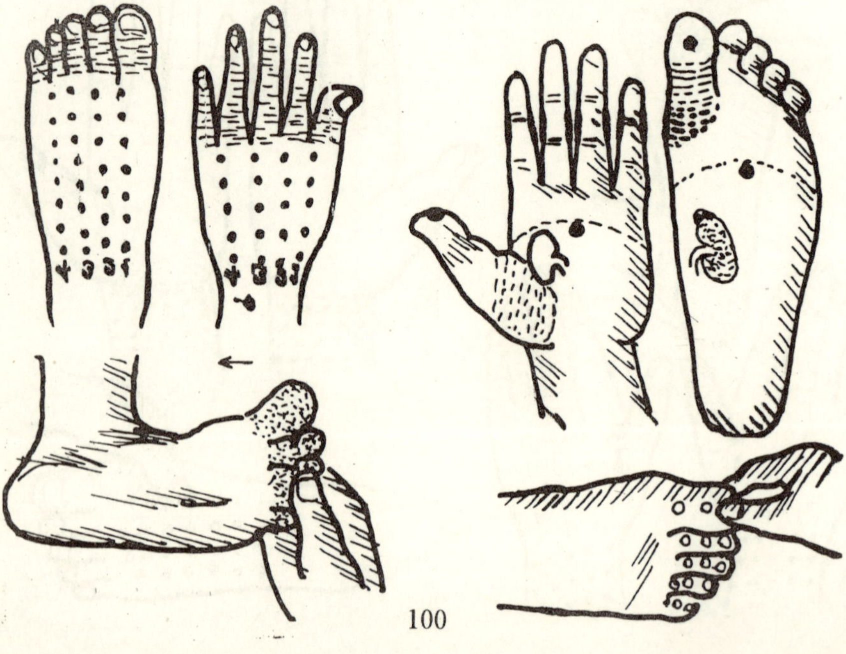

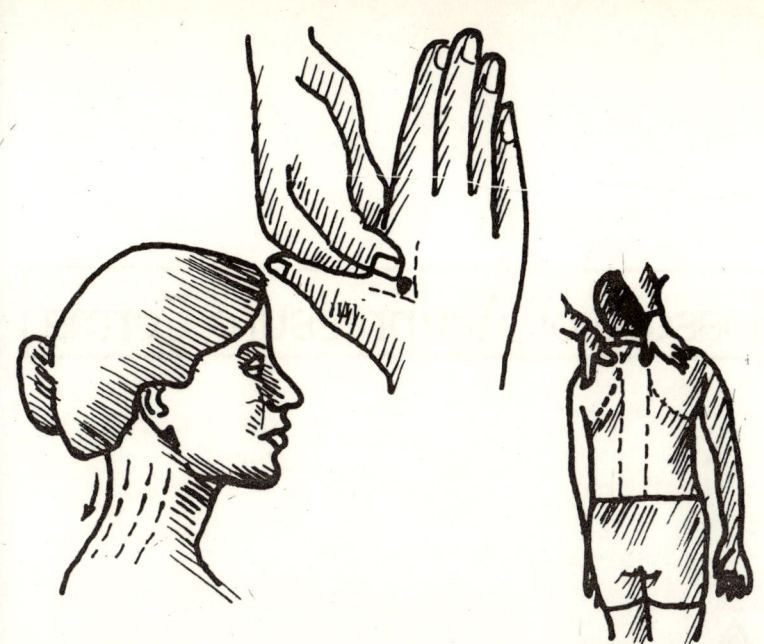

(s) Miscellaneous Physical Problems : These include hair problems, disorders of speech, weak memory, skin disease, short stature, sun or heat stroke, electric shock & faintness, hangover relief, suffocation, snake bite; wounds & cuts. The charts show the relevant pressure massage points in the same order.

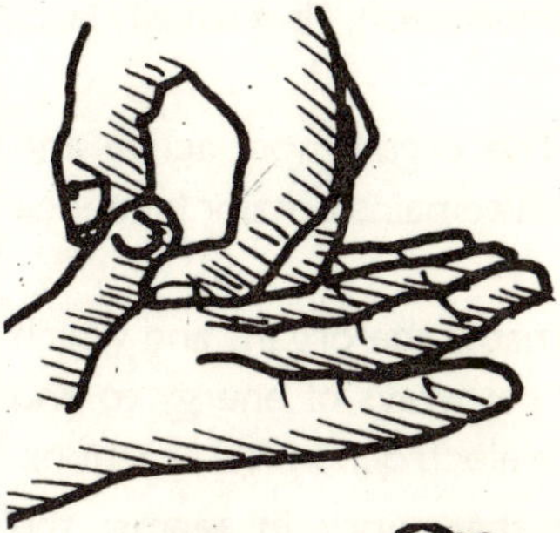

Glossary of Acupressure Terms

Acupoint (or acupressure Point):— A pin head sized area, just below the surface of the skin, that is more electrically- conducive than the surrounding flesh, and which affects an organ when triggered.

Acupressure Reaction:— A physiological response when an acupoint is triggered-usually warmth, perspiration, quecasiness, etc. May also include a longer-term "healing phenomenon," but usually lasts for only a brief period of time.

Associated Bodily-type Organ:— The organ most active and sensitive at one's moment of birth, and which remains a major influence upon his health throughout his life.

Bioenergy:— The vital force that animates the organs and which "flows"-like electricity-along meridians or pathways of energy to and fro each organ, stimulating them to produce electrochemical reactions.

Companion Organ:— Vital organs that work in teams; the companion organ is the team-mate of the organ being considered.

Contraindications:— Times when applying pressure at the fixed points should be temporarily avoided due to some other complications in the body of the subject or patient. In certain cases it may be permanently suspended.

Electro Chemistry:— The Chemical and electro-magnetic reaction produced by the body's organs and glands in action, and which is stimulated by bioenergy; this is the key to health-when our electro chemistry is properly balanced, we are said to be in good health.

Glandular/organ function:— Specifically, the "pericardium" and/or "Triple Warmer"—groups of organs and/or glands working in concert to provide complex physiological responses, such as circulation of blood and energy, digestion, sexual drive (libido) etc.

Healing phenomenon:— The cleansing and purging process which may occur in a particularly ill individual during acupressure therapy. Its typical symptoms—which may last several days—include malaise, temporary changes in bowel movements, headaches etc.

Hyperactive (organ):— An organ that is functioning too actively; it is one of the two kinds of organ mal-function (the other being underactive).

I.A.S.E.:— International Acupuncture System Equivalent. The acupressure points are also used in other types of acupuncture.

Imbalance (between Organs):— In a mated pair of organs (e.g. the heart and small intestine), one of the team functioning in a hyperactive way often creates the opposite reaction—underactivity in its team—mate (or vice-versa). Also, when any organ is malfunctioning, One or more organs "down steam" will malfunction in response to it, creating a state of imbalance.

Root Organ:— A key organ to one's health—when this/these organ's are malfunctioning, one's general health deteriorates; but as the root organ is healed, one's general health improves.

Sedating acupoints:— Acupressure points that tend to calm a hyperactive organ or glandular/organ function upon being triggered.

Testing/balancing acupoints:— Acupressure points that help to restore balance to both hyperactive and underactive organs or glandular/organ functions upon being triggered.

Underactive (organ):— An organ that is functioning too sluggishly.

Book Two
Acupuncture Therapy

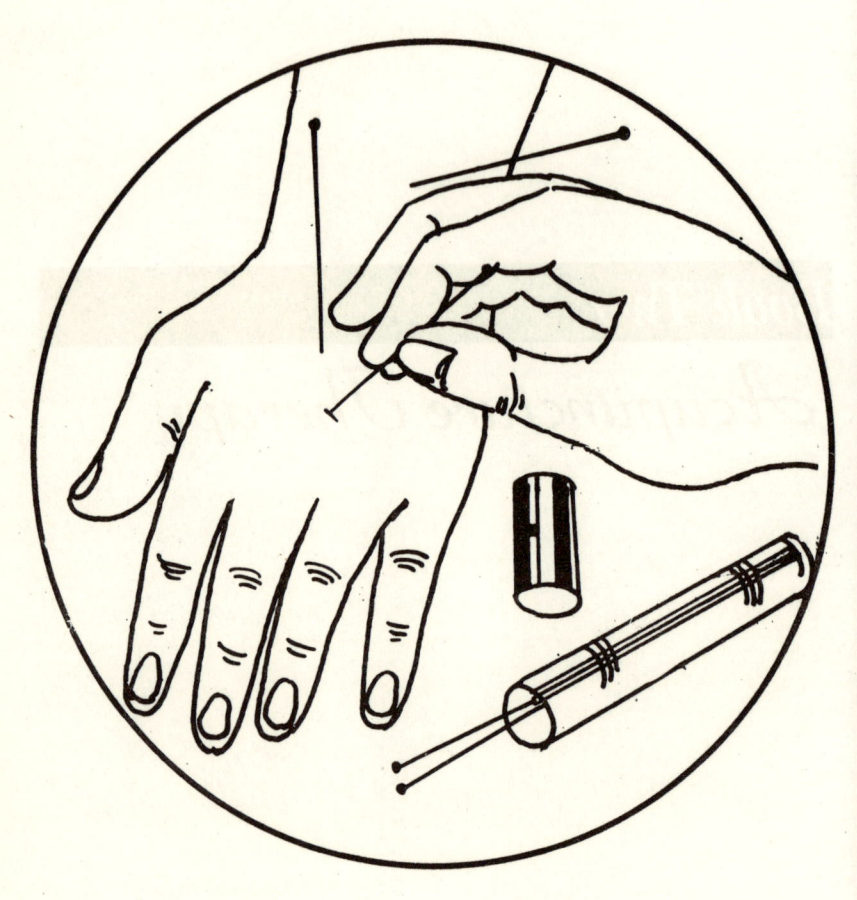

Acupuncture: A Miraculous Therapy

A popular form of treatment in the Orient for over 4000 years, acupuncture has been one of the oldest methods employed by medicine. Whatever its exact origin, acupuncture quickly became a major resource of eastern healers—and as it remain today. China claims more than a million registered acupuncturists and even the citadel of the allopathic style of treatment, America, has their number in tens of thousands.

There is no doubt that in the past doctors in the West found it difficult to believe in the acupuncture because it didn't fit in with their traditional concepts about the anatomy and the working of the human body. They wouldn't accept that diseases could be diagnosed by feeling twelve distinct pulses at the wrist or that the sum total of human illness was due to an imbalance between the opposing life forces of the YIN and YANG. Likewise, they found it impossible to place any special significance in the named acupuncture points, and couldn't believe in the idea of the circulation of 'Qi' energy along the twelve meridians or pathways which acupuncturists believe run up and down the body on either side. Nevertheless, they were forced to concede that acupuncture could, and very often, relieve pain.

However, in the recent years the west has taken a far greater interest in this ancient form of healing and today acupuncture is practised all over the world; although surgery under acupuncture analgesia, which has been researched, has scarcely been done outside China or Sri Lanka. Similarly, much of the real achievement and potential of acupuncture still remains obscure to the majority of people, including doctors. Despite this basic ignorance there is no denying the fact that acupuncture is still becoming increasingly popular. The reason is obvious. The greatest desire of the patient is to get cured irrespective of his or her deciphering the intricacies of the treatment. No one wants to be a cook to enjoy good food, isn't it? Research by a team of doctors at St. Bartholomew's Hospital, London in 1981, into the use of acupuncture in the treatment of chronic back pain, reported a cure rate of 70-75%. Similar results were obtained by the doctors elsewhere in the west which made this therapy increasingly popular. As Dr. Andrew Stanway observes in his book "Alternative Medicine", "most people who go to acupuncturists are the hopeless cases that orthodox medicine can't cure—yet 70% of them improve. This is remarkable by any standard!"

To many people it seems that modern scientific medicine, for all its accumulated learning and vast financial resources, has failed to provide the necessary knowledge as to how they should prevent ill health, nor has it provided a cure for a large number of their illness. Advance surgery may give the impression of medical and technological mastery of health problems, yet the unpalatable truth is that most operations could be avoided. Some of the many conditions for which there is no medical therapy or where it is only possible to ease the symptoms with drugs are as follows: arthritis, asthma, back pain bronchitis, chickenpox, the common cold, many types of depression, eczema, german measles, hay fever, many forms of heart disease, hepatitis, herpes, influenza, measles, migraine, multiple scleroris, muscular dystrophy, Parkinson's Disease, scitica, sinusitis and numerous ill defined problems. In a few cases of other illnesses, such as forms of cancer, the treatment is so severe and disturbing that patients have wondered if the treatment is not worse than the disease. Moreover, the state of our health bears little relationship to the ever increasing expenditure devoted to medical research and treatment.

It is in these cases the acupuncture therapy excels over other style of treatment. To the acupuncturist healing is something that transcends treatment and is difficult to analyse still in a scientific manner. It is in healing where much of the 'art' of medicine resides. Acupuncture promotes healing by its ability to harmonise the vital forces, regulate body functions and balance the emotions. Nevertheless, it cannot be successful unless the patient helps himself by regulating his own life, enhancing his vital energy and balancing his emotions. Whether the patient's prescription is a pharmaceutical drug, a herbal or homeopathic remedy or an acupuncture needle, unless he is willing to take responsibility for his own health be will never be doing what is best for himself. Acupuncture and the traditional oriental medicine teach a way of life in which staying healthy is the overpowering desire.

Acupuncture: Origin, History & Concept

Using a sharp instrument to pierce the skin at certain strategic points was a medical treatment practised at the dawn of history over a period of time a highly sophisticated form of medicine has evolved in China which incorporated this procedure, together with imoxibustion (burning a piece of dried herb over the point), herbal medicine, massage and dietary regulation. The term acupuncture is itself a very much more recent word and was probably derived from the Latin word 'acus' (a needle) and punctum (particle of the verb "pungere': to prick), although early practice was almost certainly carried out with pieces of flint, bamboo or bone. Later, gold and silver needles were manufactured and these were used to treat the nobility. When in more recent times, needles were made of stainless steel, some authorities regarded these as inferior to gold and silver, but experience all over the world with steel needles has shown that these are the best type of needles for most purposes in the acupuncture technique.

The origin of this miraculous therapy is still shrouded in mystery and legend. The three legendary Emperors Fu-Hsi, Shen Nung and Huang Ti are generally regarded as being the originators of the Traditional Chinese Medicine Fu-Hsi is sometimes called the Adam of China and is said to have taught that the cosmos is divided into two complementary, interacting parts known as Yin and Yang. Since this concept forms a vital foundation to the entire philosophy of traditional Chinese medicine it will be dealt elaborately in the next chapter. Shen Nung, who lived around 2700 BC, is regarded as the father of Chinese medicine and is said to have formulated the idea of acupuncture. He also invented the plough and is regarded as the greatest figure in ancient China. Huang Ti (C. 2697-2599 BC) is known as the Yellow Emperor and is supposed to have begun the construction of the Great wall. He is supposed to be the author of the "Nei Jing"—The Yellow Emperor's classic of Internal Medicine—which is the earliest book on acupuncture still existing and is regarded as the common of traditional Chinese Medicine. It is probable that the collective work, based upon the saying of the Emperor, may have been compiled around the third BC and antidated to enhance its authenticity. In the first part we find the dialogue between the Emperor and his Chief Minister and physician, Ch'i PO, describing their view of human physiology, the origins of diseases and how these should be treated. The importance of conforming with the laws of the universe is stressed and it is interesting to note that at the beginning of the book Ch'i PO tells his readers that 'in ancient times people patterned themselves upon the Yin and Yang and lived in harmony. He writes of harmony, temperance in eating and drinking, regular hours for sleeping and rising and life extending for 100 years. "Nowadays," he remonstrates, "people are not like this, they use wine as beverages and they adopt recklessness as usual behaviour: He goes on to say how they make love when intoxicated, dissipate their vital forces in passion, are discontented and seek amusement of the mind and donot keep regular hours. All this causes them to degenerate after the age of fifty! Have times changed at all, we might ask?

It may sound unbelievable that the author of this Chinese classic even anticipated William Harvey who first expounded the theory of the circulation of the blood in the west in the seventeenth century AD. More than 4000 years earlier Huang Ti wrote, "the blood is under the control of the heart, the heart is in accord with the pulse. The pulse regulates all the blood and the blood current flows in a continuous cycle and never stops. Apart from its teaching about the circulation of blood, NeiJing also describes some fifty types of pulses and thirty-seven different kinds of tongues: both are aspects of diagnosis which have consistently occupied a more prominent position on traditional Chinese

Medicine. Mention of the Ayurvedic style of diagnosis may not be incongruous at this place which also diagnoses the root cause of the disease following these two basic symptoms as the essential parameters: pulse and the colour of the tongue.

What is unique about Chinese traditional medicine is that it provides us with a complete explanation of how the body works, how the vital forces are formed and how they may become unbalanced. Above all, it views the human body as a vital whole, infused with energy, which is more than the sum of the workings of its various organs. This, of course, is unlike the more mechanical view of western medicine which sees the organism in purely physical pattern.

The fundamental concept of the Chinese medicine is to regard man as a miniature universe. One of the greatest stumbling blocks encountered by Westerners when studying acupuncture is caused by their failure to realise that it is based upon concepts which are still obscure to us for example, it sees man as a miniature universe—a microcosm within the macrocosm. The microcosm reflects the macrocosm and is subject to the same laws. The ancient Hindu scriptures also aver that which is in universe is also in a human body and what is not in a human body is also absent in the universe. Moreover, this concept says that the microcosm also affects the macrocosm in rather the same way that each individual member of society affects society as a whole. The course of nature is guided by Tao-the unknowable which becomes expressed in the formation of the dual forces, YIN and YANG. It is the Tao that brings about the ever recurring changes, such as day to night, the waxing and waning of the moon, light to dark, the growing and ripening of crops, summer to winter, life to death or incarnation to reincarnation, and is present in the coexistence of good and evil, male and female, sun and shade, wet and dry and hot and cold. As a part of this totality we are no less ordered by the Tao and subject to interplay of YIN and YANG than any other part of the natural world. In nature an imbalance of YIN and YANG results in draught, storm, tidal waves, earthquakes and other disasters; in our own body it results in disease. Until we can grasp this essential relationship of man and cosmos we cannot begin to comprehend the basic concepts of traditional Chinese medicine or acupuncture.

As we all know fundamental to our existence on earth is the presence of water. Its movement can be traced from the smallest spring or well to tiny brooks which become streams and cascade into lakes, which give rise to slow majestic rivers, which wind their way to the open sea. From the ocean, the water evaporates and forms vapour or mist which later become cloud. Finally, by the action of the wind and changes in temperature, the cloud condenses and falls as rain or snow upon the earth to be absorbed and, eventually, to complete the cycle. The Chinese realised that our own vital force or '*qi*', as they called it, followed somewhat similar phases within the body. These concepts of cyclical movement and change, the reflection of the universe and man in each other, and the interaction between them, are seminal to the whole of traditional Chinese Medicine. Moreover, they provide the key to the recognition and understanding of the patterns of disease or disharmony as well as to the formulation of treatment.

Acupuncture seemed to start getting recogniton the world over around the later part of the fifties. In 1959, one of the serious treatises on the subject appeared in the English language, and in 1960, a group of osteopaths and naturopaths who had studied acupuncture in France and Germany brought the famous Dr. Lavier from France who threw first light on this school of medicine. Nowadays this miraculous therapy has almost captured the hearts of patients all over the world. Its extreme popularity is on account of it being simple method of treatment. It doesn't require long list of medicines, cumbersome operations etc. and on top of it is incapable of having any adverse side effects. Even the puncture by the needle is so painless that the patients hardly feel the prick. Yet the net result is early recovery from most of the ailments/disorders for which the much vaunted and much researched school of treatment, the allopathy has no answer.

The Acupuncture Philosophy

As discussed in the previous chapter the bed-rock of Acupuncture faith is the concepts of Tao, YIN and YANG, the five elements or their transformations and the principles that identify the pattern of disharmony.

The Tao: The Way To Ideal Life

'Tao' in Chinese means the way. It is seen as the motive force which calls forth order from primeval chaos. By the activity of the two polar forces of YIN and YANG creation is accomplished out of this chaos. After creation the Tao remains as the abstract, inconceivable influence which continues to exercise government over the universe, whilst YIN and YANG, through their dynamic interplay, maintain all things in their correct and harmonious balance.

Though the Tao conforms to the ancient Hindu belief of God being formless it contrasts the Judao-Christian God in not being distinct from creation and not possessing the attributes of 'father' which lead to a possible response to prayer or intercession.

Disease Results On Account of Disharmony in YIN and YANG

Although prevalent in the ancient Indian thought wrong-doing is not seen in the moralistic sense of Indianism, Christianity and Islam in which punishment will eventually be meted out by an offended God, but is seen as something that insults creation by introducing disharmony. It therefore brings unhappiness and disease and prevents the individual from achieving the right goal or attaining perfection. The man who robs a bank for example, because he is motivated by greed can never be happy and, for all his material gain, is neverthless in a poorer state than the peasant who is contented whith his meagre gains and is happy. The man who ignores the laws of nature and over-eats, over-indulges in sex, takes no exercise, drinks excessive amount of alcohol or takes drugs, bring, disharmony to his body which manifests itself through diseases and disorders. Since the body is inseparably linked to the mind this disharmony disturbs body's inherent communion with the universe. Then the man finds himself at variance with the Tao.

In Chinese Traditional medicine it is the dualistic principle of perfect harmony between YIN and YANG that is necessary part of the creation, of being and of ideal health. It stands in stark contrast to the now rather out worn mechanistic model of Descartes and Newton which is the basis of modern science as also the modern logicality of medical science. Whilst their contribution to the material world is well known, it is also a fact that this illogical reasoning that has separated mind from body and brought human existence to the brink of spiritual baukruptcy. It has regarded man as a machine, enabling him to be repaired when things go wrong; yet it has led him to be totally oblivious to the psychic cause of the physical problem. This school of medicine has scant regard to any attempt to go beyond the physico- chemicalism to find the solution.

It is for this reason that orthodox medicine seems to be concentrating on relatively unimportant matter and failing to get to the root of problems. As long as the 1920, a certain Dr. Fraser, The Canada Lancet, demonstrated that bacteria were more likely to be the result of disease rather than its cause but seventy years later we are still floundering with the discredited germ theory of Pasteur. Overwhelming evidence has been produced to show, for example, that undernutrition, malnutrition and environmental toxins are as much more basic causes of 'infectious' diseases; yet destructive antibodies are still being employed with an abandon which is beyond belief. It has been, on the contrary, proved that acupuncture is capable of potentiating the immune response and enhancing resistance to so—called infections.

Taoist Meditation:— Taoist meditation stems from the time of legendary Huang Ti, the founder of Taoism, at a time when the mists of pre-history were hardly beginning to clear. However, the meditation which was revived by the philosopher Lao Tsu is central to the Chinese medicine as it is directed to both the improvement of physical functioning and the attainment of greater enlightment.

This sort of meditation should be done in a comfortable position with spine erect in an atmosphere of fresh air. The lotus or half lotus posture (Padmsana or semi Padmasan posture) are recommended but for those for whom this is impossible there are good alternatives. The hands are crossed and rested gently on the lower legs with the thumb of the lower hand lightly grasping the palm of the upper hand. The chest should be slightly inclined forward and the buttocks pushed slightly backwards. The mouth remains closed and the tongue should just touch the roof of the mouth to conduct PRANA (the vital air) from the nostrils to the throat. Eye should be lightly closed or semi—closed. The mind is now cleared of all thoughts and desires and is about to concentrate on nothing. Thoughts should not be actively foced out of the mind, for this is the sure way of causing them to return, but gently discouraged until they disappear. This type of meditation is an exercise in concentration but is also a method of cultivating the free movement of air within the body. The PRANA is anothoriental term which refers to the subtle energy extracted from the air which ultimately goes to form the 'qi' the harmonious distribution of which is synonymous with good health.

The readers would note that Taoist meditation is exactly the other name of the famous Yogic posture called shavasan with the difference that in the latter the aspirant keeps lying down like a corpse.

Meridian Meditation:— The Chinese also described meridian meditation which consists of visualising and concentrating upon the meridians or pathways of energy which traverse the body. Sometimes this is assisted by physically rubbing or massaging the meridians with thumb following the traditional route from the meridians associated with lungs where the flow of energy is said to commerce, via each meridian in its rightful sequence (see the chart ahead) ending with liver meridian. The tips of the fingers may be used instead of the thumb and each side of the body should be done seperately. Usually the massage is performed first, after which one mentally travels the through each meridian, sensing any blockage or disturbance of energy.

The meditation was part of what was known as the Internal Exercises which also included the three Animal Exercises taken from the deer, crane and turtle, all of which were observed to possess longevity. These exercises formed the basis of the Internal Exercises.

The Deer Exercise:— It is based upon tightening and strengthening the anal muscles, which in male strengthens the rectum and prostrate, ameliorates impotence and premature ejaculation and helps to enlarge the heed of the penis, and in female strengthens the muscles of the vagina and rectum, cures and prevents many vaginal problems and menstrual disorders and helps to maintain youthfulness and beauty by strengthening the sexual glands. In both sexes the entire glandular system is energised and balanced by this exercise.

The Crane Exercise:— In is essentially an abdominal breathing exercise and may be combined with the Deer exercise. It is particularly helpful in claiming the body and is a useful preparation for sleep.

The Turtle Exercise:— It consists basically of stretching the neck in imitaiton of the tortoise pulling its head out of its shell. It energises the spine, including the neck, strengthens the shoulders and removes stiffness from the muscles in these area. It also stimulates and regulates the thyroid and parathyroids: the very important endocrine glands sited in the neck region.

Health Versus YIN and YANG:

The ancient Chinese belief is that under the influence of Tao the original state of Chaos became organised and energy was divided into two forces, YIN and YANG, which resulted in the formation of the material world. These two polar forces maintain everything in its rightful state by their continual ebb and flow, opposition and attraction and dynamic interplay. The entire cosmos became divided into heaven (YANG) which consists of the light, ephemeral, 'pure' substance which rose upwards; and earth (YIN) consisting of the heavier, coarser material which sank below. Thus, YANG equates to the qualities of activity and function; whereas YIN is death, but even in death there is some YANG, and in traditional Chinese thinking all things have life. There can be no YIN without YANG, nor YANG without YIN!

The original explanation of YIN was 'the shady side of a hill' or the north side (at least in the northern hemisphere) and YANG was the sunny side or south. Thus, YIN refers to dark, cold and damp; whilst YANG refers to light, warm and dry; To take this theory a little further it can be said that YIN stands for night and YANG for day. The outer circle in the figure below depicts this relationship, whilst the intermediate circle depicts the relationship of YIN and YANG as determined by the cycle of the sun. From the moment of its descent from its zenith (moment of maximum YANG) the YIN force begins to increase. Conversely, from midnight, which is the moment of maximum YIN, the YANG influence begins to strengthen.

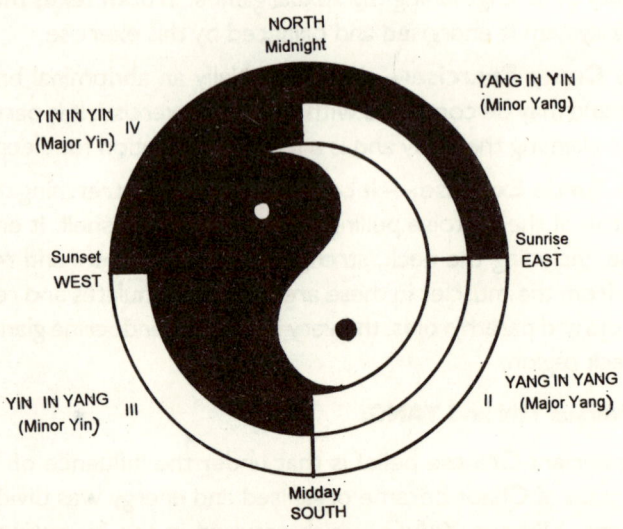

Figure 1: A schematic representation of the endless interplay of yin and yang. The outer circle represents the daily variation of yin and yang, the intermediate circle portrays the solar cycle from zenith to nadir, and the inner circle is the Chinese monad showing how all things are composed of yin and yang, that yin changes into yang and vice versa, and that there is no yin without yang or yang without yin.

TABLE I

General and cosmological correspondences to yin and yang.

YIN	YANG
Earth	Heaven
Moon (Major Yin)	Sun (Major Yang)
Night	Day
Autumn/Winter	Spring/summer
North	South
Noon-MN	MN-Noon

Completion	Incipience
Structure	Function
Passive	Active
Dark	Light
Wet	Dry
Cold	Hot
Proton	Electron
Negative	Positive
Sinking	Sising

TABLE 2

Some physiological features in terms of yin and yang.

YIN	YANG
Female	Male
Right side	Left side
Front	Back
Lower part	Upper part
Inside	Outside
Responsive	Aggressive
Transporting organs	Storage organs
Chronic	Acute
Deep pain	Superficial pain
Constant pain	Intermittent pain
Pain does not move	Pain moves around
Parasympathetic	Sympathetic
Centripetal	Centrifugal

Everything in the universe can be perceived in terms of YIN and YANG. The Table I lists some of the YIN/YANG correspondence in nature, whilst the Table 2 shows how various anatomical and physiological Characterstics may be understood in terms of YIN. The importance of this in respect of treatment should be apparent.

YIN and YANG And Physiological Considerations:—

An intermittent (YANG) pain which changes position, is superficial, aggravated by pressure and probably associated with inflammation is quite different from a constant, deep (YIN) pain which does not move from place to place, is usually relieved by pressure and probably associated with degeneration. The treatment of such pains would also be different and, on the simplest level, the first type of pain would probably be relieved by a cold application and the second type with a hot one. However, nothing in medicine, Chinese or otherwise, should be taken for granted!

Table 3 lists a number of more objective anatomical and physiological correspondences all of which help the physician to make a correct diagnosis in terms of Traditional Chinese Medicine.

TABLE 3

Yin and Yang physiological effect. In general, yang manifestations are signs of good health, but excessively yang characteristics are also undesirable.

PART OF BODY	YIN	YANG
Hair	White/Grey	Red/Black
Head	Bald	Abundant Hair
Eyes	Large, round	Long, thin
	Glazed	Sparkling
Eyebrows	Thin	Thick
Nose	Long	Short
Ears	Small	Large
	Small lobes	Large lobes
Lips	Thin or swollen	Thick (not swollen)
	Dark colour	Pink colour
Tongue	Flat	Roundish
	Quivering	Firm
	Protrudes little	Protrudes well
Joints	Stiff	Flexible
Hands	Hot/moist	Dry
	Cold & moist	Warm & dry
Nails	Long & narrow	Short & wide
	Grain across	Grain up & down
Skin	Smooth	Rough

Returning to figure 1, we can observe that the daily cycles of sunrise and sunset initiate the qualities of major YANG, minor YANG, major YIN and minor YIN. These variations of YIN and YANG are also important and are correlated to the organs and meridians.

Above all, it is the balance of these two contrasting forces which is important and it is this imbalance that changes according to the time of day, season of the year, age and sex of the individual and, even, the movement of the moon, planets and stars.

Organs vs YIN and YANG:

As mentional earlier, YIN and YANG represented the sunny and shady sides of a hill. In place of the hill we can consider a man standing with his back to the sun. The back is then relatively YANG and the front relatively YIN. Since the small intestine and bladder meridians pass over the back (including the back of the arms and legs) these are regarded as great YANG. Situated at the side are the 'three heater' and gall bladder meridians these are considered as lesser YANG. In the front, where the sun scarcely touches but its warmth is still felt, are the colon and stomach. These are sunlight YANG. In front of the body are lung and spleen; as they are in the most YIN position they are termed great YIN. A little more to the side are the heart constrictor and liver meridians which are aboslute YIN, whilst the heart and kidney are seen

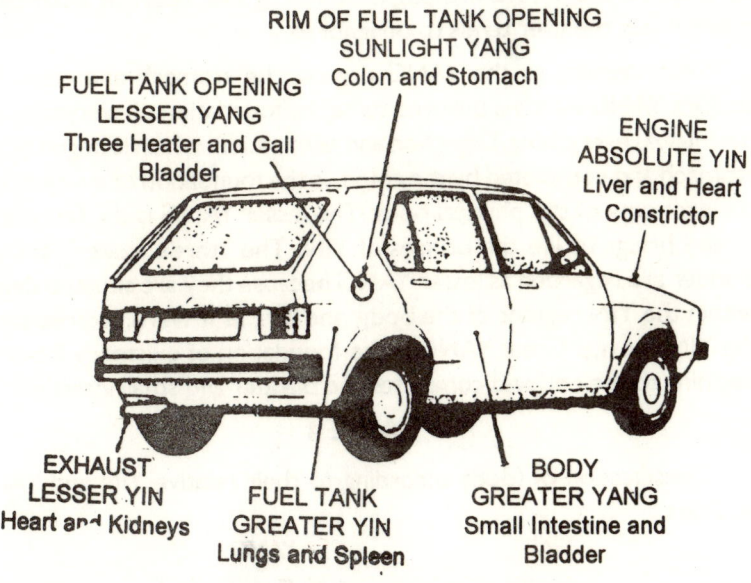

Figure 2: Quality of yin and yang in different body-areas compared with a car.

as lesser YIN as they tend to be posterior.

These relations between YIN and YANG could be explained better by taking a motor car to construct an analogy (see figure above). The outside is bathed in sunlight and is great YANG. The rim of petrol tank inlet is lesser YANG whilst the petrol cap is sunlight YANG.

As we descend into the petrol tank we pass through great YIN. The engine is absolute YIN and the exhaust, which is in contact with the outside, is lesser YIN. According to Chinese medicine the lesser YIN organs had to be deep in the body and contain rapidly flowing substance. Moreover, they had to be in contact with the outside. The two organs which fit these requirements are the heart and kidney. Absolute YIN is the linking area between lesser YIN and great YIN. Since the great YIN is the foundation of everything hidden and mysterious, the lungs and spleen were considered as great YIN, and the liver and heart constrictor as absolute YIN, which connects lesser YIN and great YIN. The liver lies between the pancreas (which is incorporated in the Chinese concept of spleen) and the right kidney, whilst the heart constrictor or pericardium undoubtedly lies snugly between the heart and lungs. The absolute YIN is the foundation of greatness and honesty. This is in contrast to the western thought which figures heart in both these qualities but the liver tends to be ignored.

With respect to the YANG organs, the stomach and colon are sunlight YANG which is believed to be the foundation of everything and permeates everything. Digestion and elimination, which is begun by the stomach and completed by the colon, is the foundation of everything in the economy of the physical body. The lesser YANG is the foundation of and brings to life the orifices of YIN. The "three heater" and gall bladder are regarded as lesser YANG because they are situated deeply within the YIN regions of the body, and are, as it were, expression of the YIN activity. Great YANG is the foundation of existence from the begining to the end and comprises the bladder and small intestine.

TABLE 4

Classification of foods according to their relative YIN and YANG qualities.

YIN	YANG
Fruits	Grains
Leafy vegetables	Root vegetables

Sugar	Salt
Fluids/juices	Herb teas
Tea/Coffee	Nuts & seeds
Alcohol	Meat/Fish/Cheese
Drugs/'Chemicals'	Eggs
Raw food	Cooked food
Yoghurt (Curds)	Miso
Spicy foods	Bitter foods

The food we eat (see Table 4) may also be analysed in terms of YIN and YANG instead of more conventional, analytical method, and it can be seen that diet will also play an important part in harmonising the YIN and YANG. An entire 'science' of nutrition termed macrobiotics has grown up around this concept and, many ideas are undoubtedly very valuable. Eating foods which are either extremely YIN or extremely YANG, such as sugar or salt, are likely to bring about imbalances: a belief shaved by all naturopaths and now fully vindicated by science. A corrollary to this theory that only locally grown food should be consumed seems to have a commonsense basis, but the application of it in our modern world is too difficult and inhibiting for most people. It may be reasonably questioned whether a rigid adherence to such a philosophy pays off. The axiom 'moderation in all things' might perhaps apply here and it can be argued that if predominantly locally grown produce is consumed, limited excursion into foods from different areas and other countries would do no harm. On the contrary, to awaken the YIN and YANG—if lying dormant—would be even better.

The Governing Laws of Acupuncture Treatment

The Chinese concept about nature is not much different from what the ancient Indian belief is that five elements rule the world. The whole world is created by them. Despite the apparent similarity there is vast difference in the choice of elements and their corelation with the human body.

The Five Elements Law:—

The traditional Chinese view is that when creation took place the YIN and the YANG brought forth the five elements water, wood, fire earth and metal[1] which made up the material substance of everything in the world. The interaction of YIN and YANG, balanced by the Tao, ensured that the proportion of these elements was correctly maintained. Even though the concept of the five elements is an oriental one, this idea of how the universe is constructed has not only stood the test of time but is a source of great insight and understanding to those who take the trouble to study it. We shall now examine the special meanings of the elements in acupuncture diagnosis and treatment by taking the elements one by one.

---

[1] The Indian concept is that these five elements are water, fire, earth, sky and air.

Water:—

As we all knopw water is the basic requirement to the existence of life on the earth. In man it is the fluids of the body which nourish and maintain the health of every cell and if these fluids become obstructed or toxic the result is disease, degeneration and, ultimately, death. It is not surprising that the kidney, which is said to store the ancestral energy, is especially linked to this element. Water is the most YIN of all the elements and is the main component of man as it is the source of nourishment that maintains the body. The movement of water in a fountain evokes a form and, in a similar way, the element of water gives form to the body. Water corresponds to the vital fluids, blood, lymph, mucus, semen and fat. Being the universal solvent it cleanses as well as nourishes. It is associated with the kidney, which nourishes the bones, with the special sense of hearing, and with head hair. It is adversely affected by cold and it manifests a dark colour of violet or black. It nourishes the wood and exercises a controlling action upon fire (see the figure 3). When in balance there will be healthy teeth and hair, good hearing and sexual vitality.

Wood

Wood represents the vegetative life within man; all the activities that continue when unconscious such as digestion heart beat, respiration and basic metabolism. In particular it relates to the activity

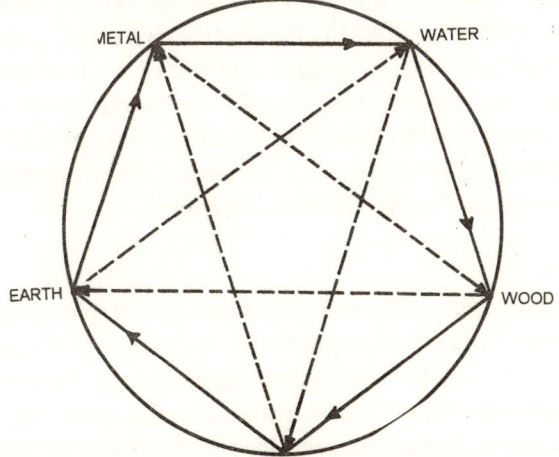

Figure 3: The five phases depicted as the five elements related by the sheng or nurtrition cycle (continuous line) and the ko or inhibiting cycle (dotted line).

of growing and increasing, and may be regarded as the "spring" phase of life. When in balance it should give the strength of a tree combined with the suppleness of a sapling. It is associated with liver which feeds the muscles, tendons and ligaments and is related to the eyes. It noursihes fire and controls earth (by covering and penetrating it). The interrelation of the elements is explained through the means of a chart.

FIRE

Fire symbolises the combustion that occurs within the body, functions which have reached a stage of maximum activity and are about to decline, and also the higher spirit of psychic aspects of man. It is associated with the heart which nourishes the circulatory system and is related to the tongue or sense of speech. When in balance there will be equanimity of spirit, a sound mind and a healthy circulation. It nourishes earth (fire creates earth by producing ash) and controls metal (by melting it). It is adversely affected by excess heat.

EARTH

Earth symbolise stability or being properly anchored. Water, wood, fire and metal all have their relative positions in respect to earth. In the macrocosm without water there would be no visible life; without wood or vegetation the earth would be barren and human life could not be supported; without fire or warmth the world would be a frozen waste; and without metal the earth would be sterile. Earth is associated with the spleen which nourishes the connective tissue and is related to the sense of taste. When in balance the individual is mentally stable, contented, and experiences physical and social well-being. Earth nourishes metal (it gives rise to the metallic elements such as sodium, potassium, magnesium, iron, zinc, calcium and other essential nutrients) and controls water by damming and filtering it.

METAL

Although symbolically, metal has a cutting and reforming action, yet it also refers to the solidifying process. In this aspect it can be seen as in opposition to fire and, clearly, the balance is again important. Metal elements are also donors of electrons and in this sense metal, although very *yin*, vivifies and produces *yang*. It nourishes water (it becomes liquid under the influence of fire, but it also dissolves in water) and controls wood (metal cuts wood). It is associated with the lungs which nourish the skin and are related to the nose and sense of smell. Those in whom metal is well balanced are strong, have healthy skins, healthy assimilation and elemination and are resistant to disease.

TABLE 5
Some correspondences to the five elements.

ELEMENT	WOOD	FIRE	EARTH	METAL	WATER
VISCERA	Liver	Heart	Spleen	Lungs	Kidneys
ASSOCIATED ORGAN	Gall Bladder	Small instestine	Stomach	Colon	Bladder
TISSUE	Muscle/ligaments	Vascular system	Connective tissue	Skin	Bone/teeth
ORIFICE	Eyes	Ears	Mouth	Nose	Genitalia/anus
SENSE REFLECTED IN	Sight Nails	Speech Complexion	Taste Lips	Smell Body hair	Hearing Head hair
FLUID	Tears	Sweat	Lymph	Mucus	Saliva
ODOUR	Rancid	Burnt	Sweet	Fleshy	Putrid
EMOTION	Anger	Joy	Empathy	Grief	Fear
SEASON	Spring	Summer	Midsummer	Autumn	Winter
ADVERSE WEATHER	Wind	Heat	Humid/damp	Dry	Cold
VOICE	Shouting	Laughing	Singing	Weeping	Groaning

Climate & Health

The ancient Chinese Considered Climatic factor to be the principal external disease causing factors and for this reason, much of their medical literature abounds with discussions about the weather. This, however, is not as odd as it appears on prima facie knowledge because a great deal of scientific investigation has now been carried out on the connection between disease and climate, season and weather and some very interesting facts have emerged. The Mistral (wind) of the Mediterranean causes migraine, insomnia, recurrence of nuralgia aggravation of tuberculosis and bronchitis. Hippocratic medicine speaks of pains which occur prior to changes in the weather and patients who can predict weather by their own sympotms are well known. Surgeons know that complications to surgery occur more frequently at certain times and a study by Dr. J. Kummal, as early as in 1936, showed that operations are more dangerous when the weather is changing. It is well established that rheumatism is aggravated by sudden falls in temperature, strong winds and the influx polar air masses, a discovery first made by the Dutch doctor, Dr. Tromp. That asthma is vunerable to the influence of weather is what even the modern researches indicate. It is probably aggravated by an increase in the relative proportion of positive ions in the atmosphere and by lowering of the barometric pressure below a certain level. It is also aggravated sometimes by pollen which may account for its high incidence in summer. Deaths from heart disease occur more often in very hot or very cold weather, in short in extreme temperatures.

To the Chinese cold was particularly harmful to the functions and organs related to water. This belief conforms to the prevalent medical concept now that cold adversely affects the kidneys and bones—hence the expressions "Chills on the kidney" and Chilled to the bone." The wood was thought to be particularly vunerable to the east wind and the invasion of wind gives rise to the aches and pains in the muscle and ligaments which tend to move around the body. Fire is aggravated by heat, earth by humidity and metal by dryness. Respiratory conditions are known to be made worse by very dry conditions and the skin is also not at its best when the weather is dry.

Emotions Versus The Five Elements:

As is also the ancient Indian concept the Chinese also believed that a healthy emotional state was indipensable condition of good general health. To them the correct balance of assertiveness, joy, calmness, sympathy and respect were essential. Excessive anger, excessive joy or excitement, obsession, prolonged or dispassinate grief and fearfulness or anxiety were the internal adverse factors which resulted in disease. More correctly, they are the manifestation of imbalances in the five elements caused by internal factors and represent a weakness or fixation in one of the elements.

Anger is related to wood and is thus reflected in our use of the word 'liverish'. Inability to express anger is seen as a weakness in the wood. Excessive joy or excitement is seen as harmful to the fire and the association between joy and fire must be more than mere imagination since the heart 'jumps with joy' and 'misses a beat' from excessive excitement. Lack of joy is a depressive state related to the fire and can often be dramatically cured by simple tonifecation of the heart meridian. The earth is related to the centre and 'being centred' or properly grounded allows us to experience empathy and calmness.

The 'grasshoper' like mentality and inability to concentrate may be caused by problems with the stomach or spleen which are related to earth. In this connection, it cannot be emphasised too greatly or too often that the Chinese were not speaking of the precise anatomical organs as we understand them today, but to physiological functions connected more with the *'qi'* or vital energy than the gross, visible material structure or corresponding physiology.

Grief, as we know has a direct bearing on the function of lungs. One gasps or holds one's breath on hearing bad news, whilst the skin conditions are well known to be aggravated by anxiety. Prolonged or disproportionate grief is recongnisable type of depression and the focus of treatment in these cases must be lungs.

The reader must be well aware of the physiological effects of excessive fear. The "butterflies in the stomach" and visit to lavatory are common occurence when one is asked to give a public performance which are the symptoms of excessive fear. Similarly, the flavour of sweetness is associated with earth which encompasses the

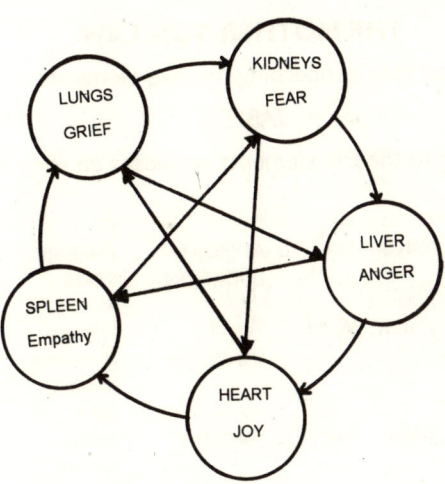

Figure 4: *The mutual relationship of the zang (yin) organs in accordance with the sheng and ko cycles and the corresponding emotions.*

spleen-pancreas. It is evident that diabetes, a disease of the pancreas, is closely related to sugar intake which has experienced an astronomical rise over the hundred years or so. During the war years in Europe, when sugar was rationed, diabetes declined at the same rate with the consumption of sugar.

It may be mentioned that according to the *ko* cycle *(shown in Figure 4)*, anger overcomes sympathy, joy overcomes grief, empathy or sympathy overcomes fear, grief overcomes anger and fear overcomes joy. How many people lead joyless lives because they are racked by anxiety or fear and how many criminals, thugs and delinquents are ill because of imbalances in their energy which could easily be put right by acupuncture and correct nutrition? Drugs, electroconvulsive therapy and prison have all been tried and found wanting but for some obscure reason no society has yet been brave enough to substitute these measures with economically sounder and more promising treatment outlined in Chinese medicine!

The acupuncture points which are particularly helpful in regulating the energy on the basis of an appraisal of the five elements are mentioned in Table 6.

THE MOTHER-SON LAW

This is a typical idea concerning the five elements

TABLE 6

Points relating to the five elements or phases on each of the principal meridians.

(1) DESCRIPTION CHINESE	(1) DESCRIPTION ENGLISH	(3) YANG	(4) YIN	(5) APPROXEN LOCATION	(6) ENERGIC STATE	(7) MOST USEFUL FOR:
Jing	Well	Metal	Wood	Tips of fingers/toes	Energy is at its most mutable point	Mental illness
Young	Brook	Water	Fire	Hands/feet	Energy is more specifically polar	Febrile illness
Yu	Stream	Wood	Earth	Hands/feet	Energy flows more strongly	Painful joints

| Ching | River | Fire | Metal | Wrist/ankle | Energy concentrates | Respiratory disorders |
| Ho | Sea | Earth | Water | Elbow/Knee | Energy emerges from or enters a deeper level | Digestive disorder |

Column 1 lists the Chinese description, column 2 gives the approximate English equivalent, column 3 and 4 tell the polarity of the meridian, column 5 notes the approximate anatomical position, column 6 shows the level or state of energy at that stage and column 7 indicates the most useful therapeutic indication. These points are most suitable for manipulating the energy and are frequently employed for treatment based upon a diagnosis of the relative state of the five phases.

Mutual relation. It would better be described as a working hypothesis rather than a law. In fact it is nothing more than the *sheng* cycle since it proposes that the liver is the 'mother' of the heart, the heart the 'mother' of the spleen, the spleen-pancreas the 'mother' of the lungs, the lungs the 'mother' of the kidneys and the kidneys the 'mother' of the liver. The same relationship exists between the gall bladder and small intestine, the stomach and colon, the bladder and gall bladder, which are the 'coupled' organs.

A trouble mainfested by any organ in the body is thought to be due to its not being properly nourished by the 'mother'. A lung disorder, for example, is seen as a failure of the heart to transmit vital energy or qi to the lungs: an explanation which is by no means inconsistent with Western medical thinking.

Rhythm Round The Clock

Normally everyday is divided into four distinct period—morning, afternoon, evening and night. These daily divisions are like miniature seasons of spring, summer, autumn and winter. Thus, the annual rhythm of life is influenced by this daily variation. The significance of this is considerable and a great many scientific papers have been devoted to this topic. The weather is also influenced by this cycle: strong winds abate in the evening and storms are more frequent in the late afternoon. All our bodily functions vary according to the time of day. For example, blood levels of melatonin, a hormone secreted by the pineal gland, are high at night and low during the day. This, in turn, causes reduction in the activity of the ovaries at night. Blood pressure and body temperature are higher in the evening than they are in the early morning— at least in healthy people. Babies tend to be born in the early hours of the morning, and it has been established that it is actually easier to give birth at that time than at other periods of the day. It is interesting that more people die at this time as well! According to Ancient Chinese Belief, there is surge of vital energy or *qi* in each organ in every two hour period of every twenty-four cycle. This starts in the lungs between 3-5 a.m. because the expansion of the lungs signifies the drawing of energy into the system. Apparently, we should be born during those hours! There is little doubt that the time of birth is significant and should be under the control of the foetus. The postponement of birth to 'office' hours is thought by traditional practitioners and modern doctors alike to be disadvantageous to the baby.

In conformity with the Chinese clock, symptoms of excess will be aggravated at the time of fullness of energy, whilst those of deficiency may be aggravated at the opposite period of the day when the organ energy is at its minimum. These periods are sued to treat the relevant

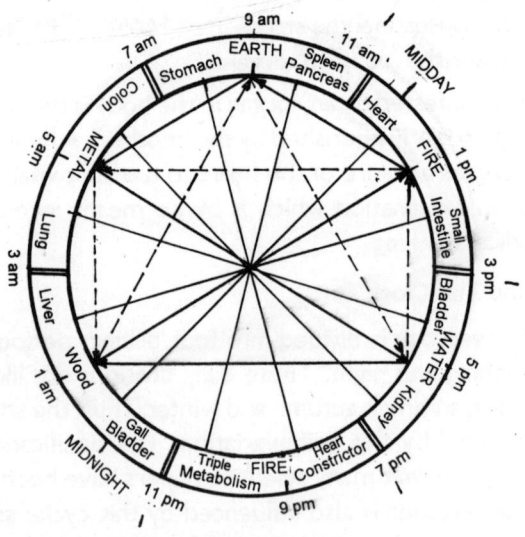

Figure 5: The Chinese Clock This indicates the periods of optimal energy in the different phases and related organs or functions. Superimposed upon this are the sheng (nutrition) cycle, denoted by the continuous heavy line and the ko (inhibitory) cycle, denoted by the intermittent line. The faint lines traversing the centre denote the Midday Midnight

organs and there are even specific points on each of the twelve main meridians or channels where this may be best carried out. These are known as horary points. On each meridian, there are points which relate preferentially to each of the five element or phases and the horary point is the one which relates to the element of that particular organ and for that reason is also known as the 'element' point. In a deficiency state the point is used at the beginning of the two hour period when the energy is starting its surge. In excess conditions the point it treated with a sedating technique at the end of the period.

The Midday-midnight Law:—

According to this law it would be inconvenient to treat the liver during its appropriate period, which is in the early hours of the morning, and even the most dedicated doctor would not take kindly to his patients turning up at 3 am to have their lungs toned up. As a rule, patients do not turn up for treatment during the hours of night which is an extremely good thing. Fortunately, according to the Midday-Midnight Law a patient who has liver problems and requires treatment between 1 am and 3 am can come and have exactly the opposite treatment done to his small intestine at the same hours in the afternoon. The Chinese doctors obviously realised that without such a law they would get no sleep, and even if it had not been discovered it would surely have had to have been invented. Figure 5 shows the Chinese clock and the implications of the Midday-Midnight Law can be easily seen from this.

It is of great academic interest that when the sheng and ko cycle relationship are placed into this picture, these both form numerous regular geometric patterns, a phenomenon which has not been previously noted. It contributes nothing to say medical or therapeutic application of these laws but enhances a little the theory that God is a mathematician.

The Husband-And-Wife Law

According to Traditional Chinese Medicine, half the organs of the body are reflected in the pulse at the left wrist and the other half at the right wrist. There are three positions and at least two levels at each pulse. These three positions are approximately one finger's width apart. The levels are superficial and deep. The superficial level can be felt by very lightly touching the skin. The deep level can be felt by pressing hard enough, almost to obliterate the pulse. Each level at each position reflect a different organ which is shown in Table 7. The organs associated with the right side are 'wife'. In health, the husband should be dominant and wife submissive. The sexist terminology is used to explain an underlying truth about the relationship between the organs. If a 'wife' dominates a 'husband', the seed of disorder has already been sown.

The acupuncturist learn a great deal about the energy in the different organs from the pulses and that is why he will somtimes spend quite a lot of time feeling the different pulses.

It may be curious to note that the pulse reading is also given much emphasis in the ayurvedic school of medicine which suggest both the styles of diagnosis being not much different.

TABLE 7

The left and right pulses slowing the related organs and the Husband-and-Wife-Laws.

Position	Level	'Husband' Left Wrist	'Wife' Right wrist
Distal	Deep	Heart	Lungs
	superficial	Small Intestines	Colon
Medial	Deep	Liver	Spleen-pancreas
	superficial	Gall Bladder	Stomach
	Deep	Kidneys	Heart Constrictor
Proximal	Superficial	Bladder	Triple Metabolism

Qi, Organs, Meridians & Acupuncture Points

Qi?

The natural query is: What is Qi? It has been already mentioned that the term 'qi' or 'Ch'i' is the name given by the Chinese to denote the subtle energic principle which activates the body and maintains it in good health.

It is often very difficult for those who have been born and brought up in a modern western society to appreciate the concept of 'qi' when all our bodily functions are described in the analytical terms of physics and chemistry. The energy within the body is only understood as heat or electricity liberated from high energy molecules.

When the working of the body as a whole is considered, perhaps the good analogy is that of radio and television receivers which operate on two type of energy. On one hand they both require electrical power either supplied by the mains or a battery; this source of power could be compared to normal food of the human being. It is interesting that neither radio nor television can work without a measured current which, incidently produces heat as food does in the body. On the other hand, and much more important to their proper function, however, are the radio and television waves which are subtle electromagnetic waves permeating the envirnonment which are 'absorbed' by the radio and television, and presented into a recognisable audible or visual display. The very existence of such waves would have been strongly denied by scientists of earlier centuries because there was no technology to recognise them. In fact, of course, many of them would not have existed since there was no broadcasting, but diffuse energy within these wave lengths has always existed, even if it remained obscure until our modern invention of the radio and television. Many other electromagnetic energies of various wavelengths abound in our universe and we can categorise these under the broad description of cosmic radiation. These cosmic energies are selectively absorbed by the human being and transmuted for his or her own benefit.

References to these invisible bodies symbolising energy are to be found in a wide variety of text originating in China, India, Egypt and ancient Greece. The Bible too refers frequently to the subtle anatomy of man, particularly in 'The Revelation of St. Jhon'. A little further on he writes about the etheric body having three basic functions.

"It acts as a receiver of energies, an assimilator of energies and as a transmitter of energies. If each of these functions is maintained in a state of balance, then the physical body reflects this interchange of energies as a state of good health! This very succinctly summarises the Chinese concept of 'qi' and even its derangement, thought by Chinese to be brought about by internal and external devils (adverse emotions and harmful environmental factors).

Qi is said to be extracted from the food after it has been properly digested. This is done by spleen but if the food is not fully digested the 'qi' is not properly refined and gross 'impure' substance will be sent by the spleen to different parts of the body where it will cause pollution, congestion and disease. This is another way of stating the fact that poor digestion is the foundation of disease. If the digestion is good, the 'qi' is transported by spleen to the lungs where it combines with ancestral 'qi' from the kidneys and 'qi' of the body. The qi is sent to all parts of the body and it permeates the entire organism, initiating and sustaining movement, protecting the body from adverse invasive factors from the outside, constituting a warp to hold everything in place, maintaining normal temperature and generating the vital substances such as blood, urine, sweat, tears and semen. According to its function the qi is distinguished in the following way.

(i)   **Organ Qi:—** The qi in each of the organ is the same but functions differently in different organs in much the same way as radio waves might produce classical music on one channel on the radio, a debate on another and jazz on a third. A closer examination of the organs and functions will be made when we shall be elaborating on the 'zang fu' phenomenon.

(ii) **Meridian Qi:**— This is the qi or energy that is transmitted via the meridian network and is responsible for sustaining the body and contributing towards its material development.

(iii) **Protective Qi:**— The Protective qi circulates between the skin and flesh and is responsible for protecting the body from adverse external influences. It controls the pores of the body, moistens the skin and is involved in the production of sweat and urine.

(iv) **Nutritive Qi:**— This is the energy which contributes to the formation of the blood and moves inseparably with the blood within the vessels.

(v) **Ancestral Qi And source Qi:**— Ancestral qi is the motivating force behind the nutritive and protective qi. It concentrates within the chest and aids the rhythmic movements of respiration and heart beat. This is the qi that moves the blood. Source qi is of congenital origin and is stored in the kidneys and is said to be the root of the twelve primary meridians and the fount of life.

(vi) **Disturbance of Qi:**— Stagnant qi : This is when the orderly movement of qi is impaired. When this occurs in the limb it mainfests itself as aches and pains. When it is in the organs it shows up in different ways as shown in the table on next page.

(vii) **Rebellious Qi:**— This implies that qi is going in the wrong direction. For example, the qi of the spleen should go upwards, and if it reverses there may be ultimately prolapse of the abdominal or pelvic organs. Another manifestation is diarrhoea. On the other hand the qi of the stomach should go downwards, and if this is rebellious there will be vomitting. Rebellious qi is a subcategory of stagnant qi.

TABLE 8

[Some symptioms of stagnant and deficient qi in the five zang (YIN organ-symptoms).]

ORGAN	STAGNANT QI	DEFICIENT QI
Liver	Distension of chest and Abdomen and menstrual disorders	Irritability, timidity, fear, incision, blurred vision
Heart	Stabbing pain in the left shoulder and feet, blueness of lips.	Spontaneous sweating, lethargy, short of breath.
Spleen	Retention of urine, fullness or distension of chest & abdomen.	Lassitude, muscular weakness, loss of appetite, oedema, diarrhoea.
Lungs	Cough, shortness of breath.	Weak cough, asthma, weakness of voice, fatigue.
Kidneys	Incontinence, oedema	Backache, reduced sexual drive shortness of breath.

(viii) **Deficient qi:**— This may affect the entire body with resulting tiredness and lethargy, or may be in a particular organ (Table 8).

(ix) **Collapsed qi:**— This is a subcategory of deficient qi and is manifested by prolapses.

BLOOD:—

It is extremely difficult to identify the difference between the Chinese concept of blood and the blood which we know circulates in our blood vessels. Infact they are much the same thing, but the Chinese concept of blood envisages a fluid which is not entirely confined to the blood vessels but even flows in the meridians. Blood is formed by the action of qi upon elements of nutrition, having been transported by the spleen to the lungs and heart. There is a close relationship between the blood and qi and it is the qi that moves the blood. If the blood is deficient the face will be pale and lustreless, and the skin may become dry. In the heart a deficiency produces a dull, pale complexion, insomnia, poor memory and palpitations. In other organs it will produce other symptoms. The blood may also be stagnated or congealed, a condition often characterised by sharp, stabbing pains. There may be swelling of organs where there is congealed blood.

BODY FLUIDS:— Known as 'Jin ye', the body fuids are secreted by the cells of the body and include tears, sweat, saliva, milk, genital secretions, intestinal secretions and, perhaps most important of all, the secretion of endocrine glands or harmones.

THE ORGANS:— 'Zung fu' is the name for the organ system in Chinese Medicine. Most of them are equated to the corresponding anatomical organs known to western science but the Chinese concepts are slightly different, much wider and embrace functions not normally attributable to the organs in Western science (see Table 9). In addition there is a triple metabolism, which is sometimes known as the "three heater", and also the pericardium, which is known as 'heart constrictior' or 'circulation sex'. The three heater refers more or less to the three types of metabolism going on in the body, namely the interchange of gases in the lungs and tissues which takes place in the upper heater, and the metabolism of elimination and sexual function which is the lower heater. The 'three heater' system is also intimately connected with what we call the endocrine system in Western physiology. The heart constrictor, as its various names suggest, is a sort of protector of the heart as well as being connected with circulation and sexual function.

TABLE 9

[The Zang-fu organs, their functions and designations as State Officials.]

ORGAN	OFFICIAL	FUNCTIONS
Liver	Military General	Seat of the soul. Controls metabolism, removes toxins, stores blood. Sends pure energy to gall bladder.

ORGAN	OFFICIAL	FUNCTIONS
Gall Bladder	Decision Maker	Receives pure energy from liver. Stores and secretes bile. Overactivity results in rash decisions; under activity in indecision.
Heart	Emperor	Seat of all powers of mind and soul. Rules blood and vessels. Stores the 'shen'(spirit).
Small Intestine	Chief Executive	Separates pure from impure. Transforms matter into pure energy and waste. If it is in disharmony the body lacks nourishment and there is stagnation of thought.
Heart Constrictor	Ambassador of joy and happiness	Protects the heart. Together with the three heater moves blood and qi throughout the body and harmonises the activity.
Three Heater	Minister of Central heating & Water ways	Controls body temperature. Together with heart constrictor enables all the other 'zang fu' function. Water ways probably refers to the lymph system.
Stomach	Official of Rotting and Ripening	Receives roots, ripens the food. Sends 'pure' part to the spleen and 'turbid' part to small intestines.

ORGAN	OFFICIAL	FUNCTIONS
Spleen	Minister of Transport and Distribution	Transports energy throughout the body. Sends energy from food to the lungs. Moves and transports water.
Kidneys	Minister of Health and Social Security	Stores ancestral energy (jing). Rules birth, growth and maturation. Rules water.
Bladder	Provincial Governor	Receive and excretes urine. Complements kidneys and lower three heater.
Colon	Minister of Drains	Removes wastes from the body. Instigates change. Disharmony of colon results in a rigid type of thinking.
Lungs	Administrators of Orderly conduct.	Controls qi. Seat of the soul which more or less refers to nervous system. They also rule water and the outside of the body.

THE MERIDIANS:— The system of meridians is called jing luo which traverse the body and acts as transmitters of qi. the twelve 'regular' meridians which are associated directly with the twelve organs are known as the main meridians. There are also eight 'extra' meridians, so called because they are ancillary to the principal meridians, although two of these which traverse the midlines of the body and have their own points are included with the other twelve main meridians. The remaining six extra meridians have transits which coincide with portions or segments of the main meridians and they lack any independent point. They are sometimes known as lesser meridians. However, another name for them is miraculous meridians.

Those symptoms that are experienced by a patient are often seen to be on a particular meridian, so it is vital for the acupuncturist to have an intimate knowledge of the precise pathway of every meridian in order that he can make a correct interpretation of such symptoms. Pain at the back of the head or in the neck or shoulders may be associated with the gall bladder or its meridian which traverses those areas; whereas pain in the face or teeth might be related to the stomach or colon meridians.

The main meridians that are connected by joining vessels known as *lo ro luo* meridians. These connect the coupled organs such as the lungs and colon and they join each meridian to its successor in the general circuit of energy around the body as portrayed by the Chinese clock (see Figure 5). So, for example, the colon meridian which ends around the nasal area is joined to the stomach meridian which originates just under the eye.

The additional meridians, are also subsidiary vessels known as tendino-muscular meridians and distinct or divergent meridians. These follow similar pathways to the major meridians.

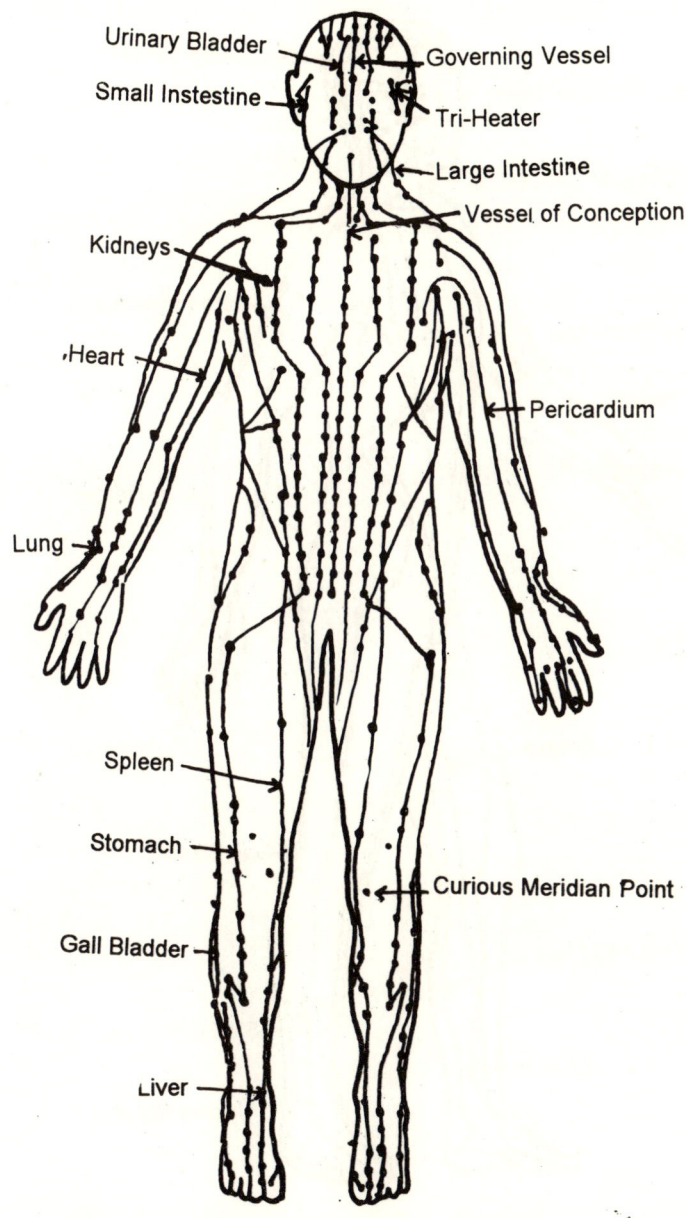

Figure 6: *The meridians and acupuncture points. (Front view)*

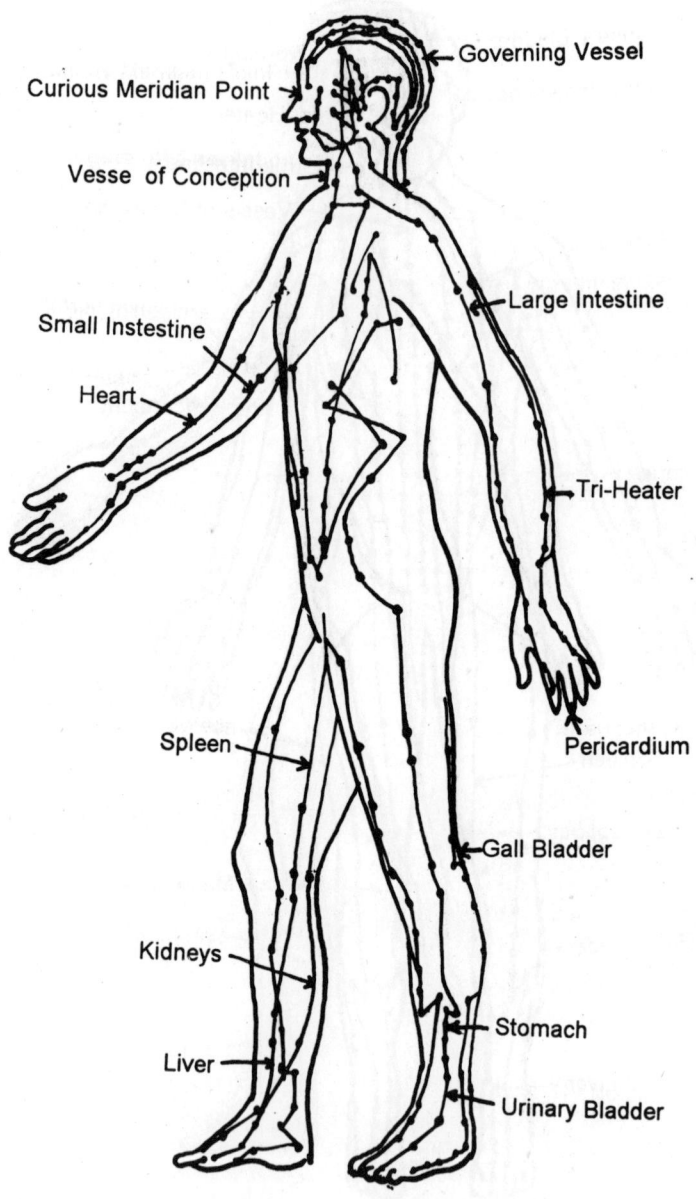

Figure 7: The meridians and acupuncture points. (side view)

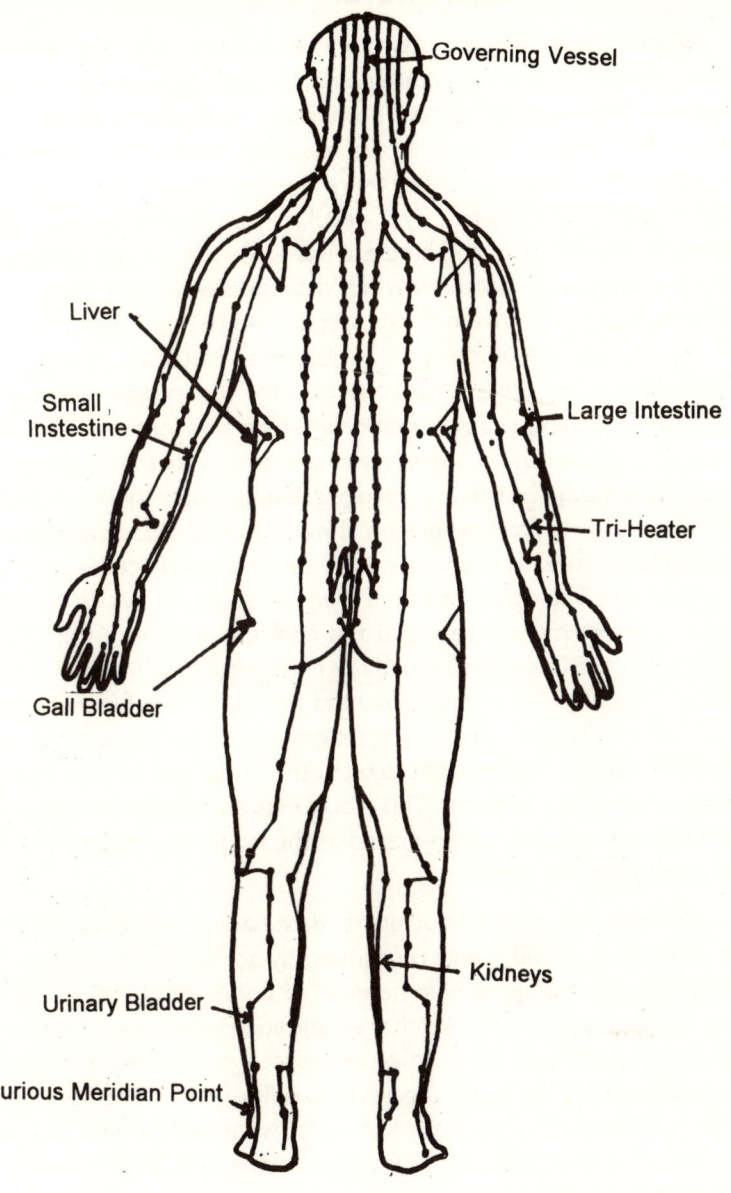

Figure 8: The meridians and acupuncture points. (Back view)

ACUPUNCTURE POINTS

Despite some scientists claim to have demonstrated the existence of the meridians and acupuncture points through tissue analysis and the assertion of this fact by Walter Thompson in his book Acupuncture as Far as We know, it cannot be asserted that this evidence is unquestionable. In all probability there are such routes within the body which are identifiable by peculiar proportions of DNA (deoxyribonucleic acid) and bioelectrical activity, and quite some time ago it was suggested that there was a 'data transfer system' much more primitive than the known nervous system, which operates on a direct current of miniscule amperage. Dr. Margaret Patterson, in her book *Addictions can be Cured*, argues the case for the existence of such a system in her attempt to give a rational explanation for the phenomena of acupuncture. It can be said with virtual certainty that there are points around the body which are recognisable through their bioelectric activity or ability to transmit electrical impulses with less resistance than surrounding tissue. The points can be termed acupuncture points or acupoints. Dr. Thompson refers to them as 'acupores' which seems to be a very much more meaningful and descriptive name. After all, it is unlikely that the Creator designed the human body with points all over it for the benefit of doctors of Chinese medicine! The function of the acupores is to receive electromagnetic energy from the environment, to transmute and transmit this around the body, and to 'excrete' the energy which is not required. This would entirely validate the traditional view that the needles, when placed in the acupores, help to regulate and harmonise the energy.

Although 365 acupores or points date back to antiquity yet there are now some, 2,000 points recognised by acupuncturists today. This figure includes a considerable number of points on the external ear, nose, hands, feet and scalp which are replications of the entire meridians and organs portrayed as micro acupuncture systems on small areas of the body: notably the sense organs. This reflex system may be used for acupuncture on the ears, nose and scalp, whilst on the feet the most common therapeutic action is massage. On the eyes, the phenomenon is utilised for diagnostic purposes only.

The Causes And Diagnosis of Various Diseases
CAUSES OF DISEASE

The conventional medical thinking lists the follwing eight factors as the potential causes of any disease.

1. Genetic. (This compares with (9) below.)
2. Nutritional. This may be under-nutrition or malnutrition.
3. Metabolic. This includes tumours
4. Infection.
5. Environmental. Includes exposure to environmental toxins and adverse climatic factors.
6. Structural. Trauma could be included under this heading.
7. Allergy. This could be regarded as a sub-category of metabolic disorder.
8. Wearing out.

Although Chinese medical thinking is not different, yet it lists them in the following order.

1. The external evil influences of wind, heat, fire, damp, dryness, and cold. (Similar to (5) above.)
2. The mental pathogens (internal devils) of anger, worry, anxiety, excessive grief, excessive fear and fright.
3. Epidemics. (Similar to (4) above.)
4. Bad foods and beverages. (Similar to (2) above.)
5. Excessive sexual activity.
6. Trauma from incidents such as animal bites and accidents. (Similar to (6) above.)
7. Visceral parasites.
8. Poisoning.
9. Hereditary factors.

The relationship between the adverse weather conditions and emotions has already been discussed in the earlier chapter. Before the discovery of microorganisms in the West, the Chinese had a remarkable understanding of epidemics and realised that they could be spread by lack of ventilation, overcrowding, infected people or animals and contaminated water. The custom of drinking a lot, of boiled water in the form of weak tea had its origins in this knowledge. Long before inoculation of smallpox was known in the West, the Chinese were using this form of immunisation against smallpox. The value of inoculation and vaccination is now uncertain, but it indicates that the Chinese displayed a considerable insight into the transmission of infections.

POOR NUTRITION

There is no doubt at all that absolute priority should be given to the provision of adequate food and clean water for all populations. This is independent of acupuncture or any other therapy. Eating wisely is an integral precept of Chinese medicine which, as expected, stresses the importance of balance. It has already been noted how excessive salt and sugar consumption can harm people; In addition to that, the modern practices of refining, adding nonnutritive chemicals, overcooking, incorrect cooking, bad preparation, freezing storing, preserving and mixing foods are all contributing daily to our ill-health. The poor nutritional quality of the food, together with other prevalent modern influences, encourages overeating—another serious and ubiquitous present-day nutritional source of disease. According to traditional medicine, food which is not properly digested in the stomach gives rise to contamination of the 'essence' or energy sent to the spleen and liver. This results in the body having to recruit exceptional methods of eliminating waste matter such as boils, skin eruptions, perspiration, etc. The condition may reach the stage where a fever is induced to 'burn up' this accumulated matter which often takes on the form of excess phlegm. The first, and best medicine is, therefore diet: either a restricted diet or a fast.

STRAIN

Strain is another cause of disease. According to the Chinese, too much walking strains the liver and gall bladder, which will be reflected in aching of the muscles and ligaments; too much looking affects the heart and small intestines and causes problems in the circulation; too much sitting injures the spleen and stomach which is noticed as sensitive flesh; too much lying down is detrimental to the lungs and colon, causing reactions on the skin; and too much standing injures the kidneys and bladder which results in aching bones.

Like the modern 'moderates', the ancient thinkers were more or less unanimous in their condemnation of excessive sexual activity, and some of their modern equivalents go as far as to say that all sexual activity if brought to the point of normal orgasm is injurious to the health as it 'saps vital energy'. Others are obsessed with the harmful effects of masturbation, though, logically, it cannot be seen that this can have any different physical effect to 'normal' sexual intercourse. It cannot be agreed as to what constitutes excess with regard to this activity but there seems little doubt that over-indulgence in sex, just as in anything else, will bring about eventual ill-health. On the other hand, sex without orgasm is often recommended as enhancing health and various techniques and postures are prescribed for different problems.

The Basis of All Diseases

According to acupuncture theory, the root casue of a disease is a disorder of vibration. Every cell in the body vibrates at a specific rate and vibration is, of course, energy. Vibrations outside the normal range are synonymous with disease. The insertion of needles aids the restoration of correct and harmonious vibration and in this way restores health.

Acupuncturist Method of Making the Diagnosis

What do you expect from an acupuncturist. How should be believe. After, I hope, making you welcome, he will listen very carefully to your history as any doctor should do. The only difference is that in addition to the usual questions asked by doctors about bowels, waterworks, appetite, sleeping habits, etc., he will ask what might seem to be some rather strange questions. No, he will not enquire about your heart constrictor or if you have a pain in your three heater, but he will want to know at what times your symptoms are worse, or for that matter better.

Suppose you wake up every morning with discomfort at about 1.30 a.m. he will suspect that you have a nattering gall bladder because, according to the Chinese clock, that is the time when the gall bladder is likely to be most vocal. He will be particularly anxious to know if you are affected in any way by the weather; especially heat, cold, damp or the wind. If you dislike the cold, or fear the cold, or your symptoms are worse in cold weather, the acupuncturist will turn his attention to the kidneys and bladder which are more vulnerable to cold than any other organs.

Of course, he will also ask you about your emotional state. If you tell him that you 'fly off the handle' easily he will suspect the liver or gall bladder; if you cry a lot he will probably think of the lungs, and if you are sad or anxious he will most likely be led to consider the spleen. He might want to know if you are attracted or repelled by any particular colour or taste because any positive reply to these questions would also be helpful in terms of assisting him to recognise a fixation in one of the elements.

The acupuncturist will take into consideration any medical tests which you might have undergone. Some of these tests are of virtually no value but many of them are extremely useful. It cannot be stressed too often that acupuncture is not opposed to other forms of medicine, and especially not to modern medical investigations. This is why it is necessary for acupuncturists to have medical knowledge. A case to illustrate this occurred in Sri Lanka when an Oriental lady working in a developed country was being tutored on an advanced course of acupuncture. She carried out an acupuncture treatment on a man with a serious heart condition in which she stimulated the kidneys. Now we have already learned in the earlier chapter that this will have a dampening effect upon the heart (water being put on the fire) and in this particular case it was obviously the wrong treatment. Had this lady been able to understand an electrocardiograph or taken the trouble to ask one of the many doctors who could explain, the treatment could have been modified accordingly. As it was, because of her ignorance and cynicism concerning Western medicine the man received a dangerous treatment. When subsequently questioned about this in her examination, the practitioner was rash enough to reply that the patient was fine after her treatment. What she did not know was that he was later taken into a coronary care unit.

It is generally believed that acupuncture (provided it is carried out by a trained acupuncturist) cannot do any harm. This is because the acupuncture cannot induce the body to do anything detrimental to itself. In other words, the needles can only encourage the body towards a balance or harmonisation. The author would agree with this principle: the problem in the case just related is that the kidneys of that particular patient did need stimulating but the important factor was the correct order or priority of treatment. It is the author's belief that the order of priority can be changed by acupuncture or even by massage or touch for that matter. In this case we are imposing upon the body a new order of correction or, put more accurately, we are directing the body's healing force to deal with compensations rather than the prime problem. Normally this does not matter too much and the very worst that happens is that the patient takes longer to recover, but occasionally it can be disastrous.

Let us concentrate again on your visit to the acupuncturist. He will also ask you about perspiration, belching, wind, sexual habits and work. Having given all the answers you will then be asked to disrobe for an examination.

Again the examination will follow usual procedures with a number of additions. These are centred mostly on the tongue, the eyes, the pulses and specific reactive points called the alarm points. He will ask you to put out your tongue and will note whether it comes out with a good thrust or goes slowly with reluctance. The first type of movement is *yang* and is a good sign. The second is *yin* and not so good. He will note if the tongue goes out a good way or not very far. The same two considerations apply. Then he will look at the colour and shape of the tongue itself. It should be a nice pink colour and slightly rounded. A very flat tongue indicates a *yin* condition. Teeth marks, cracks, or scalloping around the edges are all significant and are signs that something is not quite right. If the colour is a bright pink or red it probably indicates an excessive *yang* condition; whereas if it is a purple colour there is stagnation and probably congealed blood. Table 10 lists some of the types of tongues and moss (covering) with their respective indications. The moss should be a delicate white colour—anything else is a sign of imbalance.

TABLE 10
TONGUE APPEARANCE AND THE POSSIBLE DISORDERS.

APPEARANCE OF TONGUE	CONDITIONS
Brightened tongue	Symptoms due to heat.
Pale red tongue	Collapse of energy and blood which is often due to actual loss of blood.

Purple tongue	Stagnation of *qi* and blood or excess blood.
Pale tongue	Indication of *yin* condition. May be anaemia or malnutrition.
Cleft tongue	Deficiency of blood, *qi* or true *yin*.
Tooth marks on side (scalloping)	*Yang* deficiency or deficient *qi* of spleen and stomach
Fat tongue	Deficiency or cold
Quivering tongue	Injury to nervous system
Inability of tongue to protrude	Extreme weakness
Cracked tongue	Invasion of pathogenic heat

The moss (coating) may be white, yellow, grey or even black and the moss may be thick, thin, greasy or dry. Anything other than a thin white moss is abnormal.

Now the acupuncturist will examine your eyes. He is looking for signs in the iris which might give him a further clue to the basic problem causing your disorder. He might also carry out a normal opthalmoscopy in which he would look at the retina. He will then feel your pulses, a matter that has already been discussed in chapter 3. The ancient Chinese doctors would spend up to half an hour feeling these pulses and preferred to do it only at the crack of dawn, which are additional reasons for our placing less reliance on this now a days.

Then he may now feel your abdomen. He might do a normal abdominal examination but even if your problem has nothing to do with that area he might carry out an acupuncture examination of the abdomen. This consists of very lightly feeling the surface of the tummy for changes in temperature which can give more information about the twelve internal organs. Areas of the abdomen 'reflect' different organs and this is illustrated in Table 11.

The acupuncturist will also carry out a normal physiological examination of the part of the body concerned. If you have a pain in the shoulder, for example, he will test your shoulder by asking you to move your arm in different directions and then moving it for you to see if these 'passive' movements are easier for you. Finally, he will ask you to make the movements again but he will prevent you from actually carrying them out. This forces you to tighten your muscles without causing any movement and enables the doctor to find out if the problem is in the muscles or in the joint. He will also feel or palpate your shoulder to see if there is any swelling or inflammation.

TABLE 11

The front mu or alarm points for each of the zang fu. These points are often spontaneously tender when there is an acute disorder of the related organ.

ORGAN	ALARM POINT	APPROXIMATE LOCATION
Lungs	Zhongfu	Lower border of second rib on nipple line.
Colon	Tianshu	Two thumbs' width each side of navel.
Stomach	Zhongwang	Midway between navel and lower end of breast bone.
Spleen	Zhangmen	Free end of eleventh rib.
Heart	Jujue	On the midline eight fingers' width above the navel.
Small intestines	Guanyuan	On the midline four fingers' width below the navel.
Bladder	Zhongji	One thumb's width below guanyuan
Kidneys	Jingmen	Free end of twelfth rib.
Three heater	Shimen	On midline two thumbs' width below the navel.
Heart constrictor	Shanzhang	On the midline over the breast bone at the level of nipples.
Gall bladder	Riyue	Between 7th and 8th ribs on the nipple line.
Liver	Qimen	Two intercostal spaces directly below the nipple.

Next, he might carry out some special tests using foot zone therapy or applied kinesiology (see ahead) or he might even make use of one of the currently available diagnostic instruments. However, no practitioner is likely to do all these things and he will have selected the methods which he can do best and which he feels are the most suitable. More experienced acupuncturists are often able to make quite a rapid diagnosis with comparatively little testing. Even if your acupuncturist does not examine you at all you should not go elsewhere because he might have guessed your trouble with his long experience.

The Course Of The Treatment.

Before getting treated your predominant question will probably be, 'Is it going to hurt?' The answer is that it should be hardly painful at all. Sometimes it is so painless that a patient will not realise that a needle has been inserted, but on other occasions there is a mild burning sensation rather like a slight bee sting. If strong stimulation is sought by the doctor, you will certainly feel something as the needle is manipulated, but this should be a sensation of numbness, heaviness or tingling rather than actual pain. As it is your first visit he will probably put no more than three or four needles in, but in subsequent visits this may be increased.

Of course the acupuncturist will normally be only too pleased to talk about your problems and discuss the treatment with you he cannot concentrate on doing the acupuncture if he is being asked difficult questions at the same time—so try to keep these to a time before the treatment starts or after the needles have all been inserted.

The treatment can last from about five minutes up to half an hour and the average length of a session is about twenty minutes. It depends upon the disease and the experience of the acupuncturists.

At the conclusion of the treatment, you will probably be wondering what it will do to you and how often you will have to have further treatments. To answer the first question, it will help to harmonise your body functions so that you will probably feel very relaxed and, possibly, light and springy when you walk out of the surgery. You might experience this feeling for just a few hours or may be for the rest of the day. On the other hand you might feel very little or nothing at all. If it was a pain that took you along for the treatment it is very likely that it will already feel a little better. This lessening of the pain might last permanently or only for a short period of time. If it only lasts for a day or two or less, then you obviously require a few daily treatments or at least a few treatments on alternate days. As you get better, the treatments sould be spaced out more. This has more or less answered the second question, but the total duration of the treatments or total number of treatments will depend upon the seriousness of your condition, the length of time you have had it and your own recuperative powers.

Hering's Law of Cure

Constantine Hering, who was actually a homoeopath, always maintained that a true cure takes place from the head downwards, from inside the body to the outside, from the more vital organs to the less vital and symptoms disappear in the reverse order to their appearance. The first part of Hering's Law implies that healing starts in the mind, but sometimes symptoms do in fact literally travel down the body on their way out. If a skin lession occurs during treatment, this may very well be an indication that healing is taking place from inside out. The reappearance of long lost symptoms is a sure sign that healing is taking place. When symptoms change in reverse of Hering's Law we must ensure that they are not merely being suppressed and driven deeper into the body.

Perhaps at this times your acupuncturist might venture to give you some recommendations concerning your life style where a change would help you to be healthier. The ancient Chinese distinguished five levels of doctors. The lowest was the animal doctor who only treated animals. The next was the acupuncturist/herbalist who treated minor problems. The third level was the surgeon who treated more serious conditions. The fourth level was the nutritionist who taught people how to extend their lives and be healthier by eating correctly. The highest of all was the doctor who taught the 'laws of the universe' who could intuitively see how the patient was at variance with nature. The acupuncturist, according to the Chinese, belong to the fifth category.

The Eight Principles or Principal Patterns of Disharmony

These form the basic diagnostic system of Traditional Chinese Medicine. The eight principles or categories are:

Yin	Yang
Cold	Hot
Internal	External
Deficiency	Excess

The categories of *yin* and *yang* have already been discussed in the earlier chapter, but Table 12 lists some common disorders in terms of their *yin/yang* predominance.

COLD Vs. HOT

Normally a disease of cold is characterised by a dislike of cold, paleness, cold arms and legs or cold hands and feet, passing a lot of pale urine, thin white secretions, pain lessened by warmth, and having slow movements. The tongue is pale, swollen and with a white moss coating. There may be a desire to drink hot liquids and the patient may sleep curled up in bed.

However, a disease of heat is portrayed by quick, agitated movements, dislike of heat or hot weather, excessive thirst, desire for cold drinks, fever, constipation, small amounts of dark urine and a red tongue with a yellow moss. The pulse will be fast, whereas in the cold condition it is slow. This is also true by the Ayurvedic school of medicine.

Internal and External

This is self-explanatory. A skin problem, a common cold or a joint pain are external; whereas a generalised infection with high fever, inflammation of one of the organs or a growth or tumour inside the body are internal. Internal problems tend to be chronic and external ones acute.

Deficiency and Excess

Normally coincident with *yin* and *yang*, though deficient *yang* and excess *yin* can also occur. Also, to complicate matters, it is possible to have two different types of condition co-existing. For example, an acute infection which is both hot and *yang* can be superimposed upon a chronic, cold, *yin* condition where there is frailty and general deficiency. (See Table 12.)

TABLE 12

Some common parameters of ill-health classified in terms of yin and yang.

EXCESS YIN	EXCESS YANG
Self-conscious	Over-confident
Apathetic	Aggressive
Sad	Euphoric
Flabby muscles and tissue	Hard tissue/spastic muscles

Pale skin and complexion	Ruddy complexion
Slow metabolism	Fast metabolism
Weak pulse	Strong pulse
Slow speech/weak voice	Rapid speech/strong voice
Easily fatigued	Plenty of stamina
Low blood pressure	High blood pressure
Slow movements	Rapid movements

The Pulse

Although the most important considerations regarding the pulse have been important considerations regarding the pulse have already been mentioned, yet as the pulse is such an important feature in the Chinese diagnostic system, a list of some of the pulse findings and their implications is given in Table 13.

TABLE 13

Some common pulse readings and their meanings.

PULSE	INTERPRETATION
Superficial pulse	Early stages of disease. Invasion of external pathogens.
Deep pulse	Internal condition
Slow pulse	Cold syndrome
Rapid pulse	Hot syndrome
Weak pulse	Indicates deficiency
Strong pulse	Indicates excess
Intermittent pulse	Impairment of *qi* and blood
Wiry pulse	Insufficient liver *yin* and hyperactive liver *yang*.
Knotted pulse	Cold phlegm and stagnant blood

Conclusion

Despite the causes of disease according to Chinese medicine being similar to those recognised by modern Western medicine, greater emphasis is placed upon the role of the spirit or mind which is thought to play a part in all diseases. The influence of adverse weather conditions is given greater recognition in the Chinese system. Diagnosis is made by taking a history, asking questions, observing the patient, examining relevant parts, looking at the complexion, ears, eyes tongue and feeling the pulses. Testing for trigger points and alarm points and ascertaining any unusual odours are also important. The period of the day when the patient feels better or worse, unusual tastes in the mouth, food cravings, the nature of the voice, whether any type of weather or time of year influences the symptoms and the body type are all considered by the acupuncturist. It is also important that he is able to recognise the signs of good health because this helps in the identification of minor problems and imbalances.

The Formulation of The Treatment

Selection of The Points

Thus far we concentrated on the philosophy behind Chinese Medicine; how the Chinese described the formation of the body's energy and how it operates within the organism. We have noted how the energy may become disordered and how the acupuncturist can recognise this by his various diagnostic methods. Having made this diagnosis, how does the acupuncturist selects the points to insert the needle?

Local and Distal Points

The prime consideration of the acupuncturist should be to give the patient relief from his symptoms, particularly if there is pain. For this he usually does local and distal points. This means that he treats points where the problem actually is or, in the case of referred pain, where the problem originates. Usually, one meridian is involved and the points will be selected from that meridian. In cases of shoulder pain, where five or six meridians pass close to one another, points may be selected from more than one meridian. Next the acupuncturist will treat spontaneously sensitive points, which the Chinese call *ah shi* points, from the expression commonly used when these points are pressed. Many English students have held a quite erroneous belief about the origin of these words! The distal points are given in Table 14, but these are only the commonest ones. If possible, a distal point on the meridian being treated should be selected. The point *hegu* on the hand is often chosen in painful conditions since it is also a special point for pain. Thus, for facial pain it would serve the dual purpose of distal point and special point. The next most useful point for pain lies on the stomach meridian, on the foot between the second and third toes. This is also a distal point and is used particularly for pain in the lower half of the body. Sometimes, the end point, which might be the first or last point on the meridian, is used as a distal point. This is why, in acupuncture, we often treat a patient at the opposite end of the body. A patient, surprised that he had been given needles in his foot for pain in his head asked the nurse why this was. The nurse thought for a moment and said, 'It's like inflation, it starts low down but gradually works upwards!'

TABLE 14

The main distal points and the areas which they cover.

DISTAL POINT	LOCATION	AREA AFFECTED
Hegu	Hand	Face, special sense organs, front of head and neck
Lieque	Wrist	Back of head, neck, back of chest and lungs
Neiguan	Arm	Front of chest, upper abdomen, internal organs of chest and upper abdomen, diaphragm
Zusanli	Leg	Internal organs of abdomen, especially intestines
Weizhong	Back of knee	Low back. Genito-urinary problems
Sanyinjiao	Leg	Crutch, pelvic organs and external sex organs

Let us now cite the example Mrs. S.C. who first attended for acupuncture at the age of 47 with arthritis of the right hip of several years' duration. This lady had been advised to have a hip replacement and wanted to try acupuncture to see if she could obtain relief from her pain whilst she was waiting for surgery. She realised, of course, that acupuncture could not cure her and in her case the relief of symptoms was not only paramount but the only thing that could sensibly be done. A needle was inserted at the point near the hip which is known to be effective for hip pain and sciatica. A distal point influential for muscle and tendon was also used. Moxibustion, using the osteoarthritis technique of burning a small piece of moxa on the handle of the needle, was given to the first point and the patient reported complete relief from her symptoms after the third treatment. By a process of trial and error she discovered that the effect of the treatment lasted for about three months and at regular quarterly intervals returned for a 'top up'. This continued with amazing regularity for some five years until she moved to a distant part of the country and was given a new practitioner. During these years Mrs. S.C. had not only been pain free but had been able to postpone her hip replacement which is very helpful in a fairly young person. It should also be recorded that this lady, apart from her arthritic hip, which was brought on by an accident, was very fit and had no apparent signs of any other problems.

Selection of local and distal points incorporates two fundamentals of acupuncture; that all acupuncture points treat diseases of the local and surrounding areas, and that all acupuncture points treat disease occurring along the meridian as well as those of the pertaining organ, related tissue and connected organ of special sense (see Table 15). In this particular case we were able to use the gall bladder meridian which passed over the area of trouble and has as its related tissue the muscles and ligaments. Local, distal and *ah shi* points combine three different methods of employing acupuncture points and these are frequently used together.

TABLE 15
The influential points.

INFLUENTIAL POINT	TISSUE
Shanzong	Respiratory system
Dashu	Bone and cartilage
Geshu	Blood
Znongwan	Fu (The hollow, 'yang' organs)
Zhangmen	Zang (the solid, 'yin' organs)
Taiyuan	Vascular system
Yanglingquan	Muscle and tendons
Xuanzhong	Bone marrow

The Special Effects Points

(a) *Analgesia* Acupuncture is a powerful analgesic and the most effective analgesic points have already been mentioned.

(b) *Sedation* There are a number of points which have a specifically sedative effect; particularly *baihui* on the head, *shenmen* on the wrist, *hegu* on the hand, *fenglong* on the leg, *yanglingquan* on the leg and *taichong* on the foot. One or more of these points or pairs of points are usually combined with other points, though sometimes where the condition being treated is nervousness or anxiety they may be used alone.

(c) *Homoeostasis* This means the tendency to maintain balance within the body. Some points have a particularly homeostatic effect and help to regulate temperature, respiration, heart rate, sleep, appetite, muscle tone, acid-alkali balance, endocrine secretions, regularity of movement and secretions of the digestive tract, etc. The best points for this are *quchi* at the elbow, *zusanli* on the leg and *sanyinjiao* on the inside of the leg.

(d) *Immune Enhancing Points* Acupuncture has been used for thousands of years by the Chinese in the treatment of infection and it has been shown that certain points have a considerable effect in raising the body's defence mechanisms. The most effective of these are *dazhui* on the neck, *quchi*, *zusanli* and *sanyinjao*.

(e) *Motor Effects* These are points which are situated over the main motor points of the body which are associated with the gross motor muscles. These points are used in cases of paralysis or muscular weakness. Treatment using these points has been successfully employed in cases of poliomyelitis particularly in India.

The Points of Special Influence

There are eight influential points which have a special action on the specific tissues to which they are related. These are listed in Table 15.

The Xi-cleft Points

There is one *xi*-cleft point on each of the main meridians and these points are particularly effective in the treatment of acute conditions which are either associated with the meridian or its pertaining organ. An acute cough, for example, was treated by using the *xi*-cleft point on the lung meridian. **Xi**-cleft points can be remarkably effective when correctly chosen.

THE *MU* (ALARM) AND *SHU* (ORGAN ASSOCIATED) POINTS

The front mu points have already been described in chapter 5 and are listed in Table 11. When used in treatment they are quite often combined with the back *shu* points: though either may be used independently. The back shu points are points on the bladder meridian which are situated each side of the vertebrae from the third thoracic down to the sacrum. They relate to the outflow of the sympathetic ganglia which contribute nerves from each spinal segment to the various internal organs. These points are undoubtedly inluenced by deep massage and vertebral manipulation which is carried out by osteopaths. This is another way of explaining some of the effects of osteopathy. In acupuncture the points are treated in the usual way with needles. Moxibustion may also be applied with or without needles. Generally, acupuncturists use a toning or stimulating technique on these points as they are in direct contact with the organs. However, 'perverse' energy, which we have avoided discussing up until now, may be drawn off at these points. Perverse energy can be considered as one or other of the external disease factors which gain access to the body when the defensive energy is weak and upset the normal vibratory frequencies. It is only when this disorder reaches one of the organs that its related *shu* points would be used to calm or remove it. The *shu* points lie about one and a half thumbs' width either side of the vertebral column. The same distance away laterally is another series of points which correspond to the same organs on a spiritual or emotional level and would be used for shock, excessive grief or any disease which had its origin in such emotional trauma.

A young girl of 14 who was suffering from anorexia nervosa, which dated from the death of her pet rabbit, responded very well to acupuncture in which these points were used.

The Five Elements and The Points

Selection of the points on the basis of imbalances found in the five elements, sometimes called transformations or phases. Using the Mother-son Law, a deficiency would be treated by enhancing the transfer of energy from the 'mother' organ on the *sheng* cycle. For example, a deficiency found in the kidney could be treated by drawing energy from the lungs *(see Figure 4)*. Becuase the lungs are related to the element 'metal' the metal point on the kidney meridian would be used for treatment. The *yang (fu)* organs can be dealt with in the same way. Sometimes the influence of the *ko* cycle can be made use of and in the case of kidney deficiency this may be because too great an inhibitory influence is being exerted by the spleen (earth). In addition, there may be overactivity of the heart which is not being controlled by water. The precise treatment would depend upon the exact findings but it is possible that the 'earth' point of the kidneys might be used.

Consider an example of the use of the five elements on that of Miss. N.T. who was suffering from chronic constipation and sinusitis. The colon was found to be deficient and the simple expedient of treating the earth point *quchi* at the elbow was remarkably effective. Additional relief for the head problems was obtained by deep pressure massage on the points *fengchi* on the gall bladder meridian at the back of the skull. These points are known to be effect in the treatment of many kinds of headache and 'fuzziness' in the head.

In migraine cases, an imbalance of energy is often found between the liver and gall bladder and there is often an overactive state of these organs. Although one has to be very careful when treating the heart meridian, good results are sometimes achieved by merely treating the point *shaochong* at the tip of the little finger, for this is the wood point of the heart meridian and encourages the transfer of energy from liver to heart. Professor Jayasuriya was one of the first to do this particular treatment as previously most practitioners had used points on the liver or gall bladder or heart constrictor meridians.

Period or Horary points may be used in conformity with the Chinese clock which has already been described in the earlier chapter

The Eight Extra Meridians

These meridians are used for treatment, mostly by using what are known as the 'key' or 'confluent' points. These are pairs of points, each pair being used to bring into play one of the meridians. Two pairs of key points are normally used together, so that two of the extra meridians are employed. The normal coupling of the points, the meridians which they control and the indications for use are given in Table 16.

The Eight Basic Diagnostic Principles

As a result of a diagnosis utilising the eight diagnostic principles, points may be used for their known energic influences. In Table 17, some patterns of disharmony are listed, together with the related signs and symptoms, and the Western medical equivalents. As there are a large number of such patterns which are not listed, it is not felt appropriate to indicate the actual points which might be used and in any case these would vary in individual cases.

TABLE 16

The extra meridians, key points and areas and symptoms which they cover.

KEY POINT	EXTRA MERIDIAN	AREA OF BODY AND INDICATIONS
Neiguan	Yin Wei Mo (Yin Energy Conserver)	Heart, chest and stomach. Nervousness, Varicose veins, pain in chest, timidity, indigestion, abdominal pain, amnesia,
Gongsun	Chong Mo (Vital Energy Regulator)	Hyperacidity, heart disease, palpitations, gastric ulcers.
Houxi	Du mo (Governor)	Neck, shoulder, back and inner corner of eyes.
Shenmai	Yang Chiao Mo (Yang Energy Accelerator)	Epilepsy, febrile disease, articulatory and locomotor problems, insomnia, paranoia, obsessional neurosis, manic-depressive state, hormonal imbalance.
Waiguan	Yang Wei Mo (Yang Energy Conserver)	Area behind ears, outer corner of eyes and cheeks. Coldness, arthritis of toes, acne, boils, earache, chills, fever, tinnitus, toothache,

Foot Linqi	Dai Mo (Belt Channel)	Abdominal distension, weakness and motor impairment in the lumbar region.
Lieque	Ben Mo (Conception Vessel)	Throat, chest & lungs. Asthma, bronchitis, epilepsy, eczema, headache, hay fever,
Zhaohai	Yin Chiao Mo (Yin Energy Accelerator)	laryngitis, sore throat, urino-genital disorders, sexual weakness, difficult birth, cystitis, sleepiness, toxaemia of pregnancy, post partum pains and bleeding, bladder weakness.

TABLE 17

A few examples of patterns of disharmony in terms of Chinese medicine, the signs and symptoms and equivalent designation in Western medicine.

PATTERNS IN CHINESE MEDICINE	OBSERVATIONS AND SYMPTOMS	WESTERN EQUIVALENT
Hyperactive liver yang.	Vertigo, tinnitus, nausea, red tongue and wiry, rapid pulse.	Hypertension
Retention of damp phlegm	Fullness and suffocating sensation of chest, nausea and vomiting, white sticky moss on tongue. Slippery pulse.	
Deficient qi and blood	Lassitude, palpitation, insomnia, weak pulse.	
Wind-cold flung	Cough with thin sputum, shortness of breath, white moss on tongue, superficial pulse.	Bronchial asthma
Phlegm-heat of lungs	Rapid and coarse breaking. Thick purulent sputum thick, yellow moss on tongue and rapid pulse.	
Insufficient kidney *yang*	Pallor, dizziness, blurred vision, listlessness, lumbar soreness, frequency of urination, thready pulse.	Impotence
Wind obstructing meridians	Sore, painful joints. Pain moves around. White moss on tongue	Arthritis

Cold obstructing meridian	Painful joints, worse with movement. Pain does not move. Worse in cold.	
Damp heat obstructing meridians	Swollen and painful joints. Fever and thirst. Tongue reddish with greasy, yellow moss. Rapid pulse.	Rheumatoid athritis

Points of Junction

There points are also knwon as the junction points between the meridians of coupled organs which are heart and small intestines, spleen and stomach, lung and colon, kidney and bladder, liver and gall bladder and heart constrictor and three heater. These points are used particularly when there is an imbalance between any two organ pairs as they activate the joining vessels. These points are normally used in conjunction with the sources or *yuan* points. The use of junction points could be considered to be a subcategory of the use of the five phases.

Modern Medicine

Despite not being a desirable method acupuncture points may be selected merely in terms of the doctor's understanding of the patient's problem in terms of Western medicine. This is a 'hit and miss' affair because Western medicine takes little or no cognisance of the individuality of the patient and focuses its attention almost exclusively on the disease *per se*. For example, there are at least four different patterns of disharmony associated with bronchial asthma, two of which are illustrated in Table 17; yet Western medicine would regard them all as the same disease. Moreover, the acupuncturist will recognise nuances of energy disturbance even within those four major patterns and his treatment will be exactly tailored to the patient at every stage of his progress back to health. The Western medical approach could be even more misleading in this instance because of its preoccupation with the site of manifestation of the disease which is the lungs, rather than the *origin* of the disease which may be in the digestive system. This is a fact that has always been insisted upon by naturopaths and is in conformity with the five elements where earth (digestion) is the 'mother' or nourisher of the metal (respiration).

Auricular Acupuncture (Specialised Acupuncture)

In it the treatment is carried out on points on the external ear. This part of the ear is endowed with points which reflexly affect every part of the body (see Figure 9) and these points may be needled in conformity with the accepted rules of acupuncture. For example, a person suffering from an eye disorder might have needles placed in the 'eye' points of the ear, together with liver and gall bladder points, which are couple organs of the related element (see Table 5). The point of the bladder might be included on account of the close proximity of the bladder meridian to the eye.

The powerful effect of auricular acupuncture is well illustrated by the case of Mr. P.K. who was a young man of twenty-five suffering from severe pain in the penis whenever having an erection. He had received a variety of treatment including acupuncture, and was in a state of despair. His acupuncturist advised him to have auricular acupuncture but, not doing it himself, left the lad to find another practitioner. He ended up in a surgery and the situation more or less obliged the surgeon to treat him with auriculotherapy, even though his experience of it at that time was very little. He was treated principally with the external genital point and a press needle (see next chapter) was placed on this point and retained by the patient who was instructed to press on it every day and at any time he experienced the pain. Ten days later he reported a considerable improvement and about a week after his second treatment telephoned to the surgeon to say that the was completely cured and would like to cancel his next appointment as it entailed a long and difficult journey. It seemed almost too good to be true because this boy had been suffering for seven years, but quite by coincidence the surgeon met him two years later at an exhibition and he reported two years of complete freedom from his problem. It scarcely seems necessary to relate how grateful he was!

Auriculotherapy is an ancient form of treatment and was doubtless effective because the ear is richly endowed with nerves which have connections all over the body. This form of treatment has received a great deal of attention in modern times. In Germany the Munich Auriculotherapy Association has more than 3,000 members which is an indication of the popularity and widespread use of this form of acupuncture.

It believes that each cell in the body carries within its chromosomes a computer-like representation of all the features of the entire body and this is probably the theoretical basis for these various reflex areas. Moreover, the entire body can be superimposed on the ear (see Figure 9) and it is found that different parts of the ear are embryologically

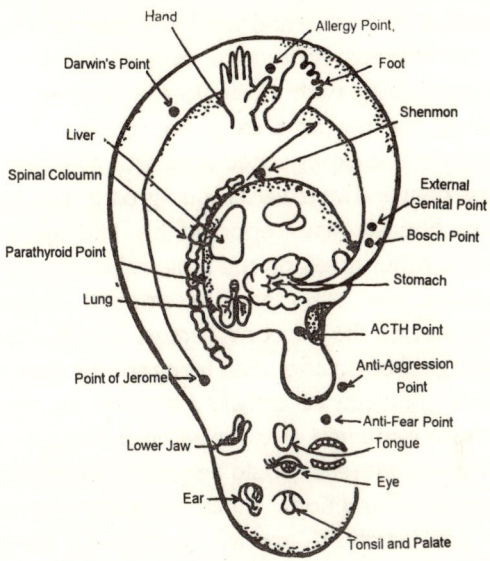

Figure 9. Some of the more commonly used acupuncture points found on the ear. Darwin's point is used for treating sleep disturbances; the Bosch point is used for psychosexual disorders; the allergy point is used for allergic conditions; and shenmen is used for emotional or nervous problems. The point of jerome is also used for relaxation purposes, and to treat sleep problems.

connected with the corresponding areas of the body superimposed upon them. Since 1966 auriculotherapy has been widely used all over China for both treatment and anaesthesia. It has been found most useful for disorders of the internal organs and may be combined with body acupuncture or other forms of acupuncture.

Scalp, Nose, Hand, Foot, Wrist And Ankle Acupuncture

These are the special reflex points covering the entire body, apart from the regular points.

Scalp

The scalp acupuncture is based upon areas of the scalp which are related to the motor areas of the cortex of the brain. These areas were mapped out by Jiao Shen-fa, a neurologist in the Ji Shan People's Hospital in the Shanshi Province of the People's Republic of China, during the time of the Cultural Revolution (1966-69). Shen-fa, who also had a good knowledge of acupuncture, took to heart the exhortation of Chairman Mao for physicians of both traditional and modern disciplines to put aside their political difference and work together for the benefit of the people, and he started work on a case of hemiplegia (one sided paralysis) by stimulating with a needle the area on the scalp which corresponded to the motor area of the cortex. The results were astonishing: the patient experienced a sensation in the paralysed limbs during the treatment and afterwards had a greater degree of movement in them. After Shen-fa had reported his findings, other workers established many other areas on the scalp relating to different cortical functions. Usually, the scalp area is situated fairly close to the corresponding part of the cerebral cortex, but the connection is an electro-physiological one rather than being strictly topographical. Since the measurement of electrical activity in the brain is regularly made on the scalp in Western medical practice when an electro-encephalogram is recorded, this phenomena should be readily understood by Western trained scientists. Conditions most frequently treated by scalp acupuncture are paralysis, mental disorders, speech disorders, cardiovascular problems and genito-urinary disorders.

Nose

It is similar to ear acupuncture in that there are points on the nose which relate to different areas of the body. As in ear acupuncture, the needle should only be inserted superficially and always on the outside or external part.

Foot and Hand

The foot and hand points may be treated with a needle or massaged. The experts generally oppose placing needles on the under-surface of the foot and feel that this is an area which should be given massage only. The reflex areas on the foot are shown in Figure 10. The reflexes on the hand or foot should be treated with a deep compression massage.

Wrist-ankle

Acupuncture at wrist-Ankle region is a comparatively new technique which started after a paper was published by the Department of Neurology of the First Teaching Hospital of the Second Army Medical College in Shanghai, People's Republic of China, in 1976. This new form of acupuncture was developed because the wrist and ankle are less

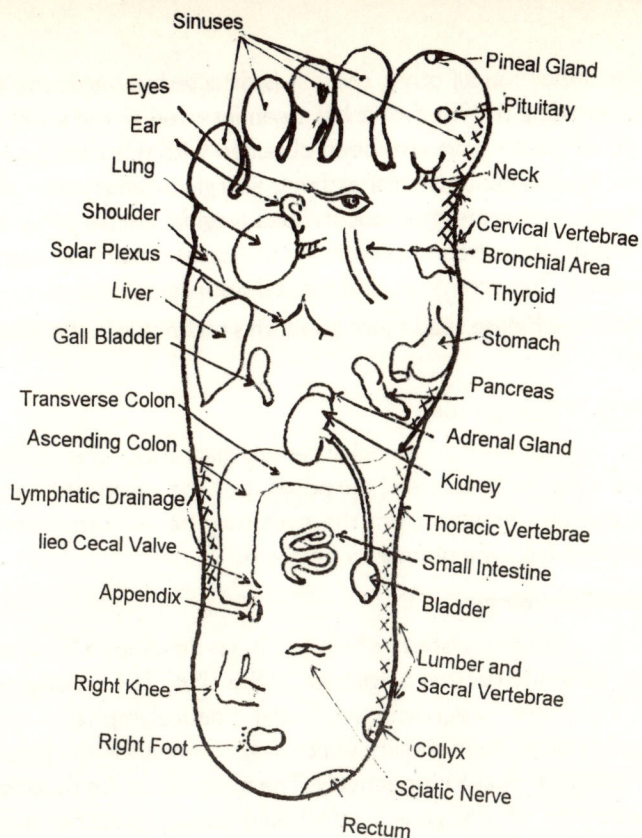

Figure 10: The right foot showing the acupuncture micro-system which is commonly termed foot reflexology. These reflexes may become simultaneously sensitive with a disorder in the part of the body to which they are related. Treatment to the reflex is usually done with a deep, compression type of massage and is often known as foot zone therapy.

sensitive areas than the hand or foot. The method is easy to learn and simple to use and is economical in terms of needles which is a consideration always relevant in the Third World. Moreover, the therapeutic results are very good. There are twelve points, six at the wrist and six at the ankle, and the needle is inserted just under the skin in a horizontal fashion. The needle is not manipulated and is retained in the position for about 20-30 minutes. The method has proved to be very effective in acute disorders such as sore throat, headaches, toothache, low back pain, neuralgia, menstrual pain and pain in the limbs. If the pain is in the hand or foot, the needle is directed towards the site of pain: in all other cases it is directed towards the elbow or knee according to whether it has been inserted at the wrist or ankle. Very good results have also been obtained with this technique in cases of nasal discharge, bronchial asthma, allergic inflammation of the gut, incontinence of urine, and leucorrhoea (vaginal discharge); whilst fairly good results have been noted in stroke cases, insomnia, disturbances of sensation, hypertension, and mental disorders.

Note:— Please read more about this technique in the Acupressure section.

Iridology (iris-diagnosis)

Iris-diagnosis is now a well accepted diagnostic science. We do not use the eyes for treatment purposes, but the diagnostic information which can be obtained from the eyes may be used to formulate the treatment which will ultimately be given.

Applied Kinesiology

This is another system which has been developed in recent times and the only one to have originated in the USA. The reflex points used were renamed 'neurovascular' and 'neurolymphatic' points in conformity with their activity which was to enhance the blood supply or lymphatic drainage respectively. The method can be used for testing the presence of allergens, undesirable foods, poisons, medication, vitamins and food supplements and it is even possible to use it to test the suitability of a proposed treatment. Some problems, such as ionisation disorders, can scarcely be found by any other method

Through and Through Acupuncture

In this method, two or more points are joined up by the insertion of the needle. The selection of points is made on the basis of the special therapeutic property of the combined points.

THE ACUPUNCTURE NEEDLES

In the ancient time acupuncture needles were made from pieces of stone and flint in 1926 several quartz needles were excavated at Chou Kou Tien near Peking (Beijing). Bamboo needles were also certainly used as the ancient Chinese ideograph for "needles" incorporated the idea of bamboo and only in later years did this become altered to imply metal. Bronze, stone and bone needles were all unearthed in 1899 at Hsio, Tun Yuan Shui, An yang county and province. According to Change Yu Min, carapace needles usually made from turtle shell were used in acupuncture treatment as early as three thousand years ago, and the stone needles from An Yang were dated about 1700 BC.

These early stone needles were called 'bian' which actually means stone to treat disease. In the late Neolithic period around 2000 BC, ceramic neeldes were introduced and by about 1600 BC in the Bronze Age metal needles were first manufactured. It was not until the Warring states period (403-221 BC) that advances in metallurgy made it possible to manufacture fine, steel needles which were ideally suited to the practice of acupuncture. Although gold and silver needles were thought to be superior the consensus of opinion is that the modern, stainless steel acupuncture needle is second to none.

Traditionally there were nine varieties of needles that were used in acupuncture therapy and they may be summarised as:

1. The 'arrowhead needle' used for drawing blood and treating hot conditions.

2. The 'round' needles used for rubbing against the skin and treating stagnant qi.

3. The 'pressure needle' which had a tip shaped like a grain of millet and was used for shallow treatment of meridians.

4. The 'sharp needle' which was round with a sharp tip and used to drain abscesses.

5. The 'sword needle which was similar to the sharp needle but larger and used for draining superficial abscesses.

6. The *round-sharp* needle which had a thin, round body and slightly expanded head and was used for elimination of obstruction.

7. The *fine, filiform needle* which had a thin shaft and was used for the elimination of cold, heat, pain and obstruction.

8. The *long needle,* similar to the previous type but longer and for deep insertion.

9. The *large needle* which had a thick body and was used for the treatment of arthritis and draining fluids.

The Present Day Needles:— Not much different from the ancient ones, they are,

1. *The filiform needle.* This is the commonest type of needle used in acupuncture and the only type used buy some practitioners. The shaft is made of stainless steel and the handle has a superimposition of copper, bronze, silver or stainless steel. By having a different metal on the handle there will be differential heating when moxa is applied to the needle and this results in a tiny electrical discharge which runs down the needle. Whether or not this influences treatment is still open to argument. The length of the needles varies from 12.7mm to 203.2mm. Occasionally, even longer needles are used and these may be threaded down the back to join up a whole series of points. The diameter of the needles varies from 0.46mm to as little as 0.19mm and the following table shows

different gauges in general use.

Gauge	26	28	30	32	34
Diameter (mm)	0.46	0.38	0.32	0.26	0.23

Gauge and corresponding diameter in mm of the commonly used acupuncture needles.

Thirty or thirty-two gauge needles are usually selected for acupuncture on the face and around the eyes, for children or cases where very little, Stimulation is required. If longer needles are used a wider gauge is usually chosen and wider gauge needles are needed for treatment requiring strong stimulation. The most popular-needle is the 38.1 mm 28 gauge which might be considered an 'all purpose needle.

2. The *embedding needle*. This is also called the press needle, intradermal needle or implanted needle. Its purpose is to be inserted and left *in situ*. The commonest design is the thumbtack type which is 2-3mm long and has a small circular head at right angles to the shaft. The head prevents entry of the entire needle. It is most frequently used for ear acupuncture and may be pressed from time to time when in position—hence the name 'press needle.' Another variety is a tiny stainless steel ball which is applied to the acupuncture point with adhesive. This is not strictly a needle and cannot be inserted through the skin. It is safer than the needle and is more pleasant for the patient. The most recent innovation is a squarer design of the ball-bearing type which is magnetised. These are now under research and it is too early to say if they are superior to non- magnetised needles.

The Longer Needles (used for deep points)

3. *The plum blossom needle*. This is also known as the 'five star' or 'seven star' needle. It consists of five or seven short needles protruding from a holder which is attached to a long handle. This instrument is used to tap along the meridians or on specific areas of skin and is used on children, weak or elderly patients, for skin conditions and for those patients who dislike puncturing or who are allergic to needles.

4. *The hot needle*. This needle is fairly thick in gauge and is made from a special alloy of silver. It is brought to red heat and plunged into certain types of superficial swellings or ganglions. The needle is immediately withdrawn so that it only remains in contact with the flesh for a fraction of a second.

5. *The prismatic needle*. This is needle with a triangular point and is

used to induce bleeding at certain points. This treatment mostly used for certain types of inflammatory conditions, acute disturbances and allergic skin conditions.

6. *Rolling drum.* This is really a variation of the plum blossom needle. It consists of a revolving drum with rows of protruding needles which can be 'run' up and down the skin over a meridian.

Sterilization of Needles

Sterilization of needles is very necessary particularly after being used. Some needles are pre-sterilized and disposable but are mostly not very suitable for acupuncture as the practitioner cannot get the full feed-back through the handle; nor can he manipulate them easily. A standard type of pre-sterilized needle has now been produced by Acumedic in the UK and these are quite satisfactory for acupuncture use. Moreover, if desired, they can be sterilized after treatment and re-used. Other needles should be fully sterilized before being used, though cleansing with surgical spirit is probably quite satisfactory.

Once a needle has been used for a treatment it must be discarded or sterilized by autoclaving or an equivalent process. After removal, the needle should be cleansed by wiping with surgical spirit or a dilute antiseptic. It should then be autoclaved and subsequently retained in a closed container until required again. The skin is usually swabbed with alcohol before needle insertion, but this does not seem to be necessary. It is important that the doctor's fingers are scrupulously clean when carrying out acupuncture. Infections being transmitted by acupuncture treatment are almost unheard of but there was a single case of an unqualified practitioner in England who managed to spread serum hepatitis becuase of his lack of training and ignorance of correct sterilization. Since then, local authorities in Britain have attempted to control the practice of acupuncture to minimise the possibility of any repetition of such an event, but no member of the public need have any qualms about this aspect of acupuncture if the practitioner is a properly qualified and registered acupuncturist.

Needles should not be repeatedly re-used as they tend to become pitted and blunted and the metal tends to get fatigued with repeated sterilizing. This means that the treatment is likely to be more painful than it should and there is a risk of the needle breaking after being inserted. After ten years of practice and thousands of acupuncture treatments the author has yet to see this happen; so one can rest assured that it is a rare occurrence. Usually it can easily be dealt with by a qualified practitioner.

How To Insert The Needles

These needles are to be used very delicately. Acupuncturists do not just push needles into bodies in the way that doctors and nurses give hypodermic injections. Apart from the fact that the point, which is less than a millimetre in diameter, has to be carefully located, the angle and depth of insertion vary at each point and have to be correctly observed. Some points are needled perpendicularly to the skin surface; many are needled at an angle of about 45 degrees and some are needled almost horizontally with the needle making an angle of 15 to 25 degrees with the skin.

Insertion with the needles should be made rapidly through the outer layers of tissue in order to make the operation as painless as possible. From then onwards, the way in which the needle is introduced depends upon the type of treatment desired. In any event the acupuncturist aims to obtain a sensation (felt by the patient!) which is termed *deqi*. This is a sensation of either numbness, tingling, heaviness, soreness, distension or a feeling of slight pain at a distance from the site of puncture. Frequently, *deqi* is felt as a radiating sensation and experienced along the acupuncture meridian often called 'latent propagating sensation along channel' (LPSC).

Acupuncturist may also pick up '*deqi*' and is recognisable as a sense of tightening felt through the needle handle which results from local muscle spasm in the patient. Some acupuncturists claim to be able to feel a subtle sensation on the hand when it is held at a distance from the needle, but this cannot yet be agreed as an objective, reproduceable phenomenon. Research in China has shown that acupuncturist's *deqi* is not felt if a muscle has lost its nerve supply.

Usually different qualities of *deqi* are obtained in different areas. Where the muscle mass is thin the feeling is usually that of local distension, whereas if the muscle is thick it is usually one of numbness or soreness. If the acupuncture point is close to a nerve trunk, the sensation is likely to be that of tingling or 'electric shock'. In some instances *deqi* cannot be obtained and this does not mean that the treatment is not working. It must be stressed that *deqi* although not pleasant is quite distinct from the sensation of pain.

The following techniques are some of those which may be used by acupuncturists to 'manipulate' the needle immediately after insertion:

1. *Raising and thrusting.* In this technique the needle is thrust up and down by a push-pull force exerted on the handle. The correct depth should first be obtained by prescience or *deqi* (or both!) and the needle then lifted just a few millimetres and immediately returned to the original depth. The amplitude of the movement may be increased for very strong stimulation, but the needle should on no account be completely withdrawn. If *deqi* is not obtained the angle of the return thrust may be very slightly varied with a view to seeking an elusive point.

2. *Twirling or rotating.* In this case the needle is introduced to the correct depth as before but is then rotated by approximately 180 degrees. This is usually repeated for about half a minute, allowing the needle to return to neutral more or less by itself. According to tradition, if the needle is rotated clockwise it invokes a stimulating process and if anti-clockwise it causes sedation.

3. *Combination of raising and thrusting with rotation.* This is more difficult manoeuvre to perform but generally gives better results. It is also thought that by thrusting the needle during the patient's out-breath and raising or lifting during an inspiration a greater degree of stimulation is obtained and, conversely, by introducing the needle during the inspiratory phase and with drawing expiration a greater degree of sedation is brought about. Manual manipulation to induce analgesia has to be done fairly rapidly and has to be sustained for the duration of surgery. Except for dental extraction which is almost instantaneous, electrical stimulation is used during surgery as it is more reliable, less tiring and more acceptable to the patient. The classical procedures are summarised in Table 18, but are not frequently used by modern acupuncturists. It can be seen from this table that the length of needle retention is also thought to influence the degree of stimulation or sedation, but this becomes very confusing since over stimulation results in sedation and the cycle of stimulation-sedation-stimulation is repetitive.

TABLE 18

The classical procedures of bu (stimulation) used mainly for yin disorders, and xie (calming) used chiefly for yang disorders.

BU (Stimulation)	XIE (Calming)
Massage point before and after needling	Do not massage
Use gold needle	Use silver needle
Insert at end of expiration	Insert during inhalation
Insert obliquely in direction of energy flow	Insert obliquely against direction of energy flow
Insert rapidly	Insert slowly
Rotate clockwise	Rotate anticlockwise
Manipulate for a few seconds	Do not manipulate or manipulate for several minutes
Withdraw immediately	Retain for 10-12 minutes
Withdraw slowly during inhalation	Withdraw rapidly during exhalation
Close exit (by finger pressure)	Leave exit open

4. Other Techniques:— Included in this category are:

(i) **Plucking:**— In this case the needle head is 'flicked' by the physician or operator's index finger.

(ii) **Scrapping:**— In this case the needle is held firmly with one hand whilst the finger nail of the index finger of the other hand is rubbed up and down the needle, sending a vibration down the entire needle.

(iii) **Trembling:**— This is a similar technique to that of raising and thursting but the amplitude is so small that the effect is a vibration or trembling of the needle.

A Necessary Precaution:— Before puncturing it is important for the physician to select the correct needles and these should be approximately twice the length of the depth of insertion. This permits good manipulation of the needle and avoids the risk of placing the needle to its full depth; which should NEVER happen under any circumstances.

The needle may also be influenced with electricity or heat. Why this might happen is explained in the chapters ahead.

The order of inserting and removing needles is important since it reflects the general rule that one should be orderly in one's activities. The general rule is to treat from above downwards but it is also in order to treat painful areas or lessions before other points.

Some acupuncturists have taken the question of sterility to ridiculous extremes by using the 'no-touch' method of needle insertion. To do this the needle is handled only with sterilised forceps and is never touched by the fingers until it has been fully inserted. This technique is valuable where very deep penetration is desired, but would seem to be quite unnecessary and even counter-productive in other cases since it renders the application of feedback from the needle impossible and negates the basic principle of acupuncture.

TABLE 19

Methods of needle stimulation most often in use today.

TYPE OF STIMULUS	METHOD	EFFECT	INDICATION
Strong	Needle is rotated, raised and thrust rapidly with a good amplitude	Sensation is strong with wide propagation along meridian.	Patients with strong constitutions. For acute pain, cramps and Excess conditions.
Mild	Needle is rotated, raised and thrust slowly with small amplitude.	Slight sensation not usually propagated.	Weak or nervous patients, those with history of fainting. For Deficient conditions.
Moderate	Between strong and mild methods	Moderate sensation which may extend along meridian.	Used in most cases

The Scientific Basis of the Acupuncture Therapy

Despite the apparent inability to explain the reasoning behind this acupuncture therapies, the Western world tried to establish many theories to establish its credibility.

Some of them are following:

(i) The Neural Theory:—

In simple words, this theory maintains that pressure or irritation on the acupuncture point transmits 'repair' messages to the brain which are relayed to the centre which monitors body repair and mobilises the appropriate mechanisms.

This process involves what is known as the cutaneo-visceral reflex. The phenomenon was first noted in the West by the British neurologist Henry Head; and subsequently formulated in Head's Law which states that, 'When a painful stimulus is applied to a part of low sensibility in close central connection with a part of much greater sensibility, the pain produced is felt in the part of higher sensibility rather than in the part of lower sensibility to which the stimulus was actually applied'. This is a rather long-winded way of saying that a dysfunction in an organ of the body can be manifested on an area of skin which is either painful or unduly sensitive. Every organ has a related area of skin which lies adjacent or fairly near to it. Inflammation of the stomach is reflected in the adbominal area above the navel; when in the small intestine the area of pain is lower; whilst when in the colon it is lower still. The alarm points in acupuncture corresponding to these three viscera are also in the three reflex areas, which would seem to indicate that acupuncture, at least to some extent, depends upon these neural connections despite the fact that the true identity of the relationship was obscure to the Chinese. Acupuncture relies upon Head's Law to 'deceive' the body into responding to a slightly painful irritation on the skin done by acupuncture by sending out repair massages to the related organ. These areas of skins are known as dermatomes and this is described as one of the methods of selecting points in the previous chapter. Some of the skin reflex areas are at a distance from the related organ, which is consistent with traditional acupuncture as well as modern medical thinking.

Almost universally agreed is the fact that acupuncture works, at least partly through the nervous system, but Dr. Robert Becker, Professor of Orthopaedic Surgery at the Upstate Medical Center, New York State, USA, postulated a complete operational data transfer system in living organsims which controls such changes as growth, healing and biological cycles. He was led to this discovery by his successful regeneration of tissue in animals and the union of fractures in humans by the use of electricity. He claimed that this system was the precursor of the nervous system and interlocked with it to provide a link between the nervous system and the cells of the body. In a personal communication to Dr. Margaret Patterson, published in her book *Addictions can be Cured*, Professor Becker wrote, 'I believe at this time I can unequivocally state that there are significant electrical correlations for approximately 50% of the acupuncture points. We have concluded, therefore, that acupuncture has a basis in reality. There is a previously undescribed system of data transmission additional to the nerves in living organisms. We believe that this system is primitive in nature, operates with an analogue type of D.C. electrical signals and is concerned with the sensing of injury and effecting its control of healing processes. We believe the system is located in the perineural cells and Schwann cells peripherally and the glia cells centrally. There is evidence at least in the glia that these cells are capable of controlling the operational level of the nerve cells themselves.

(ii) Circulatory Theory:—

When the acupuncture needle is inserted, it causes either a constriction or a dilation of blood vessels, depending upon the particular points used. This is another theory to explain how acupuncture work; though it does not fully explain how this effect is brought about in the first place. However, we do also know that acupuncture can stimulate the production of such substances as histamine and kinins, both of which are thought to be vasodilators of in other words, have the effect of causing an increase in the diameter of small blood vessels. Kinins also have an effect on muscular activity of the internal organs and lower blood pressure. On the other hand, acupuncture frequently has the effect of lowering the levels of these substances and, since they are well known to be potent causes of pain, this is another explanation for the pain-relieving effects of acupuncture.

(iii) The Gate Control Theory:—

This theory was postulated to explain the pain control mechanism of acupuncture. According to this theory, the perception of pain is controlled by a mechanism in the nervous system which alters or modulates the impulse which will later be interpreted as pain. This mechanism is called the 'gate' and its function would appear to be some sort of monitoring of impulses which are going to end up as being registered as pain. If the gate is bombarded by too many impulses it closes and prevents some of the impulses from getting through. Now it is well known that the impulses which are interpreted as pain are carried by nerve fibres of narrow gauge called C fibres, whilst impulses transmitted by large diameter fibres are not interpreted as pain. Impulses from large diameter fibres have the effect of closing the gate whilst the small diameter fibres open it. It is thought that the acupuncture stimulates the large nerve fibres which close the gate and prevent the existing impulses travelling along the narrow fibres from reaching the brain.

(iv) The Motor Gate Theory:—

This theory attempts to explain the motor recovery effects of acupuncture in a similar way that the Gate Control theory is used to explain the relief of pain through acupunture. According to the motor gate theory, there is a functional 'gate' which, when closed, prevents motor nerve impulses from reaching their target muscle. According to Jayasuriya the anterior horn cells (which initiate or relay the motor impulses) are, in many forms of paralysis, not dead but in a state of 'suspended animation' or 'hibernation'. In other words, the functional 'gate' is closed, probably as an initially protective mechanism to limit the damage from the disease. Acupuncture therapy, according to Dr. Jayasuriya, sets up a heavy inward barrage at the motor gate which is capable of partly or completely opening it. This barrage of nerve impulses travels along the large diameter fibres in a direction contrary to normal. The full explanation of the neurological mechanisms involved is fairly complicated and beyond the scope of this book, but one of the factors contributing to motor recovery is almost certainly the activation of spindle cells. These tiny, elongated capsules situated along muscle fibres are made to 'fire' when the muscle is stretched. The important fact is that they are also stimulated by gamma motor neurons which are conterbalanced by alpha motor neurons, so that at any time the muscle can be maintained in a state of correct tone. If the gamma motor neurons are stimulated by acupuncture, the discharge causes the contraction of certain fibres known as intrafusal muscle fibres. This activates the spindle cells in the same way as muscle stretching. This ultimately reinforces the effect of the counterbalancing alpha neuron which brings about muscle contraction.

(v) Augmentation of Immunity:—

It was noticed that acupuncture has an immune-enhancing action and this is brought about by a rise in white blood cells, an increase in gamma globulins and opsonins and a rise in antibody concentration.

Numerous other biochemical changes resulting from acupuncture have now been documented. These include hormones and prostaglandins which may account for respiratory improvement after acupuncture, serum triglycerides which may explain its effect on the cardio-vascular system, red blood cells which may account for improvement in cases of anaemia, and dopamine which may explain some of the results obtained in Parkinsonism and certain types of mental disorders. We are no nearer to understanding exactly how acupuncture brings about these biochemical changes, but the fact they occur has given acupuncture a scientific guise because its results can be quantified and measured by tests which are acceptable to any scientist.

(vi) Neurotransmitters

Research carried out at the Chinese Institute has shown that serotonin and noradrenaline are also actively involved in the mechanism of acupuncture in pain relief. Serotonin is an important substance that plays a role in normal brain and nervous functioning. It is possible that serotonin is produced in the pineal gland, although this is not yet proved. It is certainly released in part of the brain known as the raphe nuclei and is active in the limbic system which may be described as the emotional centre of the brain. Other neurotransmitters are also influenced by acupuncture and partly explain its action.

(vii) Endorphin Theory:—

As we all know that Endorphins eat the body's own morphine-like substances which have the effect of abating pain. The endorphin theory is the most comprehensive of all the theories so far put forward to explain acupuncture in scientific terms. It all began with the discovery in 1965 of a substance known as betalipotropin by Dr. C.H. Li and his colleagues at the University of California, San Francisco, USA. This was the forerunner of the discovery of opiate-like substances in the brain by John Hughes and Hans Kosterlitz at Aberdeen University in Scotland in 1974. The next year saw the isolation of two substances from a pig's brain by Hughes and Kosterlitz which they called enkephalins, from the Greek meaning 'from the head'. The enkephalins were shown to have a basic, composition similar to beta-lipotropin and one of them, methionine-enkephalin (abbreviated to met-enkephalin), had opiate like properties and was described as an endorphin which means, literally, a morphine-like substance from the body itself. This was a name proposed by Professor E. Simon of the New York Medical School, USA.

The discovery of endorphins at long last explained the existence of morphine receptors in the brain, which could hardly have arrived there on the off chance that man would take an extract of the opium poppy. More importantly, it provided the much needed explanation for acupuncture just at the right moment! It was of Professor of the University of Toronto, Canada, who first made the connection between endorphins and acupuncture. His primary interest had been with the field of drug addiction and he reasoned that withdrawal symptoms experienced by morphine and heroin addicts were due to the fact that the injecting of these drugs took up the receptor sites and left the body's own endorphins unoccupied. Because the body does not want too much of these substances freely moving around and having nothing useful to do it shuts off its own supply. As soon as the injections of external heroin are curtailed the body is deprived of its own source of opiates and enters a state of extreme discomfort. This is the well known withdrawal state. Pomeranz suspected that endorphins might be involved in the production of analgesia by acupuncture. It had already been established that there was some chemical involved which was transported in the blood stream. This was discovered by administering acupuncture to a rabbit, connecting its blood supply to a non-acupunctured animal and finding that the latter now had its pain threshold elevated. The other two facts that convinced Pomeranz that he was on the right track were that mice whose pituitary glands had been removed could not have analgesia induced in them by acupuncture, thus proving that the chemical concerned was produced in the pituitary and secondly, that the drug nalaxone negated the acupuncture analgesia. Since nalaxone is a well known morphine anatagonist, this suggested that the analgesia induced by acupuncture was due to a morphine-like substance.

The Methods Of Moxibustion, Cupping & Massage

Moxibustion may sound a strange word but it has interesting origin. This word is the Latinised derivater of the Japanese 'moegusa' word which is the herb Artemisia Vulgaris (mugwood or chinese wormwood). This is ignited and applied directly or indirectly to acupuncture points as a form of treatment. It is said the primitive people discovered the benefit of therapeutic heat accidentally by experiencing relief of symptoms whilst warming themselves by fire, hence it is a very ancient form of treatment, possibly antedating the use of needles. Even in prehistoric times they were practised together and this gave rise to the term 'acumoxy'. In Sri-Lanka this is termed 'vidium-pilissum'.

According to the Traditional oriental Medicine the heat from moxibustion 'Warms the *qi* and blood in the channels and is therefore useful in the treatment of disease and maintenance of health'. The herb itself is said to have a very *yang* quality and has the effect of regulating the *qi* and blood and expelling cold and dampness. When burned it penetrates the channels and is mostly used for chronic, weakened conditions where the channels have become obstructed by cold or dampness or for stimulating the movement of *qi* and blood.

To what extent the inherent medicinal qualities of the herb are transmitted through moxibustion is still a matter of conjecture. Modern simulators of moxibustion which burn no herb but emanate radiant heat from an electrically activated sapphire head, or some other type of electrically operated heating element, seem to have good effect, though some acupuncturists hold that they are very much a second best to the real thing. However, the smoke emitted by the smouldering herb does have a physiological effect—particularly on the nervous system.

The herb *Artemisia vulgaris* is found growing wild throughout most of the Far East and much of Europe and this is a possible reason for its being chosen for moxibustion. The leaves are usually dried in the sun and rendered into powdery form which is known as 'moxa punk'. Sometimes other dried herbs are mixed with the Artemisia. Different grades of moxa punk are available and selection is made according to the mode of application. The finer grades are used for making small cones which are burnt directly on the skin whilst coarser grades are more suitable for making moxa sticks which are rather like large cigars and are burned at a distance from the point.

The different ways in which moxibustion is carried out are the following:

1. **Moxibustion—Direct Method**

The moxa punk is moulded into small cones about the size of rice grains which are placed on the skin over the positions of the acupuncture points which are to be treated. Only one point is treated at a time and the moxa cone is ignited, preferably with an incense stick, and allowed to burn. If it is allowed to burn out completely, it results in a scar and this is termed 'Scarring Moxibustion'. The alternative method is to flick the cone off the skin as soon as any discomfort is felt by the patient and this procedure is usually repeated to a total of three or five cones at each locus. This method is known as 'Non Scarring Moxibustion' and is the method usually preferred nowadays, particularly in the West! However, Scarring Moxibustion has, apparently, been used successfully in the treatment of intractable allergic bronchial asthma in the People's Republic of China and the author has seen this used at an Ayurvedic research institute in Sri Lanka where it was employed with great success in the treatment of arthritis.

2. **Moxibustion—indirect Method:—**

There are three main methods of indirect moxibustion: the use of cones placed over an intermediate substance, the application of moxa to the acupuncture needle, and the use of moxa sticks or rolls. When used in the indirect method, the cones may be slightly larger than when they are ignited directly on the skin. The following substances may be used as intermediaries:

(a) *Ginger* A thin slice of ginger root about 2.54mm thick is used and the moxa cone is burnt on top of it. Very small holes may be pierced through the ginger. Care must be exercised to ensure that the heat is not so intense or prolonged as to cause blistering.

(b) *Garlic* Garlic may be used instead of ginger and is particularly indicated for cases of chronic paralysis. Garlic may also be used as a heat transmitting agent over carbuncles, in which case the carbuncle is first covered with damp paper and the garlic applied to the area that first dries out from the heat of the underlying inflammation. The garlic should be about 1/2cm thick and replaced after five cones of moxa have been burned. When used in the treatment of paralysis it is sometimes allowed to heat up beyond the point of discomfort.

(c) *Clay* This is made into a cake and used in the same way as the foregoing. It is recommended for eczema and some other skin problems. The treatment is usually continued until the patient experiences an inner warmth.

(d) *Pepper* The powdered form of white pepper is made into a paste with flour and water and spread over the point to be treated in a layer about 2mm thick. A slight hollow may be made in the centre which can be filled with a different herb such as powdered cinnamon or clove. The moxa cone is placed on the paste in the usual way and burned. The method is supposed to be good for arthritis and local numbness or stiffness.

(e) *Salt* This method is used on the navel which is filled with salt to the level of the surrounding abdomen and this is then usually covered with a thin slice of ginger. Ther moxa cone is placed on the ginger and ignited. Sometimes, it is burned directly on the salt but in this case care must be taken to ensure that the skin is not burnt. The treatment is used for abdominal pain accompained by diarrhoea or for general augmentation of energy and vitality.

(f) *Other substances* These include bean-cake, aconite cake which may be made with yellow wine or water, or other herbs. None of them is currently in common use.

The Application of Moxa to The Needle

The common method of applying moxa may be by wrapping moxa punk around the handle of the needle or chopping off a small section of a moxa roll, introducing a small hole through it and carefully fitting it on to the head of the needle. This, of course, has to be done after the needle has been inserted into the acupuncture points and therefore requires considerable dexterity to avoid inconveniencing the patient. In both these methods, the moxa is ignited, allowed to burn out completely and the process repeated two or three times. The needle should be allowed to cool between each operation. The second method is known as the 'OA' technique because it is particularly effective in many cases of osteoarthritis. It is usual to surround the base of the needle just at the level of the skin with a piece of foil or thick paper to protect the skin from any accidental dropping of the burning moxa from the handle. Needless to say, the practitioner is very careful during all types of moxibustion to ensure that the patient is not inadvertently burnt.

Moxibustion With a Moxa Stick or Roll

The most simple way of applying moxibustion and may be done over parts of the body where other methods would be unsuitable, such as points which are covered by hair. The moxa roll is ignited and coaxed into a state where the end is glowing with heat. Again, there are several methods of practical application:

(a) *Warm cauterization* The end of the moxa roll is held about 1cm away from the skin and removed when the heat starts to become unbearable.

(b) *Rotation method* This is similar to the previous method, except for the fact that the moxa roll is moved gently over a small area, such as the knee, which may require treatment. The moxa roll may also be alternated between two points, either in a continuous slow movement or by remaining over each point for a short while and then moving rapidly from one point to the other.

(c) *Sparrow-peck cauterization* In this method the moxa roll is brought slowly to within a few millimeters of the skin and more rapidly withdrawn. The process is repeated until the patient begins to feel a degree of discomfort.

(d) *Akabane method* This method was named after its Japanese exponent, Dr. Kobei Akabane, roughly at the turn of the century. It is more often used as a diagnostic test than for treatment. A thin moxa-stick or incense stick is used and the sparrow-peck cauterization method employed on the end points of the meridians (first or last points) which are situated by the nails of the fingers and toes. The joss-stick is brought within a millimetre of the point and repeated until a painful sensation is felt by the patient. The number of 'pecks' is carefully noted and each point compared for sensitivity. A point with greater sensitivity than its neighbours indicates a meridian that is out of order. The test is not used very much nowadays because the more sophisticated electrical diagnostic instruments called acupunctosocpes have largely replaced it.

3. The Hot Needle Technique:—

Despite not being a part of strict moxibustion, this is another method of applying heat specifically to a point. It is a method which has been developed during the present century because, although of ancient origin, it was modernised during the Cultural Revolution. A special needle known as *ayuan-li* is used and this has already been described in chapter 7. The needle is heated in a flame until red hot and then thrust into the point with instantanous withdrawal. It is particularly effective for benign swellings of the thyroid, other benign swellings, cysts and ganglions.

The Purpose of Moxibustion:—

It may appear obvious and that its purpose is to deliver heat to the body in order to achieve a therapeutic effect; yet that is a succinct, if not very profound summary of its purpose. Heat is well attested as beneficial for certain disorders and in 'ordinary' medicine is frequently applied for degnerative or 'cold' conditions. The precise physiological response of the body to heat has been well documented in textbooks of medicine and physiotherapy and may be summarised as an initial constriction of local blood vessels, followed by a dilation of these vessels which brings about an increase of the local blood supply in order to remove the heat. This tends to relieve pain, remove toxins and soothe nerves. In moxibustion the heat is more intense than that which is customarily applied in medical treatment, but it is also very much more specific and localised. Herein may lie part of the explanation for its efficacy because certain biologically active substances such as kinins and histamine are released into the tissue and these act as counter-irritants. The phenomenon of counter-irritation has long been employed in medicine and is the justification for the use of such medicaments as Spanish fly for the relief of pain. Roger Newman Turner and Royston Low say the it acts as a 'stressor' and they invoke the authority of Selye's concept of the General Adaptation Syndrome to better explain the effects of moxibustion. According to Selye, a stressor acting on the body elicits an 'alarm reaction' which, by activating the nervous system and the adrenal glands, leads to a 'stage of resistance'. Hormones produced by the adrenals have both anti- inflammatory and tissue healing effects and Newman Turner and Low say that, 'The initiation of a renewed General Adaptation Syndrome, by means of a target stressor at another site (moxibustion) reactivates the defensive mechanisms with a beneficial effect'. Evidence has also been adduced to indicate that other hormones are also produced as a result of moxibustion and that these include some from the pituitary. The Cooperative Research Group of Moxibustion of Jianxi Province, China, recorded various physiological parameters during and after moxibustion to the point *chihyin* which is situated at the outside corner at the base of the nail of the little toe. This point is treated when there is a malposition of the fetus. Moxibustion was found to have caused an increase in certain steroids without evidence of direct nervous stimulation and it was concluded that it worked by prompting the normal physiological process of hormone release by acting on the pituitary. The complete absence of such results when certain other points were treated with moxibustion leads to the conclusion that the point itself has a special relationship with the areas concerned and this reinforces the traditional belief correlating acupuncture meridians and points with specific tissues and functions.

The Traditional Chinese Medicine, believes that moxibustion is suited particularly for conditions of cold, dampness, deficient *qi* and stagnation. These correspond in Western terminology to such disorders as asthma, impotence, palpitations, oedema (retention of water in the tissues), poor circulation, loose stools, abdominal distension, feeling unduly cold, fear of the cold, kidney stones, tumours, withdrawn personality and diminished activity.

Moxibustion is forbidden at certain points such as in the case of points near the eyes. In the case of some of the traditionally forbidden points there seems no logical reason for the prohibition; although scarring moxibustion might cause trouble if it was done on the toes and would cause temporary disfigurement if done on the face or other commonly exposed parts. Some of the forbidden points are over superficial blood vessels and some are thought to be prohibited because of the strong effect that they can have on the body's energies. In general, moxibustion is not given to very young children, very old people, mentally disordered people, in diabetes, where there is a loss of feeling or anywhere near ulcers or inflamed areas. In all other cases moxibustion, if properly applied, is an extremely safe, comfortable and effective treatment either by itself or in conjunction with needling.

Cupping:— It is a very valuable traditional technique which also involves the use of heat, although in this case it is utilised to create a suction rather than to heat the tissues. A hollow vessel such as a glass jar or cup is used. In ancient times suction was applied to animal horns which had their tips chopped off and were inverted over the area to be treated. Nowadays, elegant glass cups are made for the purpose and these may be attached to a vacuum machine. The traditional method of using the cups is, however, still preferred and is independent of modern technology—except for the manufacture of the cups. The doctor wraps a little cotton wool soaked in surgical spirit around a pair of forceps. This is ignited and introduced for a second or two into the cup and withdrawn. The cup is then immediately applied to the patient over the area to be treated. The rapid cooling of the air inside the cup creates a partial vacuum and flesh covered by the cup is raised into the cup. An alternative method is to ignite a small piece of wool infused with alcohol on a protected area of skin and invert the cup over this. The flame removes all the oxygen which creates a partial vacuum and produces a strong suction.

The cups are retained for about five to ten minutes, depending upon the patient, time of year, area being treated and the degree of suction induced. A strong suction can become very painful after only a few minutes. The cup, having been applied, may also be moved from one spot to another without breaking the seal. If this is to be done the mouth of the cup is usually lubricated beforehand. Cupping may also be combined with normal acupuncture in which event the cup is simply placed over the inserted needle. It may also be combined with a blood letting technique in which case a special needle is used to produce bleeding and the cup subsequently placed over the small incision to induce further bleeding.

Cupping is useful in conditions of external damp invasions, stuck or congealed blood, stagnant *qi* and phlegm. These correspond to the western descriptions of coughing with phlegm, chronic bronchitis, bronchial asthma, chronic back pain or lumbago, some types of headache and sprains. It should not be used in cases of fever, convulsions, inflammation, infectious diseases, over ulcers or abscesses, over hair or in very nervous or pregnant patients.

Massage

Despite not having a direct connection with moxibustion or cupping it is considered here since it is the other traditional method of treating acupunture points besides needling. Massage may be done by pressing on the acupunture point which is known as 'acupressure' or may take the form of circular movements over the point with the finger tip. Traditionally a deep, centrifugal movement is said to disperse or sedate, whereas a light, centripetal movement has a toning effect. Pressure massage is normally done with the thumb, but may also be carried out using the palm, base of the hand, elbow, knucles or fist. Rubbing kneading, plucking, tapping, twisting, rolling and stretching techniques were also practised.

Apart from the general physiological effects of massage, which are improvement in circulation, normalising of nervous functioning, harmonising endocrine output, toning or relaxing muscles and improvement of digestion, there are also reflex effects which may be mediated via acupuncture points or by other reflex points or areas on the body which may or may not have been known to the ancient Chinese. A good example of these reflexes is that of foot reflexes described in foot reflexology or foot zone therapy *(see book one)*. This was certainly known to the Chinese and has merely been revived in the last hundred or so years in the West. The hand, too, is known to have reflex areas and the fingers are specifically related to organs or systems. The thumb is related to respiratory and liver function, the first finger corresponds to the function of assimilation and digestion, the middle finger reflects the circulation and heart function, the ring finger indicates the state of the nerves, whilst the little finger is linked with sexuality. These have been eleborated in book one.

Although reflex points are commonly treated by massage of one kind or another by osteopaths and some chiropractors yet this undoubtedly contributes to the favourable results experienced by these practitioners. It is also an integral part of the therapy connected with applied kinesiology and many forms of 'bodywork'. Manipulations of joints is also part of the traditional massage employed in Chinese-medicine and is sometimes called 'Chinese osteopathy'. this probably has the effect of breaking down adhesions, restoring full mobility, stretching contracted tissue and beneficially influencing the transmission of energy or *qi*. It may also enhance nerve function by releasing the causes of congestion in the tissue and impingement of blood supply.

Introduction of the Latest technology In Acupuncture treatment

Various advancement in a variety of fields in science have also contributed significantly in modernising the techniques used in acupuncture therapy. Following the Cultural Revolution in the People's Republic of China and the dissemination of acupunture throughout the world, the application of modern technology to the ancient practice of acupuncture has been eagerly embraced both inside China and in the world. The close cooperation of traditionally trained physicians and Western trained doctors in China has been particularly fruitful in both introducing new technology and researching the effects of acupuncture in a controlled environment. Many acupuncturists in the West are unable to participate in this kind of research because they are shunned by authorities who control the means of carrying it out. Innumerable experiments which are virtually useless are regularly carried out at enormous public expense; yet vitally important research into 'natural' treatments which involve comparatively little, cost are not even considered. Research which has a prospective and profitable end-product which can be sold by manufacturers excites the multi-national companies to sink vast sums into pharmacological development, but no company, even if it did happen to have an altruistic board of directors, is prepared to spend money when the probable outcome is not merely going to be a financial dead end, but would actually lead to a loss of exciting sales as needles, or other inexpensive items began to replace profitable drugs.

A new technique of needling called periosteal acupuncture was first described by Eelix Mann in Britain and subsequently developed by several people, particularly Geoff Greenbaum in Australia. It is useful for painful conditions but they should only be used as a last resort.

The surgical suture embedding techinque, whereby a piece of catgut about 1 cm. long is introduced into the tissues, was developed in China during the 1965-70 Cultural Revolution period itself. This technique produces prolonged stimulation of the point or points and is useful in chronic cases of bronchitis, asthma, gastric or duodenal ulcers, impotence, low back pain and the chronic effects of diseases like poliomyelitis.

The Technique of Electro-Acupuncture:—

Some famous doctors in the west have simultaneously discovered the use of electricity for pain control way back in 1857-58. Francis used a galvanic current to induce analgesia for tooth extractions. In the same period the College of Dental Surgeons convened a conference to investigate the technique and the members unanimously agreed that no local analgesic effect could be detected.

Since then, and particularly in the last twenty years, a great number of workers have reported both the analgesic and therapeutic effect of different kinds of electrical stimulation. The publication of the Gate Theory *(see previous chapter 8)* stimulated even greater interest in electrical methods of bringing about pain relief. In China, doctors of acupuncture were already using electrical stimulatioln to replace manual manipulation of needles to induce analgesia for surgery and it was an article by James Reston, the journalist who accompanied President Nixon to China in 1971, that brought this to the attention of the West. The details of his experience have been given in the first chapter.

The first surgical operation to be carried out under acupuncture analgesia in China was a tonsillectomy in 1958 in Shanghai. Since then, almost every kind of major surgery has been undertaken under acupuncture; though it is generally agreed that it is not very successful for orthopaedic surgery. It is particularly recommended for abdominal surgery and for childbirth.

In order to obtain analgesia, a weak current of a few microamperes is used generally in the form of a biphasic spike wave of a frequency ranging from 5-2,000 Hz. The higher frequencies are used for surgical analgesia, but lower frequencies are normally employed for routine acupuncture. Today, electro acupuncture is extremely popular all over the world, including China, and there are many instruments of varying sizes and complexity which can be used for treatment, electro-analgesia for surgery and for testing purpose. For this, a probe is fitted to the appropriate outlet of the apparatus and is used to test an area of skin surface. When an acupuncture point is encountered, a dial on the instrument will indicate an elevated electrical conduction through the skin. A device is usually attached which emits a high pitched sound to coincide with finding the point. These instruments vary considerably in their accuracy and depend upon careful control of a number of variables such as pressure of the probe on the skin, relative dampness of the skin and emotional changes of the testee. It is very important that the operator is thorough conversant with the location of the points before attempting to use such an instrument. Its greatest value lies in the detection of points on the ear where they lie so close together that it is not difficult even for an experienced practitioner to needle the wrong point unless great care is taken.

Sometimes, electrical treatment for pain is carried out without acupuncture and the commonest form of this is TENS which refers to transcutaneous electro-neural stimulation. That pain could be relieved by stimulating peripheral nerves with an electric current. In Britain and North America this has become a recognised treatment by osteopaths, physiotherapists and chiropractors.

Normally the treatment is given without acknowledging its origin in acupuncture and sometimes the treatment is euphemistically described as electro-acupuncture without the needles! The only problem with this is that it may give the impression that acupuncture is being practised which may delude some patients into thinking that there is nothing more to this than a having an electric current passed through them. Moreover, if a patient thought that he had been receiving acupuncture he might mistakenly be deterred from seeking a treatment he really needs.

The Constraints In The Use of Electro-Acupuncture

There are a score of contra-indications to the safe employment of electro acupuncture as well as a number of special precautions to be taken. It should not be used on small children or very old persons, nor should it be used on any person who suffers from epilepsy or other convulsive states. It should not be used in mentally ill people, non-cooperative patients, or those with excess *yang* state. Patients suffering from fever or shock or who are restless and anxious should not normally be given electro-acupuncture.

There are some points which should not be stimulated with an electric current and the current should not normally be passed from one side of the body to the other. *Yin and yang* points should not be interconnected and it goes without saying that the current should be started at zero and increased very cautiously. Ideally, a battery-operated instrument should be used so that there can be no possibility of a mains current passing through a patient.

Laser Treatment and Acupuncture:—

LASER is an acronym. Signifying Light Amplification by the Stimulated Emission of Radiation. Following the conception of this idea by Einstein, in 1923, the Russian biologist Alexander Gurvich noticed that cell division in one culture stimulated a similar proliferation in an adjacent culture, despite there being no direct contact. He termed this process 'biological induction' and observed that the phenomenon was inhibited by a glass barrier, whereas a quartz one did not effect it. This led him to conclude that some electromagnetic energy in the ultraviolet range must be involved, since quartz freely allows the passage of ultraviolet radiation, but glass does not. The evidene that a few photons could induce biological activity gave rise to the idea that this form of radiation might be useful as a therapeutic tool.

By the late 1950s, Schawlow and Townes demonstrated the practical possiblity of laser and, in 1963, Theodore Kaiman of the Hughes Aircraft Company, USA, made the first ruby laser. However it was accidentally discovered in Hungary that laser increased the supply of blood to wounds, burns and skin ulcers in both animals and humans. Studies in Sweden showed that laser can fortify damaged muscle and improve muscle tone and it was this that encouraged some beauticians to make use of laser on the face in the hope that it would remove wrinkles.

The specific qualities of laser are minimal divergence or coherence, which means that the light is in a beam that hardly spreads out at all; single wavelength or monochromatism, which means that it is an extremely pure light; and projectability over a long distance. There are various laser producing materials including argon, carbon dioxide, gallium, helium, neon and ruby, but the optimal laser for a acupuncture or therapy seems to be the helium-neon laser. Treatment with heliumneon laser helps to modify its resonace. 632 nm is also the wave length of oxygen and it would seem that this is another explanation of the particularly good effect of helium neon laser. Laser has been shown to be capable of promoting haematopoiesis (activation of bone marrow), assisting the regeneration of skin and damaged nerves, reducing pain and counteracting arthritis. It has also been shown to be capable of inactivating viruses.

Researchers investigated laser with a view to using it instead of the acupuncture needle, and the Mecherschmidt Co. in Munich developed the first helium-neon laser. Research in Alma Ata has also shown that acupuncture points are specific loci of energy exchange between the living organisms and the surrounding environment and that the application of laser to acupuncture points has unique advantages in treatment. The points are stimulated from a few seconds up to about a minute.

The laser may also be used for direct treatment of lesions and one of the most fascinating of such application is its use in many kinds of eye disease where the laser beams is directed on to the eye itself, including the pupil and retina. Good results have been obtained in cases of iritis, conjunctivitis and cataract.

The use of laser in acupuncture or for therapy should not be confused with its application in surgery where it is employed for its heating and cutting effect. In this case a very much more high-powered beam is used. For acupuncture purposes it is 25 milliwatts or less and sometimes as little as 2 milliwatts. It may be used for virtually any condition for which acupuncture might be suitable, but Table 20 gives some of the conditions which respond most readily to laser.

Laser is particularly suitable for infants and children, or nervous people who are frightened of needles. The enormous interest in laser is demonstrated by the fact that there are dozens of instruments now on the market and symposia are held several times a year on lasertherapy alone. The other type of laser most often used in acupuncture therapy is the infra-red laser which is particularly favoured by Dr. Nogier and the French school. One limitation of this laser is that it is dangerous if directed on the eye. As far as their therapeutic value and effectiveness in stimulating acupuncture points is concerened the argument between proponents of each kind of laser continues unabated. Much more work needs to be done before we have a good understanding of lasertherapy, but in the meantime it appears to be a safe, effective and painless alternative to needles.

TABLE 20

Some conditions for which lasertherapy is suitable. Those marked were internationally recommended as suitable for acupuncture treatment by the World Health Organisation at a session in Beijing in 1979

Migraine and cephalalgia (headache)	Sinusitis
Trigeminal neuralgia	Vertigo
Intercostal neuralgia	Hyperemesis
Arthritis	(excessive vomiting)
Claudication (circulatory weakness)	Bronchial asthma
Ulcus cruris (leg ulcer)	Colitis
Menstrual disorders	Insomnia
Duodenal ulcer	Nervousness
Constipation	Abnormal tiredness
Hypertension	Heart-burn
Epilepsy	Overweight
Haemorrhoids	Underweight
Diabetes	Nose-bleed
Irritability	Iritis
Hives	Glaucoma
Cataract	Emotional problems
Conjunctivitis	Skin problems

Cymatics:—

This technique uses the mixed frequencies of audible sound. According to his theory, the vibration or resonance of the cell is upset and this is what we term disease. By irradiating the cell with corrective frequencies, the harmonious resonance of the sick cells can be re-established. The instrument used in cymatics computerises the various frequencies which are recorded on a normal audiotape. This is then played back through a vibrating head which is held against the area to be treated. As in the case of laser, it may be applied to acupuncture points or directly to the lesioned areas.

Applied Kinesiology

Although this has already been described as a diagnostic method in the earlier chapter, it may also be used for treatment. Strictly speaking, applied kinesiology is purely diagnostic, but it has as it were appropriated to itself certain treatments which have been elaborated using the technique to evaluate them in the process. It uses a touch technique whereby the therapist merely connects pairs of acupuncture points by touching them simultaneously instead of inserting needles into them. It has also demonstrated that certain disorders of energy may interfere with the acupuncture treatment and are best corrected by simple procedures prior to any acupuncture. Many acupuncturists, however, regard findings as speculative. Such disorders include lesions of the hyoid bone, imbalance in the body's ionisation plant which is connected with alternate breathing through right and left nostrils and disorders in the gait reflex which is connected with the neurological administration of muscular activity during normal walking.

Magnetotherapy:—

This new method of therapy has fascinated man and it use probably one of the most elusive and least known types of energy which is currently scrutinised by science. It would appear that magnetism has a profound effect upon the development and health of both animals and man. The earth's magnetic field deflects low-energy cosmic rays which are the most prevalent of cosmic radiation and this probably changes at different parts of the earth's surface. Researchers have found that north pole magnetism has effects of slowing down growth and producing nervous, fastidious and unhealthy animals, whilst south pole magnetism accelerates growth and produces animals which are dirty, aggressive and sexually promiscuous. A balance is what is always required but in disease states there may be an indication for either south or north pole magnetism. The application of magnetic poles to acupuncture points is still in the research stage but some interesting results have already been reported.

Sonopuncture:—

Using ultrasonic vibrations is sonopuncture. This is a standard treatment in physiotherapy. In acupuncture, an instrument is used which focusses the ultrasonic energy on to a very small area in a similar way to when it is used by dentists for descaling teeth. Good results have been reported by some proctitioners who use this method but it is not a procedure that is thought by the author to be ideal.

Aquapuncture:—

Using water or fluid for acupunctures, this is a particular form of acupuncture in which a small volume of fluid, usually a vitamin solution or distilled water, is injected into the site of the acupuncture point. The rationale for this is that it stimulates the microcirculation.

Microwave:—

Microwave technique is quite in vogue now. There is virtually no limit to the imagination and a device which delivers a microwave impulse at the point of the acupuncture needles has now been manufactured in Australia and, according to reports, has been found to be very effective.

Homoeopuncture:—

This technique is joining two therapies for common good. This is a clever combination of acupuncture and homoeopathy which has now been practised in Sri Lanka for several years. When a particular homoeopathic remedy is seen to be indicated it is administered to the patient at the tip of the acupuncture needle. This obviates the problem of the remedy being antidoted by being taken with a meal or too near a cup of coffee, etc. It is thought to be the best way that the remedy can be introduced into the body. Initial results appear to be very encouraging but it takes a long time to analyse a treatment where two different therapies are being administered together.

Ginseng:—

This is another name for Chinese herbal therapy. The use of ginseng has been so consistently and inextricably woven into Traditonal Chinese Medicine that no treatise on acupuncture can be considered to be entirely complete without some mention of it. It is, of course, only in the West that the use of ginseng can be considered a new method of treatment. One of the reason for its special place in Chinese medicine is that it assists and potentiates acupuncture treatment, probably through its favourable influence on the endocrine system and its ability to establish harmony and encourage homoeostasis;

It would be nonsense to claim that ginseng is a cure-all; yet there is scarcely an illness that cannot be helped by this herb. What is even more interesting and valuable is its proven ability to enhance health and prevent disease. It is, as it were, a general immunizer, and it is in this capacity that it is particularly in tune with the basic philosophy of Traditional Chinese Medicine.

The ginseng plant is only found growing wild in two small areas of the globe—on the rugged slopes of Manchuria and South Korea. So avid is the collection of this plant that it is doubtful if it can now be found at all, except in very small amounts in remote parts of Korea. Cultivated ginseng is found in China, Korea, Japan, Russian and USA. The best quality plant comes from Korea and can be recognised by the redness of the root after it has been steamed. Beware of the lucrative practice of the passing off old, hardened carrots as top quality ginseng!

With almost magical properties, it is not surprising that many legends sourround the origin of ginseng. One such legend from Kirin Province proclaims that the plant of ginseng was born one summer night in the cedar forest when lightning struck a mountain stream. The stream was transformed into the ginseng root. Thus, all the elements of creation—fire, earth, metal, water and wood, are represented and balanced in the ginseng root, making it veritable panacea for all illnesses.

Evolite:—

This technique uses polarised light of a lamp. This is therapy first used in 1981 by Dr. D.Stacker, Medical Director of St. Joseph's Hospital, Bremerhaven in West Germany and Drs Andersson and Einarsson at the Department of Surgery, Eksjoklinik, Eksjoe Sweden. It was their contention that the biostimulatory effect of laser was due to its being polarised, and they found that a lamp emitting polarised light produce the same benefits as the laser. Its chief advantage over the laser seems to be that it is easier to apply and is more effective when used directly on lesions rather than acupuncture points. Research into the biochemical effects of evolite treatment has been carried out at Semmelweis University, Budapest, Hungary and preliminary results seem to indicate that it is a useful therapy.

Some Typical Case Histories

Having told all about acupuncture treatment, concerning the miraculous treatment and the various scientific theory to explain the intrecacies of this theory, it is found neccessry to include some of the typical case histories called from the various medical records. These are not all successful cases as the physicians couldn't cure some of them. But since the secret of success becomes clearer in failures than achievement of the desired goal, some such cases have also been included. Especial attempt has been made to select the cases from all walks of life and from the widest possible range of the age groups. Needless it is to emphasise that for professional reasons their names and identites have been kept as closely guarded secret.

Mr. A.B., Age 77

This aged man came for treatment for a pain in the right shoulder which radiated across upper right side of the back and down the right arm. He complained that his fingers were sometimes affected with tingling or numbness. This problem had been with him intermittently for 15-20 years. In addition, he had been suffering for three years from a pain in the right buttock, which extended down the lateral side of his right leg as far as the knee. He also had acute gout. He had his gall bladder removed seven years previously and was now on Indocid (a drug used in cases of inflammation, rheumatoid arthritis, gout and pain.) Examination showed him to have a chronic underactivity of the stomach, wasting in the leg muscles, stiffness and pain in the right hip joint. He was diagnosed as having an obstruction of the circulation of *qi* and blood, known as a *bi* syndrome. This was thought to be the type known as *fixed bi*. Moxa with needling was applied to a point on the hip and electroacupuncture was given to points on the back. The leg and buttock pain (sciatica) responded immediately to the treatment. Needles were also given for the shoulder pain but this was very much slower to respond and never seemed to clear completely. The patient discontinued treatment, after only a few sessions, much improved but certainly not cured. In this case moxa was used to remove the dampness since this type of disorder is thought to be due to the invasion of damp which obstructs the channels.

MISS S.Y., Age, 19:—

A comely lady she complained of long-standing migraine which started as a pressure pain behind the eyes and radiated to the temples. Typically, there were prodromal symptoms of blurred vision and feeling 'vague' lasting for about half an hour before onset of pain. Sometimes there would also be nausea which would start after the pain. She also complained of frequent 'ordinary' headaches and variable pain in the knees. The diagnosis was mainly an obstruction of *qi* in the gall bladder. A faulty ileocaecal valve was also diagnosed and corrected. The patient was found to have an allergy or intolerance to instant coffee and advised to withdraw this from her diet. This is quite a common problem and it is hard for many people to realise that such simple changes in diet can have dramatic effects upon health. This girl made a good recovery with four treatments.

Mr. C.M., Age 48:—

This is a case history of a business tycoon. This man, who had a sedentary occupation, complained of impotence of several years' duration. Investigation found no organic cause, though questioning the patient indicated that it was not purely psychological as he reported that he never woke up with an erection. The tongue was pale and swollen and the pulse 'thready'. He was diagnosed as deficient kindey *yang* and given moxibustion to the point *guanyuan*, situated half way between the pubic bones and the navel. Acupuncture was done at the associated point for the kindey and at *taixi*, which is a point on the kidney meridian behind the inner ankle. *Baihui* was used to reinforce the treatment and to induce calmness. After five weekly treatments the patient reported a successful outcome.

MASTER KITTOO., Age 11

This young boy was an interesting case because he met the physician purely by chance whilst he was treating someone else. He told him he suffered from asthma and asked if anything could be done to help him. It was with some trepidation that the physician treated him without asking his parents' permission but it seemed that the opportunity would be lost if it was not taken immediately. Of course, acupuncture was out of the question, so acupressure was used, particularly the touch type described in applied kinesiology. The boy was told that if he wanted any further treatment he would have to have his parents' consent. The next morning, quite early, his mother was shouting down the telephone. The physician thought for a moment that he was about to be at the receiving end of a lot of criticism for treating a child without his parents' permission but was relieved and happy to hear her say that the previous night had been the first for ten years that the boy had slept without waking up with an asthma attack. The boy was given a few more treatments, including lasertherapy, after which he was completely free from his asthma. Unfortunately, when the mother subsequently visited the family doctor and he politely enquired about her son's health, she announced that he had been cured with acupuncture. The doctor then protested, 'Acupuncture can't cure asthma', whereupon Mrs. N., a very forthright lady, said, 'Well it bloody well has,' and, as a final flourish declared that she had more faith in 'That man than the whole of Queen Mary's Hospital!' Not exactly a piece of conversation calculated to endear acupuncture to the heart of a sceptical medical practitioner! Alas, for all her rantings, there was no further contact with either mother or child; though the boy was seen by chance four years later. He was still free of asthma but had become considerably overweight. The case has to be described as a failure since the 'magic bullet' was merely replaced by the 'magic touch' and no alteration to life style was ever considered.

Mr. B. K., Age 41

Mr. B.K. complained of joint-pain. The problem here was osteoarthritis of the knee of traumatic origin and of several years duration. The man was overweight, had frequent drinking bouts, lived on a very bad diet of predominantly tea, chips and white bread, smoked excessively and, amongst other things, suffered from schizophrenia. He was on regular medication to keep this illness under control, but inwardly rebelled against it, saying that deep down he wanted to return to his natural (schizophrenic) state. It was obvious to me that his poor nutrition, aggravated by overindulgence in alcohol and cigarettes, was partly responsible for his mental as well as his physical state but it was quite impossible to get him to make the slightest alteration to his life style. The most recent comment in his hospital notes made by the orthopaedic surgeon was, 'This man will be back within six months begging for an operation'. The man had asked me what I could do for him and in view of his refusal to cooperate he had to be told 'not much'. Nevertheless, with acupuncture, massage and foot-zone therapy, he was kept going for five years until we ran into trouble with DHSS. On my advice he had stopped carrying heavy weights and had subsequently become unemployed. After much correspondence with the local authorities he had been placed on a government retraining scheme but due to his impetuous nature had not lasted as long as a day! Actually, from his description of what went on he could not really be blamed as it seems he was treated rather like a twelve-year old. The outcome of all this was that he was told that unless he had the recommended surgery he would have all his benefit cut off: a threat that scared him into agreement. He asked my advice which I was loathe to give so I prevaricated and told him that it was entirely up to him. He agreed in the end to have the operation subject to my willingness to continue treating him subsequently. The surgery was a failure and he was left in a far worse state than before the operation. At one stage his thigh muscles had wasted considerably and the hospital told him that it was because he was not doing the exercises which they had prescribed. The poor man had been doing his best, despite the fact that it was very painful and he was given some electrical stimulation for the muscles from me which, I told him, should be done by the hospital. Little did I realise that he was going to relate this statement to the superintendent physiotherapist who passed the message on to the surgeon who went into a fit of rage and told the patient that if he had anything more to do with me he would, 'wash his hands of him completely'. It seemed like a heaven-sent opportunity to retire from the scene—an opportunity I took without a second though!

Mr. S.C., Age 68:—

Despite being of advanced age. Mr. SC. was a charming man who would probably not have complained if he was on his death bed. His main problem was high blood pressure due to deficient liver *yin*. He was treated with acupuncture to *ququan* at the knee and three ear points namely, liver, kidney and *shen men*. Special points on the ear for lowering blood pressure were introduced at the second visit. When the needles were removed the patient wondered if his ear might play a tune in the wind as he walked out of the surgery. He had a great sense of humour which I am sure aided his recovery. His blood pressure returned to within normal limits for a man of his age and the vertigo which he had also complained of disappeared completely.

Mr. M.B., Age 31:—

This man's main problem was psoriasis which occurred in a few discrete patches mainly on the arms and legs. In his case the technique of 'surrounding the dragon' was used, together with two or three other points. Surrounding the dragon consists of making shallow insertions with about five needles around the perimeter of the lesions. It is a variation of local treatment. It is often very effective and was so in this case. After about ten weekly treatments the lesions were almost gone and some had completely disappeared, a few more treatments at monthly intervals completed the process, but at this stage the technique of surrounding the dragon had been entirely replaced by *baihui*, (for calming and sedation), *hegu* (for elimination), *quchi* (for its powerful homoeostatic effect), *xuehai* (for its anti-allergic effect) and *lieque* (to simulate the lungs which feed the skin).

Mrs. C.K., Age 52:—

Although quite busy, this lady complained of insomnia due to cramp which occured chiefly in the calf muscles. The point *houxi* on the hand and *neiguan* on the forearm were used as key points to activate the governor and *yin wei mo* which are helpful in spasms and cramps. In addition, they increase the activity of the parathyroid glands which help to maintain correct calcium levels in the blood. Cramps are often the result of lowered serum calcium levels. The point *yanglingquan* was used for its effect on muscles and tendons and, finally, the parathyroid point on the right ear was given a press needle. After one week and a single treatment no further cramps were being experienced and Mrs. S. was sleeping through the night without waking. (The reason for using the right ear is, you may remember, because women are always right!)

Mrs. K.D., Age 58:—

This is a case of smoking aggravating the problem. This lady was smoking sixty cigarrettes per day and, in the words of her friend, was 'Never seen without a cigarette in her mouth'. She asked if she could have acupuncture to stop her smoking and seemed like the most hopeless case imaginable. She had been smoking since the age of fifteen and in forty old years had never been without the habit. Experience has shown that the most difficult smoking cases are women in the 25-45 age group who smoke less than twenty per day, but this case looked just like the proverbial exception. She was given acupuncture to the lung and addiction points in both ears which were electrically stimulated for twenty-five minutes. After the removal of the needles, a press needle was placed in the lung point of the right ear and the patient instructed to press on it at least three times per day and whenever she felt the urge to smoke. Not only did she never smoke again but, about six weeks later, when she brought a friend along for a similar treatment, she maintained that after the acupuncture she felt 'as though she had never smoked'. At that time she was feeling immeasurably fitter and was adamant that she would never return to the domination of Lady Nicotine.

Mrs. R.S., Age 56:—

This case relates to pseudo-cancer problem. This lady was suffering from severe post-operative pain after a total mastectomy undertaken for a malignancy. She had been enduring this pain for several months and was scarcely able to sleep at night or carry on a normal life. She was given acupuncture to local points and *hegu* on both sides, from which she obtained considerable relief. However, the pain returned after three days, though with less intensity. She was given a second treatment and a TENS (transcutaneous electroneural stimulation) instrument to take away and apply every day. She asked if she could use it more often and was told that she could. On some days she used it as often as three times but as the days passed by she needed it less and less. After three more weeks she was able to return the instrument but asked if she could purchase a new one in case the pain returned.

The Possible Dangers and Pitfalls in Acupuncture

Despite the tall claim that acupuncture is an extremely safe form of treatment with no side effects, it would be more than surprising if such a potent therapy was entirely devoid of all risk. In the first place, needles must be sterile and, although this can be taken for granted when the treatment is done by a medical doctor or a properly qualified acupuncturist, it is surprising how much ignorance there is about what constitutes adequate sterility. Even if rigid sterilisation procedures are adhered to, it is possible for a needle to be misplaced unless priority is always given to ensuring that this does not occur.

Secondly, there are 'prohibited areas' such as the scalp of infants before the closure of the fontanelles, the nipples and breast tissue, the umbilicus and the external genitalia. However, moxibustion may be done at the umbilicus, some expert acupuncturists have also used points round the base of the penis in their treatment for impotence.

Next, there are the dangerous points which should only be treated by experienced acupuncturists. These are points around the eye, some points on the neck which lie over vital structures such as arteries, baroreceptors, mediastinum (chest wall) and spinal cord, points on the chest which are not protected by bone or cartilage, one points on the abdomen which lies over the gall bladder, points which are close to large blood vessels and any other points which lie close to vulnerable structures.

There are a few points, such as those at the tips of the fingers and toes and on the palms of the hand or soles of the feet, which are painful when needled. For this reason very fine needles are usually selected for those particular points as well as the face which is also rather sensitive.

Bleeding and bruising may occur at the site of the acupuncture and this can be annoying if it is on an exposed part of the body such as the face. Fortunately, it very seldom occurs but only a day or so ago one of my patients telephoned me as she was very worried because her thumb was bruised after acupuncture treatment. Massaging the point and applying some tincture of arnica ointment is the best treatment for this problem if it does occur.

A broken or stuck needle is a complication which the author has, fortunately never encountered; though this does, apparently, happen occasionally. Never inserting needles beyond two-thirds of their length is the best precaution against this as needles, if they do break, usually do so at the junction of the handle and shaft. Repeated sterilisation tends to weaken the metal and for that reason needles should not be retained for a very long time.

The forgotten needle is something that worries every busy practitioner. Once when this was discussed by a group of senior acupuncturists none could declare that he was free from guilt in this respect. Although it has seldom happened in the author's practice, Murphy's Law had to ensure that it happened to the same patient twice!

Fainting or Leaving Your Conciousness in Extreme Nervousness

If you are prone to fainting or are of a nervous disposition you should ensure that you are lying down if you have acupuncture treatment. As this is the normal practice in most Western countries fainting is not a frequent complication. It is said to be a good sign, however, as it indicates that the treatment is likely to be effective. One or two sitting patients have come over faint in the author's practice but this is an eventuality that can easily be dealt with. The needles are withdrawn and a special point for recovery is massaged.

Addiction to Acupuncture:—

There is no denying the fact that this is the only true side effect of acupuncture. But it is both rare and harmless. It is scarcely ever seen when treatment has to be paid for and can therefore be described as a largely unaffordable luxury. One interesting case occurred in Sri Lanka where the patient would turn up from time to time and after careful appraisal of the situation would seek out the most incompetent doctor or student from whom he would solicit treatment. It seemed that the more painful the needle insertion the better it fulfilled his need!

When You Should Not Receive Acupuncture (or When Caution Is Necessary)

1. *If you have any sort of malignancy.* This is because acupuncture is said to have no curative effect on malignant disorders. However, acupuncture treatment may be received for the secondary effects of the disease, such as pain, depression or insomnia. Despite this admonition it should be said that some cases of malignant growth have seen successfully treated with acupuncture, including a nine month old baby in Sri Lanka with a brain tumour which had been pronounced incurable. The infant was given six months to live and the mother, in desperation, had begged for him to be given acupuncture. When the author last saw him the child was doing fine and had already made considerable progress towards normal functioning.

2. *If you have a serious infection.* Antibiotics are normally the treatment of choice in such cases, although acupuncture may be combined with drug treatment. It may also be used if there is allergy or intolerance to the antibiotic.

3. *When you require an operation.* This includes those cases where accidents have resulted in dislocation or fracture of bones or injury to vital organs or blood vessels. Other cases for surgery include congenital malformations, mechanical obstruction or appendicitis. The latter condition has, however, been successfully treated by acupuncture in the People's Republic of China.

4. *In the initial stages of pregnancy.* Problems associated with pregnancy are regularly treated with acupuncture but these

months are to be avoided if possible. At all stages of pregnancy there are certain acupuncture points which are not used; neither is strong stimulation or electroacupuncture given. Even this advice is only cautionary and the author himself recently gave very strong stimulation to one of these points during the last month of pregnancy. This was done with a view to getting a malpositioned foetus to turn. Unfortunately, although the treatment did cause considerable movement, the baby was unable to turn completely, but the outcome was a successful breech delivery.

5. *If you are being treated for some typical illness.* These include diabetes, thyroid problems or high blood pressure where caution is required before acupuncture treatment as it may be necessary to adjust the dose of your drug in order to compensate for the effect of the acupuncture. In this eventuality it is highly desirable that the doctor who prescribed the drug should be involved in this process. If you take drugs for 'social' reasons or if you are under the influence of drugs or alcohol it is extremely important that you inform the acupuncturist before treatment. Acupuncture can be used to help you withdraw from such drugs but, in the last analysis, self determination is absolutely essential. The same thing is true for smoking as acupuncture can be very helpful if you want to stop, but it will not actually stop you.

Glossary of Acupuncture Terms

Acupuncture:—Insertion of a needle in to a predetermind and specific point on the body with a view to enhancing the '*qi*' and improving the general state of health.

Acupuncture Analgesia: – Term referring to the elevation of pain threshold by the use of acupuncture.

Acupuncture Points (acupoint) :— Point of low electrical resistance on the body surface where the '*Qi*' is capable of being influnced by various kinds of treatment, notably the insertion of a needle. The acupoints are probably loci where cosmic (eletro-magnetic) energy is absorbed and eliminated by the body.

Ah Shi Point :— A point on the surface of the body which is painful when pressed. These points arise spontaneously.

Alarm Points :— Also known as '*mu*' points, these are acupuncture points which are situated on the foot of the body and often became sensitive during illness. Most meridians have one such point.

Allopathy:—The western school of Medicine, based upon the principle of curing disease by creating a different disease.

Associated Affect Points :— These are a series of points found upon the urinary bladder meridian which runs down the back of each side of the spine. They are also known as '*shu*' points.

Ayurveda:—The indigenous Indian school of medicine based upon the principle that any disease in the body is the outcome of viciatoin of the equilibrium of the three basic humours of the body, viz, vaat (wind), Pitta (pile) and kuff (phlegm).

Ayurvedic Medicines:— The medicines mostly prepared by the natural products like herb roots and bulb of the plants.

Cupping:— Procedure in which a vacuum is created over a small area of the body by the use of cups. Particularly helpful in cases of pain and congestion as it improves local blood supply.

Deqi :—(Pronounced as 'derchee'). Sensation often felt by the patient when an acupuncture needle is inserted or manipulated.

Distal Points :—These are points which lie at the extremities of the body, below the elbow or knees. Their use reinforces the action of points near the other end of a meridian. Certain points are known to be very effective when employed in this manner.

DNA :—Deoxyribonucleic acid. This is a substance that Carries genetic information or memory.

Eight Principles :—These are the categories such as hot or cold, in which an illness or patient can be described.

Endocrine :— Glands which release secretions into the body.

Endorphin :—Morphine like substance which is generated within the body.

Five Phases or Transformations :— Sometimes known as five elements these phases refer to the cycle of life and are linked to the seasons, climate or emotions. They provide a useful framework for the interpretation and treatment of disease.

Gate Control Theory :—Theory which manitains that nerve impulses pass through a 'gate' which, if closed, prevents a sensation reaching the brain.

Governor :—The central meridian running up the back and over the head.

Homeopathy :— System of medicine based upon the principle of producing another similar disease or diathesis.

Homeopuncture :—Method of applying a minute dose of homeopathic remedy with acupuncture.

Homoeostasis :—Condition of equilibrium or harmony where everything is in balance.

Horary Point :—A point on each meridian which refers to the element to which that particular meridian is particularly related. It is a point which is usually treated at the two hour period when the meridian or organ is energised or depleted.

Harmone :—Chemical Produced by endocrine glands which acts as a messenger to control other organs or tissues in the body.

Jinglo :—System of acupuncture meridians which permeates the entire body.

Junction Points :—These are points on a meridian from which there are direct connections to the coupled meridians (e. g. colon and lung) or to the next meridian on the 24 hour clock (e. g. colon joins stomach)

Ko Cycle :—This is the control or inhibiting cycle which depicts the 'government' of one of the 'zang fu' or organs over another.

Local Points :—Acupuncture points which are situated over or around an area of pain or pathology.

Meridians :—These are lines joining acupuncture points which may or may not have a real physiological existence. It is said that the 'qi' is transmitted primarily along the meridians.

Mother-son-law :—States that antecedent organ on the 'sheng' or mounishing cycle is often the cause of a problem rather than the organ which appears to be affected.

Motor Gate Theory :—Similar to the gate control Theory but points a 'gate' which prevents a motor impulse from reaching its target.

Moxibustion :—Application of heat, traditionally by burning a dried herb to an acupuncture point.

Mu Points :—Similar as alarm points.

Naturopathy :—System of treatment based upon the principle that structure and function are intimately related and that disorder should be treated by correcting structural problems.

Qi :—(Pronounced as chee) :—Bioenergy or vital force which by its vibratory and spiral movements give life to the body and maintains its health.

Shu Points :—Similar as 'associated affect points'

TAO (Pronounced as Dow) :—The unknowable way by which all things are governed and which is expressed in creation by the two complementary forces YIN and YANG.

Xi Cleft Points :—Sometimes called accumulation points, these are points on each meridian which are particularly useful in the treatment of an acute condition of the pertaining organ.

Yin and Yang :—Polarised energy which brings all things into existence and maintains them in harmony.

Yuan Points :—Also known as source points, these are points on each meridian which have a direct effect upon the pertaining organ.

Zang Fu :—Name given to the organs and their related functions in chinese medicine.

Zymotic :—Refers to fermenting process and therefore to diseases which are caused by bacteria which 'ferment' either in the body or in the environment.

OSHO BOOKS
From
DIAMOND POCKET BOOKS

SUFI THE PEOPLE OF THE PATH
*Singing Silence 150.00
*A Lotus of Emptiness 150.00
*Glory of Freedom 150.00
*The Royal Way 150.00

PHILOSOPHY & UPANISHAD
* I am the Gate 150.00
* The Great Challenge 150.00
*A Cup of Tea 150.00
The Mystery Beyond Mind 50.00
Towards The Unknown 50.00
A Taste of the Divine 50.00
The Alchemy of Enlightenment .. 40.00
Be Silent & Know 40.00
A Song Without Words 50.00
Inner Harmony 40.00
Sing, Dance, Rejoice 35.00
Secret of Disciplehood 40.00
The Centre of the Cyclone 40.00
The Greatest Gamble 35.00

MEDITATION
*Meditation-The Art of Ecstasy 150.00
Love & Meditation 40.00
Meditation : The Ultimate
Adventurer 50.00
*The Psychology of the Esoteric 150.00

PATANJALI YOGA SUTRA
*Yoga - The Alpha and The Omega-I
(The Birth of Being) 95.00
*Yoga - The Alpha and The Omega-II
(The Ever Present Flower) 95.00
*Yoga - The Alpha and The Omega-III
(Moving to the Centre) 95.00

JESUS AND CHRISTIAN MYSTICS
* I say unto You - I & II .... Each 150.00

ZEN & ZEN MASTERS
*Zen and the Art of Living 150.00
*Zen and the Art of Enlightenment 150.00
*Zen : Take it Easy 150.00
*Zen and The Art of Meditation .. 150.00

OSHO ON KABIR
*The Divine Melody 150.00
Ecstasy : The Language of
Existence 50.00

BAUL MYSTICS
Bauls : The Dancing, Mystics 40.00
Bauls : The Seeker of the Path 40.00
Bauls : The Mystics of Celebration 40.00

TANTRA
Tantra Vision : The Secret of the Inner
Experience 40.00
Tantra Vision : The Door to Nirvana 40.00
Tantra Vision : Beyond the Barriers
of Wisdom 40.00

VEDANTA
Vedanta : The Ultimate Truth 40.00
Vedanta : The First Star in the
Evening 40.00
Vedanta : An Art of Dying 35.00

OSHO'S VISION FOR THE WORLD
*And the Flowers Showered 150.00
Be Oceanic 50.00
One Earth One Humanity 50.00
Freedom form the Mind 50.00
Life, A Song, A Dance 35.00
Meeting the Ultimate 35.00
The Master is a Mirror 50.00
From Ignorance to Innocence 35.00
Eternal Celebration 40.00
Laughter is My Message 50.00

BOOKS ABOUT OSHO
Dr. Vasant Joshi, Ma Chetan Unmani
*New Vision for the New
Millennium 100.00
Swami Chaitanya Keerti
* Allah To Zen 150.00
Swami Arvinda Chaithnya
Our Beloved Osho 195.00
Ma Dharm Jyoti
One Hundred Tales for Ten
Thousand Buddha 95.00

Order books by V.P.P. Postage Rs. 20/- per book extra. Postage free on order of three or more books, Send Rs. 20/--in advance.

◆ DIAMOND POCKET BOOKS (P) LTD.
X-30, Okhla Industrial Area, Phase-II, New Delhi-110020.
Phones : 51611861-65, Fax : (0091) -011- 51611866, 26386124

DIAMOND POCKET BOOKS PRESENTS
ASTROLOGY, VAASTU, PALMISTRY & RELIGION BOOKS

Shashi Kant Oak
* Naadi Prediction 95.00

Dr. Bhojraj Dwivedi
* Hindu Traditions and Beliefs : A Scientific Validity (Question & Answer) 150.00
* Feng Shui : Chinese Vaastu Shastra 195.00
* Pyramid and Temple Vaastu .. 195.00
* Yantra, Mantra, Tantra and Occult Science 195.00
* Thumb! The Mirror of Fate ... 150.00
* Astrology & Wealth (Jyotish Aur Dhyan Yog) 95.00
* Jyotish Aur Rajyog 95.00
* Jyotish and Santan Yog 75.00
* Remedial Vaastushastra 200.00
* Sampuran Vaastushastra 200.00
* Commercial Vaastushastra 200.00
* Environmental Vaastu 150.00
* The Mystique of Gems & Stones (4 colour) 200.00
* Kalsarp Yoga Aur Ghatvivah (in Press) 200.00
* The Mystical of Palmistry (in Press) 250.00
* Study of Omens 95.00
* The Astrological Analysis of Earthquake 60.00

Pt. Gopal Sharma, Dr. D.P. Rao
* Pyramid Power & Vaastu 195.00
* Advance Feng Shui (For Health and Happiness) 195.00
* Sri Sai Science of Griha Vaastu 195.00
* Vaastu and Pyramidal Remidies 195.00

Pt. Gopal Sharma
* Comprehensive Vaastu 75.00
* Wonders of Numbers 60.00

Acharya Vipul Rao
* Hypnotism 95.00

Cheiro
* Cheiro's Language of the Hand (Palmistry) 95.00
* Cheiro's Book of Numerology 60.00
* Cheiro's Astro Numerology & Your Star 95.00
* Cheiro's Book of Astrology 95.00

B.R. Chuwdhary
* Speed Palmistry with Memory Tips 95.00

A. Somasundaram
* Future is in Our Hands 90.00

S. K. Sharma
* The Brilliance of Hinduism 95.00
* Sanskar Vidhi (Arya Samaj) ... 95.00

Dr. B.R. Kishore
* Hinduism 95.00
* Rigveda 60.00
* Samveda 60.00
* Yajurveda 60.00
* Atharvveda 60.00
* Mahabharata 60.00
* Ramayana 60.00
* Supreme Mother Goddesses Durga (4 Colour Durga Chalisa) ... 95.00

Manish Verma
* Fast & Festivals of India 95.00

Manan Sharma
* Buddhism (Teachings of Buddha) 95.00
* Universality of Buddha 95.00

Anurag Sharma
* Life Profile & Biography of Buddha 95.00
* Thus Spake Buddha 95.00

Udit Sharma
* Teaching & Philosophy of Buddha 95.00

Order books by V.P.P. Postage Rs. 20/- per book extra. Postage free on order of three or more books, Send Rs. 20/- in advance

DIAMOND POCKET BOOKS (P) LTD.
X-30, Okhla Industrial Area, Phase-II, New Delhi-110020.
Phones : 8611861- 865, Fax : (0091) -011- 8611866.

A Mantra to Develop Brain

Biswaroop Roy Chowdhury, an authority in brain and learning techniques and National Memory Record holder, combines ancient wisdom and latest scientific Key Techniques of Memory (KTM), as a way to memory development. In his book **'Dynamic Memory Methods'**, the young Memory Consultant has given tips regarding the use of scientific memory techniques for memorising faster and retaining it longer.

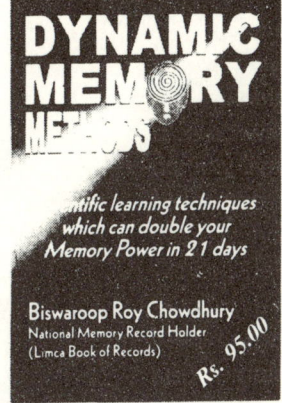

Based on mnemonics (artificial aids to learning) and laws of controlled association, the simple mental exercises mentioned in the book enhances reader's observation and concentration in an amazing way. The regular practice of various techniques mentioned inculcates the habit of using creative (Right) part of brain and thus the brain's capacity is optimized owing to balanced use of both logical (Left) and creative part of the brain. The book teaches 100 memory codes of memory language which help the reader in developing mental catalogue so that they can make their recalling and remembering effective.

The book is useful for all, a business person or a student, young or old; as familiarity with the memory language also helps in remembering telephone numbers, vocabulary, names and faces, speeches and anecdotes more efficiently.

Some of the interesting features of the book include:

- Making learning a fun
- Advanced Mnemonic System
- Curing absent-mindedness.
- Increase in intellect and positive mental attitude
- How to study smarter and not harder
- Preparing for competitive exams
- Remembering long answers of history.
- Memorising geographical maps & biological diagrams

RECEIVE BOOKS AT HOME BY VPP POSTAGE Rs. 10.00 (Extra)
ON ORDER OF THREE OR MORE BOOKS POSTAGE FREE

DIAMOND POCKET BOOKS

X-30, Okhla Industrial Area, Phase-II, New Delhi - 110 020
Phone No. : 011-6841033, 6822803, Fax : 011-6925020

'डाइनैमिक मेमोरी मेथड्स' हिन्दी एवं बंगाली में भी उपलब्ध है। प्रत्येक का मूल्य 60.00

Eureka!!!
At last the formula for ultimate success is found
A mirror for you to see yourself..
Evaluate, are you really successful?

Rs. 195/-
Add Postage 20/-

Also Available
in Hindi & Bangali

FUSION BOOKS

X-30, Okhla Industrial Area, Phase-II, New Delhi-110020. Tel: (011) 8611861-5, 6383679
Fax: 011-8611866, 6386124 Email- mverma@nde.vsnl.net.in

Available at all leading Bookshops

DIAMOND POCKET BOOKS PRESENTS
RELIGION & SPIRITUALITY BOOKS

B.K. Chaturvedi
- Gods & Goddesses of India 150.00
- Shiv Puran 95.00
- Vishnu Puran 95.00
- Shrimad Bhagvat Puran 75.00
- Devi Bhagvat Puran 75.00
- Garud Puran 95.00
- Agni Puran 95.00
- The Hymans & Orisons of Lord Shiva (Roman) 30.00
- Sri Hanuman Chalisa (Roman) 30.00
- Pilgrimage Centres of India 95.00

S. K. Sharma
- The Brilliance of Hinduism 95.00
- Sanskar Vidhi (Arya Samaj) 95.00

Dr. B.R. Kishore
- Hinduism 95.00
- Rigveda 60.00
- Samveda 60.00
- Yajurveda 60.00
- Atharvveda 60.00
- Mahabharata 60.00
- Ramayana 60.00
- Supreme Mother Goddesses Durga (4 Colour Durga Chalisa) 95.00

Manish Verma
- Fast & Festivals of India .. 95.00

Manan Sharma
- Buddhism (Teachings of Buddha) 95.00
- Universality of Buddha 95.00

Anurag Sharma
- Life Profile & Biography of Buddha 95.00
- Thus Spake Buddha 95.00

Udit Sharma
- Teaching & Philosophy of Buddha 95.00

Dr. Bhojraj Dwivedi
- Annual Horoscope 2003 (12 Zodiac Signs in one book) .. 95.00
- Hindu Traditions & Beliefs 150.00

Dr. Giriraj Shah
- Glory of Indian Culture 95.00

F.S. Growse
- Mathura & Vrindavan, The Mystics Land of Lord Krishna .... 495.00 (8 Colour photoes)

R.P. Hingorani
- Chalisa Sangrah (Roman) .. 40.00

Acharya Vipul Rao
- Srimad Bhagwat Geeta (Sanskrit & English) 75.00

Dr. Bhavansingh Rana
- 108 Upanishad (In press) ... 150.00

Chakor Ajgaonkar
- Realm of Sadhana (What Saints & Masters Say) 30.00

Dr. S.P. Ruhela
- Fragrant Spiritual Memories of a Karma Yogi 100.00

Yogi M.K. Spencer
- Rishi Ram Ram 100.00
- Oneness with God 90.00

Eva Bell Barer
- Quiet Talks with the Master 60.00

Joseph J. Ghosh
- Adventures with Evil Spirits 80.00

K.H. Nagrani
- A Child from the Spirit World Speaks 10.00

Religious Books in Hindi, English & Roman
- Sanatan Dharm Pooja 95.00
- Sudha Kalp 95.00
- Shiv Abhisek Poojan 25.00
- Daily Prayer (Hindi, English French, Roman) 25.00
- Sanatan Daily Prayer 25.00

Acharya Vipul Rao
- Daily Prayer 10.00

Shiv Sharma
- Soul of Sikhism 125.00
- Soul of Jainism 125.00

Gurpreet Singh
- Ten Masters 60.00

Order books by V.P.P. Postage Rs. 20/- per book extra. Postage free on order of three or more books, Send Rs. 20/- in advance

DIAMOND POCKET BOOKS (P) LTD.
X-30, Okhla Industrial Area, Phase-II, New Delhi-110020.
Phones : 8611861 - 865, Fax : (0091) -011- 8611866.

DIAMOND POCKET BOOKS PRESENTS

Dictionaries   Price
Diamond English-English-Hindi Dictionary 180.00
Diamond English-Hindi Dictionary 150.00
Diamond Hindi-English Dictionary 150.00
Diamond English-Hindi Dictionary 60.00
Diamond Hindi-English Dictionary 60.00
Diamond Hindi Dictionary 100.00
Diamond Hindi Dictionary 75.00
Diamond Hindi Dictionary 50.00
Diamond Dictionary (Student Edition) 40.00
Diamond Hindi-English Dictionary (Student Edition) 40.00
Diamond English-Hindi Dictionary (Student Edition) 40.00
Diamond Anglo-Assamese Pocket Dictionary (2 coloured) 60.00
Diamond Anglo-Assamese Pocket Dictionary 30.00

Language Series
Diamond English Speaking Course (Hindi) 70.00
Diamond English Speaking Course (Bengali) 70.00
Diamond English Speaking Course (Assamese) 70.00
Diamond English Speaking Course (Nepali) 70.00
Diamond English Speaking Course (Gujarati) 50.00
Diamond English Speaking Course (Marathi) 50.00
Learn and Speak 15 Indian Languages (by P. Machwe) 40.00
Learn English in 30 Days 30.00
Learn English through Bengali 20.00
Learn Nepali through English 20.00

DIAMOND POCKET BOOKS
X-30, Okhla Industrial Area, Phase-II,
New Delhi-110020
Ph. No.6841033, 6822803-4, Fax : 91- 011- 6925020
E-mail : mverma@nde.vsnl.net.in
Website : www.diamondpocketbooks.com